# ATTRACTING
# Attention

This book is part of the Peter Lang Media and Communication list.
Every volume is peer reviewed and meets
the highest quality standards for content and production.

PETER LANG
New York • Bern • Frankfurt • Berlin
Brussels • Vienna • Oxford • Warsaw

# Andi Stein

## Promotion and Marketing for Tourism Attractions

PETER LANG
New York • Bern • Frankfurt • Berlin
Brussels • Vienna • Oxford • Warsaw

**Library of Congress Cataloging-in-Publication Data**
Stein, Andi.
Attracting attention: promotion and marketing for tourism attractions / Andi Stein.
pages cm.
Includes bibliographical references and index.
1. Tourism—Marketing.  I. Title.
G155.A1S666    910.68'8—dc23    2014047064
ISBN 978-1-4331-2415-0 (hardcover)
ISBN 978-1-4331-2414-3 (paperback)
ISBN 978-1-4539-1513-4 (e-book)


Bibliographic information published by **Die Deutsche Nationalbibliothek**.
**Die Deutsche Nationalbibliothek** lists this publication in the "Deutsche
Nationalbibliografie"; detailed bibliographic data are available
on the Internet at http://dnb.d-nb.de/.

Cover photo courtesy of Kennywood Amusement Park


The paper in this book meets the guidelines for permanence and durability
of the Committee on Production Guidelines for Book Longevity
of the Council of Library Resources.

Printed in the United States of America

This book is dedicated to my parents, René and Mort Stein.

# CONTENTS

# ACKNOWLEDGMENTS

This book was inspired by a Marketing/Communications roundtable session I attended at the IAAPA Attractions Expo in 2012. Thanks to those who shared their stories and experiences and highlighted the valuable contributions they make to the promotion and marketing of tourism attractions.

I am especially appreciative to the following individuals for their insightful observations and comments about the attactions industry: Kathy Burrows, Hershey Entertainment & Resorts; Tina Hatcher, 3i Advertising/Public Relations; and Matt Heller, Performance Optimist Consulting.

Many thanks to Jeff Filicko and Kennywood Amusement Park for the fabulous cover photo and additional pix.

Thanks also to Katie Frassinelli, National Corvette Museum, and Mark Hoewing, Give Kids the World, for the photos they contributed.

A big thank-you goes to Bernadette Shade, director of production, Peter Lang Publishing, for all her work on the book's production.

Finally, I offer my heartfelt thanks to Mary Savigar, senior acquisitions editor, Peter Lang Publishing, who has been so supportive of my work and who has steadfastly encouraged me to keep writing books.

# CHAPTER ONE

# Introduction

When the Wizarding World of Harry Potter—Diagon Alley opened at the Universal Orlando Resort in the summer of 2014, members of the media could barely contain their excitement. Television and newspaper reporters heralded the opening of the resort's latest addition. Industry magazine writers marveled at its ingenious design. Bloggers lavished readers with tips on how to make the most of their visits.[1]

The much-anticipated attraction was the sequel to the wildly popular Wizarding World of Harry Potter—Hogsmeade, which had opened at the resort to similar fanfare just four years earlier. Both brought to life the scenes, characters, and stories from the acclaimed Harry Potter franchise inspired by the books of author J.K. Rowling. The successful launch of Universal Orlando's Diagon Alley was a picture-perfect scenario for attraction promoters and marketers. It was a prime example of what can happen when years of planning, development, marketing, and promotion come together, resulting in a perfect blend of over-the-top media coverage, customer enthusiasm, and, ultimately, increased ticket sales.

*Figure 1.1: Roller coasters and other thrill rides add to the excitement of the attraction experience.*
(Photo Credit: Photo courtesy of Kennywood Amusement Park)

## Creating Memorable Experiences

Attractions comprise a major segment of the tourism industry. Author John Swarbrooke describes them as the "main motivators for tourist trips" and "the core of the tourism product."[2] Theme parks, zoos, museums, aquariums, national parks, casinos, and iconic attractions such as the Eiffel Tower and Las Vegas Strip are only some of the many different types of attractions that draw millions of visitors each year. In addition, "attractions generate a ripple effect of economic activity," that impacts hotels, retailers, and restaurants, according to a study from Oxford Economics.[3] In 2011, for example, "the U.S. attractions industry generated a total economic impact of nearly $219 billion."[4]

Regardless of type, attractions share one common denominator—they are intended to provide visitors with memorable experiences. "Every single day millions of people visit attractions across the globe. These visits break down into hundreds of moments that inform our personal experience," explain authors Christian Lachel and Rich Procter. "Certain moments are so powerful that they become part of our emotional DNA. We not only remember them, we crave to experience them again and again."[5]

Attraction experiences can include the sense of wonder inspired by a theme park show or the thrill and excitement generated by an amusement park roller coaster ride. They can be culturally enriching, as with a visit to an art museum, or peacefully gratifying, as with a stroll through a national park. "The range of experiences provided by attractions is very wide and in each case reflects the resource that the site provides and its interaction with the interests and personality of each visitor," explain authors Victor Middleton et al.[6]

## Showcasing Attractions

With so many available options for travelers and tourists, promoters and marketers work diligently to make their attraction experiences stand out from the crowd. Their goal is to showcase what their attractions have to offer in order to convince customers to make them part of their vacation destinations or weekend leisure activities.

Promotion and marketing are essential components of attraction management. They serve as a means of telling an attraction's story through words, images, and events. When a new ride, exhibit, or feature such as Diagon Alley is introduced, for example, marketers and promoters begin preparing for its debut many months and even years before the attraction opens. They generate buzz with the media that will ideally result in advance press coverage about the attraction. This will in turn capture the interest of customers who will want to come see what the fuss is all about—and who will tell their friends about it using social media.

> ### *Attraction Fun Fact*
> There are approximately 400 amusement and theme parks in the United States.

## Maintaining Customer Interest

Even without something new to promote, marketers need to keep their attractions fresh in the minds of their audiences. They accomplish this through strategically placed advertisements, blog postings highlighting daily attraction activities, or contests promoted through social media and designed to direct traffic to their websites.

Attraction marketers also rely on special events and festivals to bring people through their turnstiles. Holiday events such as Hong Kong-based Ocean Park's Halloween Fest and the annual Holiday Lights Show held each December at the Kennywood amusement park in Pittsburgh, Pa., have become increasingly popular with attraction visitors, for example. Haunted houses, light displays, specialty shows, and holiday music are staples of these kinds of crowd-pleasing events.

Events with unusual themes also work well to attract customers. The Maritime Aquarium in Norwalk, Conn., for instance, sponsors an annual Chocolate World Expo that attracts more than 6,500 visitors. The event features tastings, cooking demonstrations, and sales of fine chocolates and specialty foods.[7]

Promotional incentives are another way of reaching customers. These include discounts or coupons intended to boost business during an attraction's off-season. Likewise, logo-bearing merchandise can help customers recall the good times they had at an attraction and subtly remind them to make a return visit.

## Providing Added Services

Part of effective promotion involves making the visitor experience memorable by providing outstanding customer service that leaves a lasting impression with guests. The development of the Walt Disney World Resort's MyMagic+ system, for example, redefined the customer experience when it debuted in 2014. According to reporter Jeremy Schoolfield, MyMagic+ enables resort guests to make restaurant reservations, reserve Fast Passes to avoid ride wait times, receive alerts for show start times, and synchronize their own itineraries with those of friends or family members by using a digital platform that included a website and mobile app.[8]

The debut of MyMagic+ resulted in a vast amount of positive media coverage for the Walt Disney World Resort in both popular and trade press because of the multi-faceted capabilities of the technology behind it. This essentially transformed what started as a state-of-the-art guest service into an important promotional tool for the attraction.

Technology has prompted many innovations and changes that have affected the attractions industry. Digital media, Internet marketing, and social media have all become commonplace terms in the attraction marketing vocabulary. The increased reliance on electronic media has led to the development of new communication strategies and tactics. Today's attraction promoters are constantly experimenting with a variety of communication channels and social media platforms as they try to determine the best way to reach their audiences.[9]

Promotion and marketing extend far beyond simply bringing customers to an attraction's gates. Keeping employees informed about day-to-day happenings is an important part of an attraction's activities. Knowing how to communicate during a crisis is crucial in an industry where one small misstep or malfunction can potentially affect hundreds of people. In today's globally conscious society, many attractions are also making corporate social responsibility and sustainability a routine part of their business. Consequently, communicating these activities to the public has become part of the promotion and marketing mix.

## Overview of the Book

This book offers information about how to promote and market tourism attractions for maximum results. It looks at different approaches, strategies, tools, and techniques attraction marketers can use when promoting their organizations to the public. In addition, it includes a variety of examples from attractions that have implemented successful promotion and marketing activities.

The book is intended as a resource for those working in marketing, public relations, advertising, guest relations, and other communication positions for attractions and tourism-related organizations. It also offers valuable information for students enrolled in tourism, hospitality management, and communications programs who are interested in learning about the promotion and marketing practices of the attractions industry. Following is a description of the topics addressed in each chapter.

## Types of Attractions

Within the tourism industry, there are many types of attractions that appeal to a wide range of audiences. Among these are cultural and educational organizations, heritage sites, sports venues, and commercial entertainment attractions such as amusement and theme parks. Chapter 2 offers an overview of different types of tourism attractions and looks at some of the promotion and marketing strategies that work well to bring customers into these venues.

### Top 25 Tourism Attractions

| Attraction | Annual Visitors in Millions |
|---|---|
| 1. Las Vegas, Nevada | 39.67 |
| 2. Times Square, New York, NY | 39.2 |
| 3. Central Park, New York, NY | 37.5 |
| 4. Union Station, Washington, D.C. | 32.85 |
| 5. Niagara Falls, New York/Ontario, Canada | 22.5 |
| 6. Grand Central Station, New York, NY | 21.6 |
| 7. Faneuil Hall Marketplace, Boston, MA | 18.0 |
| 8. Walt Disney World's Magic Kingdom, Orlando, FL | 17.54 |
| 9. Disneyland, Anaheim, CA | 15.96 |
| 10. Forbidden City, Beijing, China | 15.3 |
| 11. Grand Bazaar, Istanbul, Turkey | 15.0 |
| 12. Tokyo Disneyland, Tokyo, Japan | 14.85 |
| 13. Notre Dame Cathedral, Paris, France | 13.65 |
| 14. Golden Gate Park, San Francisco, CA | 13.0 |
| 15. Tokyo Disney Sea, Tokyo, Japan | 12.66 |
| 16. Disneyland Paris, Marne-la-Vallée, France | 11.2 |
| 17. Epcot, Orlando, FL | 11.06 |
| 18. Sacré Coeur Basilica, Paris, France | 10.5 |
| 19. Tsim Sha Tsui, Hong Kong | 10.09 |
| 20. Pike Place Market, Seattle, WA | 10.0 |
| 21. The Zocalo, Mexico City, Mexico | 10.0 |
| 22. Disney's Animal Kingdom, Orlando, FL | 10.0 |
| 23. Disney's Hollywood Studios, Orlando, FL | 9.91 |
| 24. Universal Studios Japan, Osaka, Japan | 9.7 |
| 25. Great Smoky Mountains National Park, TN | 9.69 |

2014 Data
Source: Statista, http://www.statista.com/statistics/303351/most-visited-tourist-attractions-worldwide

## Attraction Development

Effective attraction promotion begins with a good idea. Chapter 3 provides information about the steps needed to create and develop a successful tourism attraction. It includes details about how to evaluate the potential for a viable attraction, identify target markets, assess financing needs, and determine management responsibilities. The chapter also includes approaches to establishing different kinds of attractions, which can then be effectively promoted to the public.

## Promotion, Advertising, and Marketing

The right mix of promotional materials can be crucial in attraction promotion. Chapter 4 talks about the roles advertising and marketing play in creating promotional materials that will have a lasting impact with the public. The chapter discusses how attractions can advertise their facilities across different platforms such as print, broadcast, and online media. It also addresses various traditional and digital resources that can be used for marketing purposes.

## Media Relations

While the landscape for generating publicity has changed in recent years, traditional media are still valuable resources for highlighting what an attraction has to offer. Chapter 5 addresses the role the media can play in helping to promote tourism attractions. The chapter discusses the importance of developing good working relationships with journalists. It presents tips on the kinds of stories that are likely to attract media attention and offers suggestions on how to pitch them to reporters and editors.

## Social Media Marketing

Social media sites have become a regular part of an organization's promotion and marketing mix. Chapter 6 assesses the roles social media and the Internet now play in the promotion and marketing of tourism attractions. Information is provided about how attractions use Facebook, Twitter, Instagram, and other social media platforms to develop a following with potential customers. The chapter offers guidelines for maximizing the use of social media to engage customers and get them to help spread the word about an attraction's offerings.

## Sales Promotions and Merchandising

Sales promotions rely on the use of special incentives, gimmicks, and other techniques to encourage sales. Merchandising falls under the umbrella of sales promotion and serves as a way to stimulate sales through the on-site or online purchase of products and services. Chapter 7 provides information on sales promotions that have proven effective for attractions. It also looks at different kinds of merchandise that can be used to reinforce an attraction's brand.

## Special Events

Special events are another means of drawing attention to an attraction. Chapter 8 offers an overview of the many different types of special events that can be used to promote tourism attractions. The chapter discusses the steps involved in putting together crowd-pleasing events that drive traffic to an attraction. It also provides suggestions for how to best promote these events to the media and public.

## Guest Relations and Customer Service

Building goodwill with customers is an important element of an attraction's promotion and marketing activities. Chapter 9 discusses the roles that guest relations and customer service play in the overall success of a tourism attraction. The chapter looks at how attraction managers can promote a culture of service throughout their organizations. It also offers approaches attractions can take to reinforce customer satisfaction and encourage repeat business.

## Employee Relations

An attraction's employees are the heart and soul of its operations. Chapter 10 addresses the value of developing an employee relations program. The chapter presents different ways of recruiting, training, motivating, and communicating with employees in order to acknowledge their contributions and keep them engaged in the organization.

## Crisis Communications

Even the most well managed attraction can be susceptible to crisis at any time. When this happens, attraction personnel need to know how to respond and how to communicate information about the crisis to the public. Chapter 11 addresses the potential crises that can affect tourism attractions and the role effective communication plays in keeping people informed during a crisis. The chapter discusses steps involved in developing a crisis plan, working with the media, and using electronic resources to communicate during times of crisis.

---

### *Attraction Fun Fact*
The oldest zoo in the United States is the Philadelphia Zoo. It opened in 1876.

---

## Social Responsibility and Sustainability

Many attractions are making a commitment to their communities and the environment a routine part of their promotion and marketing activities. Chapter 12 explains how tourism attractions can be socially responsible and sustainable in their day-to-day practices. The chapter offers examples of attractions that are conducting business in a socially responsible manner through philanthropy, volunteerism, and conservation. It also offers suggestions for how organizations can communicate these efforts to the public.

*Figure 1.2: Attractions can incorporate sustainable practices such as wildlife conservation into their promotion and marketing activities.*
(Photo Credit: Andi Stein)

## Conclusion

Blockbuster attractions like the Wizarding World of Harry Potter may not come along every day. Nonetheless, attractions all over the world regularly introduce new rides, exhibits, shows, facilities, and characters, to name just a few. They also offer their customers opportunities for fun, excitement, relaxation, and happiness on a daily basis just by the mere fact of their existence. This is what creates memorable experiences.

"The visitor experience at managed attractions begins with anticipation," note Middleton, et al.[10] It is up to attraction promoters and marketers to create this anticipation—to convey the promise and excitement of memorable experiences in ways that "speak to the hopes, dreams and desires of audiences."[11]

Whether in the form of a news story, television commercial, brochure, website, Facebook posting, or special event, attraction promotion and marketing have the potential to show customers the possibilities that await them. This book addresses the many different ways to reach this potential. It explains how to make the most of promotion and marketing to bring people into an attraction and keep them coming back for more.

## Notes

1. See, for example, Dewayne Bevil and Sandra Pedicini, "Potter Wait Over! Now Get in Line," *Orlando Sentinel*, July 9, 2014, A1; Ken Wallingford, "Caught Up in the Magic at Universal Studios' Diagon Alley," *Toronto Star*, July 10, 2014, T1; Paul Ruben, "Diagon Alley: The Wizarding World of Harry Potter, The Next Chapter," *Park World*, August 2014, 32; Jeremy Schoolfield, "All Aboard," *Funworld*, August 2014, 40; and "Wizarding World of Harry Potter Diagon Alley Review and Touring Tips," *TouringPlans.com*, http://blog.touringplans.com/2014/06/30/wizarding-world-harry-potter-diagon-alley-review-touring-tips.
2. John Swarbrooke, *The Development and Management of Visitor Attractions, 2nd ed.* (Burlington, MA: Elsevier Butterworth-Heinemann, 2005), 3.
3. "New Study From Oxford Economics Outlines Economic Impacts of the Amusement Park and Attractions in the United States," *Tourism Economics*, July 2013, 1.
4. Ibid.
5. Christian Lachel and Rich Procter, "Experiences That Matter," in *Attractions Management Handbook 2013–2014: The Global Resource for Attractions Professionals*, http://www.attractionshandbook.com.
6. Victor T.C. Middleton, Alan Fyall, Michael Morgan, and Ashok Ranchhod, *Marketing in Travel and Tourism, 4th ed.* (Amsterdam: Butterworth-Heinemann, 2009), 413.
7. "Aquarium Hits Sweet Spot with Chocolate World Expo," *Funworld*, April 2014, 20.
8. See Jeremy Schoolfield, "Changing the World," *Funworld*, July 2014, 60.
9. See Jim Futrell, "The Changing Face of Attraction Marketing," *Funworld*, July 2010, http://www.iaapa.org/news/newsroom/news-articles/the-changing-face-of-attraction-marketing-funworld-july-2010.
10. Middleton, Fyall, Morgan, and Ranchhod, *Marketing in Travel and Tourism, 4th ed.*, 413.
11. Lachel and Procter, "Experiences That Matter," http://www.attractionshandbook.com.

# CHAPTER TWO

# Types of Attractions

## Introduction

Tourism attractions come in a variety of shapes and sizes and appeal to different types of audiences. They can range from large-scale venues like national parks, which attract millions of visitors each year, to small, specialized locales such as offbeat museums that have a core of followers interested in a particular collection.

Some attractions are designed to excite and dazzle customers with their jaw-dropping thrill rides and effects-laden shows. Some focus on educating their audiences, providing them with a sense of history or an appreciation for art or culture. Still others hold appeal because of their ability to evoke nostalgic memories or impress visitors by their sheer beauty or grandeur.

Depending on the nature of an attraction, the promotional activities used to bring visitors to these sites may be tailored to appeal to these varied audiences. This chapter offers a description of different types of attractions and provides examples of promotional activities that have proven successful with these venues.

## Cultural and Educational Sites

Cultural and educational attractions have the ability to both educate and entertain their audiences. They encompass museums, zoos, aquariums, science centers, and galleries, to name just a few. These venues are often promoted as ideal destinations for families, as they offer something for people of all ages.

*Figure 2.1: Visitors to the Route 66 Museum in Clinton, Okla., have a chance to learn about "The Main Street of America."* (Photo Credit: Andi Stein)

## Interactivity and Diversity

Museums have evolved over the years from their origins as static repositories that housed collections of artifacts for people to look at. Today, many museums have been transformed into facilities where visitors can learn by doing and become actively engaged through a variety of interactive exhibits and programs. The *New York Times* characterizes this new approach as "a 21st-century movement to use games and interactive digital experiences to help museumgoers learn."[1]

The Hockey Hall of Fame in Toronto, Canada, for instance, combines this approach of looking and doing for its patrons. Visitors can stroll through the halls of what reporter James Careless refers to as "Canada's Cathedral" to view artifacts such as the Stanley Cup, as well as the "sweaters, skates, and assorted memorabilia from the game's stars."[2] They can also try their hand at the game themselves by shooting pucks at and playing goaltender to computer simulations of some of hockey's greats such as Ed Balfour and Wayne Gretsky.

Some museums have broad appeal because of the diversity of their collections. Perhaps the most well known is the Smithsonian Institution in Washington, D.C., which houses a complex of 19 museums and galleries as well as a zoo. The facility's offerings cover art, history, science, nature, and popular culture.[3] Other museums feature specialized collections that attract individuals who are fascinated by the offbeat or obscure, such as the Museum of Bags and Purses in Amsterdam, the Netherlands; Center for Puppetry Arts in Atlanta, Ga.; and Spam Museum in Austin, Minn.

*Innovative Approaches to Promotion*

One of the challenges for museums from a promotional standpoint is to maintain patron interest to generate repeat business. Rotating exhibits from a museum's collection and short-term special exhibits can help rekindle the interest of previous visitors. In 2014, for example, the Spielzeug Welten toy museum in Basel, Switzerland, featured a special exhibit of Japanese dolls to celebrate Japanese-Swiss diplomacy and friendship.[4] The exhibit complemented the museum's permanent collection and offered previous customers a reason for a return visit.

A growing trend in the museum industry is the concept of "pop-up museums." These include everything from "buses transformed into mobile museums to reproductions of famous works displayed in public spaces, with exhibits lasting from a few hours to a few months," according to reporter Jodi Helmer.[5] Much like the popular food truck phenomenon, these pop-up museums have the ability to move from place to place and offer large groups of people exposure to their exhibits.

Some museums develop programs and attractions that are intended to reach out to specific audiences. The Penn Museum in Philadelphia offers specialty "touch tours" for the visually impaired, focusing on the tactile rather than the visual. They provide a hands-on opportunity for patrons who may not be able to see the museum's collection with their eyes to experience it from a different perspective.[6]

*Specialized Programs*

Zoos and aquariums have also evolved into attractions that offer visitors more than a passive viewing experience. Today's zoos feature educational programs and interactive exhibits where patrons can learn about animal welfare and conservation. Aquariums have also come into their own as tourism attractions say authors Roy Cook, et al. In some cases, this has been with the help of the cities that support them.

> Many cities, such as Camden, New Jersey, and Long Beach, California, have funded aquariums to help revitalize waterfront areas by attracting tourists and residents to oceanside regions of these cities. One of the most successful aquariums, Baltimore's National Aquarium, helped ensure the success of that city's redeveloped Inner Harbor.[7]

As part of their promotional activities, some zoos and aquariums have even added programs for families who want to have a more up-close-and-personal experience with the animals. At the National Zoo's Snore and Roar program in Washington, D.C., for example, a zookeeper takes visitors on a two-hour tour of the facility along with a night hike to look for nocturnal critters. The walk through the zoo is followed by a sleepover in a tent camp on Lion/Tiger Hill and concludes with breakfast the next morning.[8]

---

### *Attraction Fun Fact*

The Washington, D.C.-based Smithsonian Institution has two of its 19 museums and galleries in New York City.

---

## Historic Sites and Heritage Attractions

Like museums and cultural attractions, historic and heritage sites have the potential to provide visitors with a chance to learn in an entertaining manner—in this case, to learn about history. These sites include historic houses, battlefields, memorials, and living history centers. They can even include neighborhoods within a particular city such as the French Quarter in New Orleans. According to Cook et al., "More and more communities and countries are taking steps to preserve historic treasures and attract visitors through active restoration and interpretive programs. New life and uses are even being found for old industrial sites."[9]

### Living History Sites

Some historic sites and heritage attractions generate public interest because they give visitors a sense of what it was like to experience life during a certain time period. Colonial Williamsburg, for example, is a living history center where visitors interact with people dressed in 18th-century costumes and hear their stories of the past.[10]

### Dark Tourism Sites

Other historic attractions are intended to denote the occurrences of tragic events. These attractions are called "dark tourism" sites because of their somber natures. They include facilities such as the Oklahoma City National Memorial and Museum, which pays tribute to the 168 victims of the 1995 bombing of the Alfred P. Murrah Federal Building. Other well-known attractions in this category include the USS Arizona Memorial—more commonly known as Pearl Harbor— and the Auschwitz concentration camp in Poland.

The terrorist attacks on New York City's World Trade Centers on September 11, 2001, had a life-altering impact not only on the residents of New York City but on the world at large. Because of this, the memorial and museum built on the site where the towers once stood attract visitors from all over the globe. In the first three years after the memorial was built, more than 12 million people flocked to see the simple but powerfully moving design of twin reflecting pools etched with the names of those who lost their lives in the attacks.[11] The opening of the museum in 2014 generated 300,000 visitors in its first month alone.[12]

### Lesser-Known Historic Sites

While sites like the 9/11 Memorial automatically attract visitors because of their internationally known acclaim, lesser-known historic sites may need more of a boost with their promotional efforts to draw a crowd. Special events or tours are an effective way to attract visitors to these locales.

At the Eastern State Penitentiary in Philadelphia, for example, a special Halloween-themed program called "Terror Behind the Walls" allows guests to experience a "fright night" at the former prison, now deemed a U.S. National Historic Landmark. The program generates enough revenue each Fall to support year-round ongoing tours of the penitentiary.[13]

The Hollywood Forever cemetery in Los Angeles is the final resting spot for a number of stars of the silver screen. As part of its community awareness efforts, the cemetery runs a summer film series where guests can bring a picnic dinner and watch movies shown on the wall of a mausoleum for a small fee.[14]

An interest in popular culture can also contribute to the appeal of historic and heritage sites. The actor Andy Griffith is perhaps best known for his portrayal of a sheriff in the fictional town of Mayberry, N.C. Although Mayberry never existed, Griffith's hometown of Mount Airy, N.C., has become a thriving tourist attraction, thanks to nostalgia and reruns of the TV show that have kept his memory alive. Townsfolk make the most of this by sponsoring an annual "Mayberry Days" event, which draws between 25,000 to 30,000 visitors to Mount Airy each fall. The event, the town's Andy Griffith Museum, and the overall popularity of Griffith have contributed to making tourism the second largest industry in Mount Airy after agriculture.[15]

## Commercial Entertainment Attractions

Commercial entertainment attractions are sites that have been developed purely for the purpose of leisure. They offer opportunities for relaxation and escapism, often through the creation of artificial environments. Among the most popular attractions within this category are amusement parks, theme parks, and casinos.

### Amusement Parks

Amusement parks evolved from European "pleasure gardens," which date back to medieval times. These gardens were created as a source of recreation where people could gather on a Sunday afternoon to play games, watch live entertainment, and enjoy a picnic with their loved ones.

Many of these pleasure gardens also featured primitive amusement rides.[16] In keeping with this tradition, today's amusement parks are generally family-friendly environments that provide a day's outing for residents of the local communities they serve. They typically feature rides, concessions, and picnic grounds.

### Theme Parks

Theme parks grew out of amusement parks, largely thanks to Walt Disney, who pioneered the idea of the modern-day theme park when he opened Disneyland in 1955, in Anaheim, Calif.

"This theme park changed the amusement park business considerably because it expanded the concept of amusement parks from simply rides and carnival barkers to include shows, shops, and restaurants in theme settings with immaculate cleanliness, promising adventure, history, science fiction, and fantasy," explain authors Charles Goeldner and J.R. Brent Ritchie.[17]

While some of the earliest theme parks like Disneyland and SeaWorld encompass broad entertainment genres, some of today's parks have become extremely specialized. Legoland parks in Europe, Asia, and North America, for example, are designed around the theme of the popular children's building-block toys. Sesame Place in Langhorne, Pa., is based on the PBS show *Sesame Street*.

---

## Top 25 Theme/Amusement Parks Worldwide

1. Magic Kingdom at Walt Disney World, Orlando, FL
2. Tokyo Disneyland, Tokyo, Japan
3. Disneyland, Anaheim, CA
4. Tokyo Disney Sea, Tokyo, Japan
5. Epcot at Walt Disney World, Orlando, FL
6. Disneyland Paris, Marne-la-Vallée, France
7. Disney's Animal Kingdom, Orlando, FL
8. Disney's Hollywood Studios, Orlando, FL
9. Universal Studios Japan, Osaka, Japan
10. Disney's California Adventure, Anaheim, CA
11. Islands of Adventure at Universal, Orlando, FL
12. Ocean Park, Hong Kong
13. Hong Kong Disneyland, Hong Kong
14. Lotte World, Seoul, South Korea
15. Everland, Gyeonggi-Do, South Korea
16. Universal Studios, Orlando, FL
17. Universal Studios Hollywood, Universal City, CA
18. Nagashima Spa Land, Kuwama, Japan
19. SeaWorld, Orlando, FL
20. Europa Park, Rust, Germany
21. Walt Disney Studios Park, Marne-la-Vallée, France
22. SeaWorld, San Diego, CA
23. Tivoli Gardens, Copenhagen, Denmark
24. De Efteling, Kaatsheuvel, Netherlands
25. Yokohama Hakkeijima Sea Paradise, Yokohama, Japan

2013 Data
Source: AECOM 2013 Theme Index, Themed Entertainment Association

---

While most amusement parks typically attract local residents as their primary customer base, many theme parks are seen as vacation destinations and draw visitors from all over the world.

Consequently, some areas such as Southern California, Orlando, Fla., and Sentosa Island in Singapore, have become theme park hubs, enabling visitors to take in multiple parks during a single vacation.

To stay competitive, amusement and theme parks are constantly developing bigger and better rides and shows to entice customers to their gates. Part of their promotional efforts focus on marketing these new attractions to the public. Many amusement and theme parks are seasonal because of their locations in cold weather zones, so these promotional efforts begin months before the debut of a new attraction at the start of the season. These efforts are designed to build excitement and generate customer interest for the park's opening.

*Casinos and Gaming Establishments*

Casinos are also considered commercial entertainment attractions and have long been associated with venues like Las Vegas, Atlantic City, and Monte Carlo. In the last two decades, however, the development of casinos on federal Indian reservations, the proliferation of riverboat casinos, and the legalization of organized gaming in a number of U.S. states has expanded the potential of casinos as standalone tourism attractions.

According to Cook et al., "The increasing availability and ease of access to gaming locations just in the United States has resulted in more Americans visiting casinos than attending major league and collegiate football games, arena concerts, symphony concerts, and Broadway shows combined."[18] On an international scale, the casino business in Macau, a special administrative region of China, has transformed the small island in Southeast Asia into the largest legalized gambling venue in the world.

Themed décor and special events have helped promote the casino business as the market has become more competitive. Visitors to Las Vegas, for example, will find casinos that replicate famous places around the world such as Paris, Venice, and New York City. A number of standalone Indian casinos like the Viejas Casino in Alpine, Calif., have also added adjacent hotels or even outlet malls to their properties. These extra features encourage customers to make a visit to the casino more than just a day trip.

Many Atlantic City casinos operate free buses for patrons from nearby cities, often throwing in coupons for meals or slot machine play to entice customers. Some casinos have established customer loyalty programs, similar to airline reward programs, to encourage repeat business. These also serve as a means of collecting customer data that can be used to assist with targeted marketing efforts.[19]

# Natural Sites

Beaches, mountains, parks, gardens, and hot springs all fall under the umbrella of natural sites. Included in this category are for-profit enterprises such as commercially managed botanical gardens. Also included are public lands overseen by governmental agencies such as the U.S. National Park Service (NPS). According to Goeldner and Ritchie:

U.S. National Parks host over 285 million visitors a year…. The NPS administers 393 national parks, plus hundreds of other recreation areas, preserves, natural landmarks, battlefields, historical sites, lakeshores, monuments, memorials, seashores, and parkways, which encompass more than 84 million acres of land and another 4.5 million acres of water.[20]

Some natural sites are protected by laws designed to preserve and safeguard them from destruction. Ironically, this can make them especially attractive to tourists, according to authors David Weaver and Laura Lawton. "The fact that an area has been designated as a National Park… confers status on that space as an attraction, since most people assume that it must be special in order to warrant such designation."[21]

> ## *Attraction Fun Fact*
> Yellowstone National Park, established in 1872, was the first park in the U.S. National Parks system.

This can occasionally cause a conundrum for those managing the sites. They may want to promote the natural sites as tourist attractions but at the same time need to ensure the sites are not damaged by overuse or overzealous visitors.[22]

### Educational Features

Some natural sites may incorporate educational components as part of their public offerings. An exhibit called "California State Parks, 150 Years: A Gift from the People to the People" at the California State Railroad Museum featured historic photographs of the California state park system. The railroad museum was chosen as the venue for the exhibit because it is part of the Old Sacramento State Historic Park. As the museum is one of the most popular attractions in the Sacramento area, drawing 500,000 visitors a year, it was an ideal locale to house an exhibit promoting other attractions within the state park system.[23]

Visitor centers and museums strategically placed within the boundaries of a park or beach area can add to the attraction experience. The Sutro Baths was an elaborate swimming establishment and popular recreational attraction for San Francisco residents in the late 19th and early 20th centuries. Perched on the edge of the Pacific Ocean and encased in glass, the baths once attracted thousands of visitors each year. Today the remnants of the Sutro Baths are part of the Golden Gate National Recreation Area. In 2012, the Golden Gate National Parks Conservancy opened the Lands End Lookout Visitor Center on the cliff above the Sutro Baths, where visitors can learn about the history of the Baths and their surroundings.[24]

## Iconic Attractions

Tourism venues such as the Grand Canyon, Mount Rushmore, Leaning Tower of Pisa, Big Ben, and the Eiffel Tower can be classified as iconic attractions. Known for their sheer grandeur, natural beauty, or architectural ingenuity, they are considered iconic because of their status as universally recognized attractions. Iconic attractions are often included as routine stops on escorted tours.

*Figure 2.2: The city of Paris is an iconic attraction populated with well-known sights like the Eiffel Tower.*
(Photo Credit: Andi Stein)

Iconic attractions include scenic highways and byways such as Route 66. Once a main artery for travelers making their way from Chicago to California across eight states, in its heyday, Route 66 was known as the "Main Street of America." The route was eventually replaced by interstate highways that enabled travelers to make the cross-country journey in a fraction of the time. Nonetheless, local state associations promote and celebrate the existence of Route 66 through the preservation of cultural attractions along the old highway that continue to draw visitors.[25]

## Cities as Icons

Some cities such as Paris, New York City, and Las Vegas fall into the iconic attractions category and conduct ongoing promotional campaigns to encourage tourism. Known for glitz, glamour, and neon, Las Vegas attracts close to 40 million domestic and international visitors annually.[26] Over the years the city has been the setting of classic movies like *Viva Las Vegas* and the original *Oceans 11*, as well as more contemporary films such as *21* and *The Hangover*.

The Las Vegas Convention and Visitors Authority has developed a number of promotional campaigns and slogans in the last few decades to attract visitors. In the late 1980s and early 1990s, for example, Las Vegas tried to position the city as a family-oriented vacation destination. Several casinos began developing attractions designed to encourage families with children to visit the city. The Mirage Casino installed "Siegfried & Roy's Secret Garden and Dolphin Habitat," for instance, while the MGM Grand constructed a theme park behind its hotel/casino.[27]

A few years later, the family-friendly marketing approach to Las Vegas was abandoned for a full-blown concentration on the adult gambler market with promotional campaigns such as "What Happens Here Stays Here." By 2014, the city had also become known for high-quality restaurants and attractions such as The LINQ, a shopping and entertainment district in the heart of the Las Vegas strip aimed at Gen X and Gen Y patrons.[28]

## Retail Venues

In today's consumption-oriented society, even retail venues are considered tourism attractions. Shopping centers such as the Mall of America in Minneapolis, and West Edmonton Mall in Canada are touted as vacation destinations in their own right. Likewise, bazaars and markets like the Grand Bazaar in Istanbul or the Stanley Market in Hong Kong are routinely listed as places to visit in tourist guidebooks. Discount or outlet malls also count as viable attractions, pulling in millions of customers each year. Sawgrass Mills in Sunrise, Fla., for example, is considered the second most popular tourism destination in the state behind Walt Disney World.[29]

These retail venues often contain much more than just places to shop. The Mall of America, for instance, features stores, restaurants, a movie theater, aquarium, and a theme park called Nickelodeon Universe® within its walls.[30] The centerpiece of the West Edmonton Mall in Canada is a network of giant water slides called "Sky Screamer Extremes."[31]

Shopping malls may even be incorporated into large-scale hotels such as the Marina Bay Sands in Singapore. This kind of arrangement allows for cross-promotional efforts between the mall and the sponsoring hotel. Customers can check into their rooms, then head to the mall to purchase something to wear to dinner at one of the hotel's five-star restaurants.[32]

### Shopping Malls as Destinations

Shopping vacations are popular with international visitors, according to Cook et al. "Ontario Mills Mall, located 60 miles east of Los Angeles, California, attracts over 20 million shoppers each year. About 40% of these shoppers are tourists, coming from as far away as Australia, Hong Kong, Japan, Malaysia, and the Philippines."[33] The Mall of America is the number one attraction in Minnesota, drawing over 40 million visitors a year. Four out of 10 visitors are tourists.[34]

The popularity of these retail venues has prompted some of them to develop their own resources for promotion. At Ontario Mills, according to Cook et al., "The mall has an office of tourism and marketing staff targeting not only countries but also tour operators, airlines, and other travel industry representatives.[35]

Werner Escher is the director of domestic and international markets for South Coast Plaza in Costa Mesa, Calif. His outreach efforts in promoting the center as an "international destination" have taken him around the world and have been particularly successful with the Chinese market. "South Coast Plaza currently enjoys a prized reputation amongst Chinese tourists as *the* destination for luxury shopping," according to a post on the *AttractChina* blog. "Escher attributes this to what he calls 'word of mouth and word of mouse': Chinese tourist shoppers spreading the word of their positive experiences on the Internet."[36]

## Sporting Events and Venues

Sports are an extremely popular pastime and, as a result, sporting events and venues have earned their place within the attractions industry, according to Cook et al.

> Modern-day professional and intercollegiate sporting events such as football, soccer, baseball, basketball, and hockey draw millions of visitors each year to regularly scheduled games and playoffs. Special sporting events such as the Super Bowl, the Stanley Cup Championship, the World Cup, the Pro Rodeo Championship, the Indianapolis 500, and the College World Series, to name just a few, attract international attention and vast numbers of spectators to host communities each year.[37]

Major sporting events like the Olympics or the World Cup have become tourism attractions of their own. These large-scale productions draw thousands of spectators from around the world. They provide opportunities not only for the event sponsors but for the host city or country of the event as well. Individuals who patronize a major sporting event often make time or extend their stays in the host locale to take advantage of nearby attractions.

Sporting venues like stadiums and arenas can also double as tourism attractions. A number of former Olympic host cities, including Lake Placid, N.Y., Beijing, China, and Vancouver, Canada, for example, now offer visitors tours of the facilities built for their Olympic games. The city of Atlanta, Ga., even built a 20-story Ferris wheel on the site of Centennial Olympic Park, which was originally created to be the gathering place for the 1996 Summer Olympic Games.[38]

Some teams offer their fans opportunities for tours of their favorite ballparks or stadiums, especially during the off-season. Philadelphia Phillies fans, for instance, can take a 90-minute tour of the facilities at Citizen's Bank Park, where they visit the dugout, broadcast booth, and Hall of Fame room.[39] Several sports websites even offer prospective travelers tips for making ballparks tourist destinations.[40]

## Alternative Tourism Sites

While the previous sections cover the main categories of tourism attractions, the list is by no means exhaustive. In recent years, options for tourism venues have expanded beyond the attractions previously discussed. Seasoned travelers in particular have developed interests in pursuing travel and leisure activities outside the traditional tourism box. This has led to the development of attractions designed for those wanting to enjoy a unique vacation experience.

Alternative attractions consist of venues such as religious shrines, dude ranches, wineries, spas, and wellness centers, among others. They include music venues such as Branson, Mo., and Nashville's Grand Ole Opry. They can also encompass industrial sites like the Ben and Jerry's ice cream factory in Waterbury, Vt., or the Crayola crayon factory in Easton, Pa.

## Attraction Categories

### Cultural and Educational
Museums
Zoos
Aquariums
Science centers
Art galleries
Craft centers

### Historic and Heritage Sites
Living history centers
Open-air museums
Historic houses
Ethnic neighborhoods
Waterfronts and marinas
Castles
Cathedrals and churches
Railways
Battlefields
Memorials
Cemeteries

### Commercial Entertainment
Amusement parks
Theme parks
Water parks
Family entertainment centers
Casinos
Racetracks

### Iconic
Monuments
Roadside attractions
Cities
Municipal towers

### Natural
National and state parks
Botanical gardens
Beaches
Caves
Waterfalls
Hot springs
Lakes and rivers
Mountains
Rainforests
Hiking Trails

### Sports-related
Olympics
World Cup
Tennis tournaments
Sports arenas
Ski resorts
Golf courses

### Retail
Shopping centers
Mega-malls
Bazaars and markets
Factory outlets

### Alternative
Wineries
Spas
Dude ranches
Music venues
Factory tours
Religious shrines
Farms

# Conclusion

Within the attractions industry, there are many different types of venues that provide entertainment and pleasure for visitors. Some of these, such as museums, zoos, and aquariums, are designed to educate audiences. Others provide a sense of history by preserving and showcasing treasures and stories from the past.

A number of attractions such as theme parks and casinos exist solely for commercial entertainment purposes. Some appeal to visitors because of their natural beauty, iconic status, or their ability to evoke nostalgic memories. Still others provide recreational entertainment for audiences like shopping or the viewing of sporting events.

Regardless of the type of tourism attraction, all of these venues need to be carefully planned, developed, and marketed in order to attract the attention of visitors. The next chapter will look at some of the elements that go into developing a successful tourism attraction, one that can easily be promoted to potential customers.

# Notes

1. Chris Suellenthrop, "At Play in Skies of Cretaceous Era," *The New York Times*, March 19, 2014, F4.
2. James Careless, "Canada's Cathedral: A Look at the Hockey Hall of Fame," *Funworld*, September 2012, 64.
3. See "Smithsonian," Smithsonian Institution, www.si.edu.
4. See "Spielzeug Welten Museum Basel," Spielzeug Welten Museum, http://www.spielzeug-welten-museum-basel.ch/en/special-exhibitions/current-exhibitions/konnichiwa-and-grueezi.
5. Jodi Helmer, "Museums on the Move," *Funworld*, March 2013, 60.
6. Kathy Matheson, "Pa. Museum Tells Blind Visitors: Please Touch!" *Associated Press*, December 3, 2013.
7. Roy A. Cook, Cathy H.C. Hsu, and Joseph J. Marqua, *Tourism: The Business of Hospitality and Travel, 5th ed.* (Boston, MA: Pearson, 2014), 212.
8. "Sleepover at the Zoo, the Museum or the Aquarium," *WTOP.com*, August 12, 2013, http://www.wtop.com/41/3419564/Sleepover-at-the-zoo-the-museum-or-the-aquarium.
9. Cook, Hsu, and Marqua, Tourism: *The Business of Hospitality and Travel, 5th ed.*, 211.
10. See "Colonial Williamsburg," The Colonial Williamsburg Foundation, http://www.history.org.
11. "Facts and Figures," 9/11 Memorial, http://www.911memorial.org/facts-and-figures.
12. "9/11 Museum Tops 300,000 Visitors," *Orange County Register*, July 6, 2014, 3.
13. "Eastern State Penitentiary Thrives on Ingenious Business Model," *Funworld*, March 2012, 15.
14. Malcolm Jones, "Tombstone Tourism," *Newsweek*, October 22, 2012, 11.
15. Martha Waggoner, "Visitors Come to Mount Airy Looking for Mayberry," *Associated Press*, August 16, 2012.
16. See Andi Stein and Beth Bingham Evans, *An Introduction to the Entertainment Industry* (New York: Peter Lang, 2009), 132.
17. Charles R. Goeldner and J.R. Brent Ritchie, *Tourism: Principles, Practices, Philosophies, 12th ed.* (Hoboken, NJ: John Wiley & Sons, Inc., 2012), 175.
18. Cook, Hsu, Marqua, Tourism: *The Business of Hospitality and Travel, 5th ed.*, 218.
19. Ibid., 220.
20. Goeldner and Ritchie, *Tourism: Principles, Practices, Philosophies, 12th ed.*, 182.
21. David Weaver and Laura Lawton, *Tourism Management, 2nd ed.* (Milton, Queensland: John Wiley & Sons, Australia, 2002), 137.
22. See, for example, Bart Melton, "YES: Bill is Bad News for Yellowstone and Grand Teton National Parks,"

*Denver Post*, April 6, 2014, D4; and Charles Pezeshki, "NO: A Little Paddling Isn't Going to Harm the Yellowstone Experience," *Denver Post*, April 6, 2014, D4.

23. See Tillie Fong, "Railroad Museum Exhibit Marks 150 Years of California's State Parks," *Sacramento Bee*, December 21, 2013, http://www.sacbee.com/2013/12/21/6020579/railroad-museum-exhibit-marks.html.

24. See "Lands End Lookout," Golden Gate National Parks Conservancy, http://www.parksconservancy.org/park-improvements/past-accomplishments/lands-end-lookout.html.

25. See "Legendary Route 66," Legends of America, http://www.legendsofamerica.com/66-main.html.

26. See "Visitor Statistics," Las Vegas Convention and Visitors Authority, http://www.lvcva.com/stats-and-facts/visitor-statistics.

27. See James Careless, "Hit, Stay, or Fold?" *Funworld*, October 2013, 42.

28. See "High Roller: It's Here and Revolving in Las Vegas!" *Park World*, May 2014, 22.

29. See Kenny Malone, "Sawgrass Mills Mall Draws Tourists to Florida," *Marketplace*, http://www.marketplace.org/topics/business/next-america/sawgrass-mills-mall-draws-tourists-florida.

30. See "Mall of America," Mall of America, www.mallofamerica.com.

31. See James Careless, "Go Big or Go Home," *Funworld*, October 2012, 78.

32. See "Marina Bay Sands Singapore," Marina Bay Sands Singapore, https://www.marinabaysands.com/index.html.

33. Cook, Hsu, Marqua, *Tourism: The Business of Hospitality and Travel, 5th ed.*, 222.

34. "Mall of America By the Numbers," Mall of America, http://www.mallofamerica.com/about/moa/facts.

35. Cook, Hsu, Marqua, Tourism: *The Business of Hospitality and Travel, 5th ed.*, 222.

36. "South Coast Plaza's Road to Success with Chinese Tourism," *AttractChina*, July 1, 2014, http://www.attractchina.com/blog/south-coast-plazas-road-success-chinese-tourism. See also Mary Ann Milbourn, "He Made South Coast Plaza a Tourist Beacon," *Orange County Register*, April 29, 2013, http://www.ocregister.com/articles/escher-506270-south-coast.html.

37. Cook, Hsu, Marqua, Tourism: *The Business of Hospitality and Travel, 5th ed.*, 222.

38. See "Welcome to Skyview," Skyview Atlanta, http://www.skyviewatlanta.com.

39. See "Ballpark Tours," Phillies, http://philadelphia.phillies.mlb.com/phi/ballpark/tours/index.jsp.

40. See, for example, "Ballparks of Baseball Roadtrip Guide," *ballparksofbaseball.com*, http://www.ballparksofbaseball.com/roadtrip.htm; and Alon Mass, "How to Plan a MLB Road Trip: 30 Parks, One Summer," *The Art of Manliness*, http://www.artofmanliness.com/2011/10/12/how-to-plan-a-mlb-road-trip.

# CHAPTER THREE

# Attraction Development

## Introduction

Although it may sound simplistic, the key to effective attraction promotion and marketing is to start with the well-planned creation and development of the attraction itself. A successful attraction depends on an innovative idea and ample resources to develop, construct, promote, and maintain it.

The right amount of research and planning can be instrumental in guiding the attraction development process. It can ensure the attraction is viable and designed to reach its intended audiences. Research can gauge customer interest and shed light on factors such as existing competition and industry trends. Planning can help with the process of attraction design, financing, management, and marketing, among other elements.

Attraction development covers a wide range of approaches, ranging from creating an attraction from the ground up to reconfiguring an existing attraction and making it seem like new. This chapter examines the factors that need to be taken into consideration when planning a successful attraction as well as the different approaches used to develop them.

## Formulating an Idea

At the core of a successful attraction is a good idea. This can be a brand new concept that is different from what competitors are offering. It might be a twist on an already existing attraction that gives it a fresh look and infuses it with an element of newness. A good idea provides a starting point for the design, implementation, and promotion of an attraction. It can generate enthusiasm among those working on the attraction's development as well as customers anticipating its completion.

There are many potential sources for attraction ideas. Popular culture trends based on movies or books have served as the basis for blockbuster attractions such as Universal Studios' Wizarding World of Harry Potter, for example. A niche interest in a particular topic has prompted the development of many specialty attractions, including the Route 66 Museum in Clinton, Okla., or New York City's Museum of Television and Radio. A commitment to animal conservation has spawned attractions such as the Lindsay Wildlife Museum in Walnut Creek, Calif., and Theater of the Sea in the Florida Keys.

The authors of *Strategic Management for Travel and Tourism* advise, "For most organizations, the most important source of new ideas will be the customers."[1] Soliciting feedback from customers through surveys or focus groups can generate ideas that are likely to have built-in appeal. "There will be a market for the products that result because they are specifically requested by the customers."[2]

*Figure 3.1: Attractions like the Titanic Museum in Branson, Mo., feature specialized collections that offer something unique for visitors.*
(Photo Credit: Andi Stein)

## Aligning with the Mission Statement

Once an idea for an attraction has been formulated, its development should be grounded in the company's mission statement. An organization's mission is its reason for existence. It characterizes what the company stands for and hopes to accomplish. The mission drives the decision-making process and serves as a focal point for growth and development[3]

Mission statements are used in both the for-profit and non-profit sectors. Nigel Evans, et al., observe, "Some organizations attempt to frame their mission in a formal statement, which is often to be seen adorning office walls, printed on employee identity cards and published in annual reports."[4]

A mission statement should communicate a company's intentions and philosophical approach and can help guide the attraction development process. An addition to an existing attraction, for example, should be designed to reflect the overarching goals outlined in the company's mission statement. If an attraction is a start-up, those at the helm of the organization should spend time crafting a mission statement that provides direction for the project.

A company's mission statement can be incorporated into its promotional and marketing materials. Language taken from the mission statement may be used in press releases issued to the media or referenced in advertising campaigns. The mission statement should also be instilled into employees as part of an organization's internal communications activities. This can be accomplished by incorporating a discussion of the organization's mission into an employee orientation or training program.

## Conducting a Feasibility Study

The next step in the attraction development process is to conduct a feasibility study. The purpose is to determine whether or not the attraction is viable and worth the time, effort, and expense of its construction and development. A feasibility study can also be considered an analysis of the internal and external factors that may influence an attraction's potential for success. It may be conducted by an organization's in-house staff or by outside consultants who specialize in this type of work.

According to author John Swarbrooke, there are advantages and disadvantages of both approaches. In-house staff already understand the purpose of the organization and the attraction. They may also be aware of the available resources that can be devoted to it. However, their eagerness to develop the attraction may cloud their ability to be objective when conducting the study. As Swarbrooke notes, "In some cases the study is designed to legitimize a decision that has already been taken, based on other factors such as the views of stakeholders."[5]

On the other hand, outside consultants may have specialized expertise based on their experiences conducting similar feasibility studies for other companies. They have the ability to be objective in their analysis and are likely to identify issues that may be missed by in-house staff. However, these same consultants may not be fully aware of the overall purpose of the organization or have a true understanding of the projected benefits of the proposed project. As a result, they may overlook more subtle factors that are likely to have a positive impact on the attraction's success.

In putting together a feasibility study, a number of factors should be examined to determine the viability of an attraction. These include finances, potential markets, competition, and industry trends.

## Finances

Having sufficient financial resources can be crucial to an attraction's success, particularly if the attraction is a start-up. "Money, or the lack of it, is central to the strategic development of all organizations, large or small. It is one of the key resource inputs and cannot be ignored," explain Evans et al. "The most original strategies and the most complex plans for the future of a business are meaningless unless management has considered the financial position of the organization at the outset."[6] The costs of building, maintaining, staffing, and promoting the attraction all need to be taken into consideration during the development process.

Museums and galleries, for example, need sufficient capital to establish and maintain collections that will appeal to potential audiences. Theme parks need enough funds to add new rides at regular intervals in order to stay competitive and generate repeat business. Natural sites like beaches and parks may require financial resources that can be used for recovery purposes in the event of a crisis precipitated by an act of nature, such as a hurricane, earthquake, or tornado.

Start-up attractions in particular are especially vulnerable when it comes to having sufficient funding. According to the Small Business Administration, "About half of all new establishments survive five years or more and about one-third survive 10 years or more."[7] A number of these businesses don't make it because they are underfunded. Swarbrooke cautions, "Attraction operators need substantial financial resources to allow them to support the attraction in its early years, when it may be losing money, before becoming profitable."[8]

Resources also need to be allocated for the marketing and promotion of an attraction. The best attraction on the planet can go belly up if nobody knows about it. Having enough money set aside for the promotion of an attraction can have a significant impact on how the public perceives and responds to it.

## Markets

A feasibility study can help identify what the potential markets are likely to be for a new or enhanced attraction. These markets may be multi-dimensional. One area of the market consists of the customer base, those who are likely to patronize the attraction. Depending on the nature of the attraction, this customer base may be primarily local in nature or could expand to a national and/or international audience. Different segments of the customer base may be influenced by different aspects of an attraction—entertainment value, cost, location, overall quality of the experience, etc.

Another type of market is what's known as the resource market. This encompasses the external groups that provide materials and services to an attraction. These resources might include suppliers, laborers, and distributors, among others. A theme park that sells different types of fast food, for example, needs to be sure there are adequate suppliers to provide enough variety of these foods to satisfy customers. A limited number of suppliers of a particular product can mean higher prices for the attraction and its customers.[9]

If there are a number of similar facilities in the area, and all are relying on the same external vendors to keep their businesses running, the competition for these resources can be fierce—and sometimes costly. If a ride at an amusement park breaks down, for example, and there are only a handful of sources nearby where the parts needed to fix it can be obtained, the wait time to fix it may be extensive. This can result in increased costs and angry, frustrated customers.

Human resources fall under the umbrella of this market segment as well. Some attractions such as national parks and theme parks typically rely on high school and college students as sources of inexpensive labor. For seasonal attractions this works out well, as students become available to work at the start of the season and are ready to return to school as the season is ending. In warm-weather areas where attractions can stay open year-round, the availability of personnel can be more challenging as the students who are free to work in the summer may have more limited time the rest of the year.

## Competition

Another factor that can be determined in a feasibility study and that can influence the decision to launch or develop an attraction is the nature of the competition. This includes other businesses providing similar or identical products or services. It can also include businesses offering different products and services but drawing from the same pool of customers.[10]

One challenge of opening a business where others like it already exist is trying to get potential customers to give up their existing brand loyalty to the competition. To gain a foothold, a new attraction needs to offer something of added value to consumers to convince them to consider shifting their loyalties to the new attraction. Discounts, promotions, and kick-off events can all help build awareness and generate potential customers.

Sometimes a little competition can be good for business. Orlando, Fla., is known for its multitude of attractions. With the Walt Disney World Resort as its anchor, the area is filled with everything from theme parks such as Universal Studios and Legoland to smaller, niche attractions such as the WonderWorks museum and Gatorland animal park.

Although Disney may be the big draw for many visitors who make the pilgrimage to Orlando, nearby attractions offer alternatives for those who come for a longer stay and want a change of pace. In this case, some of the smaller, more unique attractions can offer visitors something completely different from the larger ones, rather than competing with these mega-attractions outright.

## Industry Trends

An evaluation of industry trends should also be included in a feasibility study. Swarbrooke explains that trends have the potential to influence consumer interest, which in turn can dictate the direction of an attraction's offerings.

"In recent years there have been dramatic changes in culture and consumer behaviour which are influencing attractions," he says. "For example, the interest in healthy eating has made attractions rethink what they offer in terms of catering, while many…have been keen to be seen to be responding to the growing concern with green issues."[11] An analysis of industry trends may also indicate whether they are on the upswing or the decline. This could influence the potential for the viability of an attraction based on the likelihood of sustaining long-term customer interest.

## Developing an Attraction

Once a green light has been given to go forward with an attraction, decisions need to be made about a variety of elements that will contribute to its success. Among these are attraction design and construction, management, and marketing and promotion.

### Design and Construction

The design of an attraction can influence how the public perceives it, which in turn can impact ticket sales. An attraction with an unusual or aesthetically pleasing design may draw attention because of its striking nature. A design that invites or encourages participation or interaction is more likely to appeal to visitors than one that appears foreboding or intimidating.

An attraction's design includes its external appearance, layout, accessibility, and strategic placement of features such as shops, restaurants, and parking lots. When constructing the attraction, safety also needs to be taken into account. It's essential to ensure there is nothing inherent in the attraction that could potentially cause harm to customers such as shoddily constructed rides or potentially hazardous construction materials.

---

### *Attraction Fun Fact*
The first Las Vegas casino/hotel was the Golden Gate Hotel and Casino, opened in 1906.

---

### Management

Management involves the overall, day-to-day operations of an attraction. Roy Cook et al. characterize management as "a unified approach to planning, organizing, directing, and controlling present and future actions to accomplish organizational goals."[12] On a day-to-day level, management responsibilities involve overseeing a variety of tasks. These include recruitment and training, facility maintenance, construction, customer service, promotion and marketing, staff scheduling, and retail operations, to name just a few.

Typically, one person is appointed as an attraction's CEO or director and is charged with general management of the entire facility. Reporting to this individual will be multiple managers who are responsible for different areas within the organization, such as operations, finance, human resources, marketing and promotion, food services, etc. In developing attractions, careful thought should be put into how these areas will be structured and staffed.

### Marketing and Promotion

According to Swarbrooke, "Perhaps the most crucial aspect of attraction management, and often one of the most ignored, is marketing. Successful attractions are usually those which have a systematic, professional approach to marketing."[13]

Marketing and promotion activities for attractions include developing advertising campaigns, working with media, engaging customers through social media platforms, and developing customer service and employee relations programs. Subsequent chapters in this book will address all of these topics in depth and explore the roles they play in the successful development and operations of attractions.

## Approaches to Attraction Development

There are several different approaches to take when developing a successful attraction, and each has its own set of challenges. Options include developing a new attraction from the ground up; reconfiguring an existing attraction; adding to an existing attraction; turning the unlikely into an attraction; and installing a new attraction on the site of an old one.

### Top 20 Museums Worldwide

1. Louvre, Paris, France
2. National Museum of Natural History, Washington, D.C.
3. National Museum of China, Beijing, China
4. National Air and Space Museum, Washington, D.C.
5. British Museum, London, England
6. Metropolitan Museum of Art, New York, NY
7. National Gallery, London, England
8. Vatican Museum, Vatican, Italy
9. Natural History Museum, London, England
10. American Museum of Natural History, New York, NY
11. National Museum of American History, Washington, D.C.
12. Tate Modern, London, England
13. National Palace Museum, Taipei, Taiwan
14. National Gallery of Art, Washington, D.C.
15. Centre Pompidou, Paris, France
16. Shanghai Science & Technology Museum, Shanghai, China
17. Musee D'Orsay, Paris, France
18. National Museum of Natural Science, Taichung, Taiwan
19. Science Museum, London, England
20. Victoria and Albert Museum, London, England

2013 Data
Source: AECOM 2013 Museum Index, Themed Entertainment Association

## Developing a New Attraction

Developing a new attraction from scratch requires a solid idea, good business plan, substantial bankroll, and well-planned marketing campaign. Some new attractions begin with the acquisition of a collection or a piece of property. This was the case with the house where Walt Disney was born. For many years the birthplace of Walt Disney was simply a private residence in a Chicago suburb until a couple with a background in attraction development purchased the property. In 2013, the duo announced plans to turn the house into a museum called the Walt Disney Birthplace.

The new owners unveiled a Kickstarter website campaign to raise funds for the project. As a means of raising awareness of their endeavors, they formally announced their plans to the press, which generated publicity in *The New York Times* and other media outlets nationwide.[14] The results of the publicity efforts provided the momentum needed to begin remodeling the facility and turn it into an attraction.

Some start-up attractions may be mired in the development stages for years before they are finally brought to life. The Neon Museum in Las Vegas officially opened to much fanfare in 2012. However, the idea for it was conceived 16 years earlier in 1996. What started with some leftover relics of neon signs from defunct Las Vegas casinos grew into a lot called The Boneyard filled with pieces of the past.

The process of turning the collection into an actual museum began with occasional guided tours of the lot. A fundraising campaign allowed for the restoration and placement of some of the collection's neon signs in downtown Las Vegas. Finally, in 2012, enough funds had been raised to open a formal visitors center for the collection, according to reporter Edward Rothstein, "providing a small store, display screens surveying Las Vegas history, and a place where visitors could meet guides for a 45-minute tour."[15]

Sometimes a new attraction can go far beyond the hopes and dreams of its creators. Graceland in Memphis, Tenn., is the former home of rock and roll legend Elvis Presley. After his death in 1977, his wife Priscilla transformed the home into a tourist attraction with an investment of $500,000. Before Graceland opened to the public in 1982, many who worked on the project predicted the attraction would have a limited lifespan, according to reporter Michael Lollar. They expected it to draw a crowd for a few years until the memory of Elvis had faded away.

More than 30 years later, Graceland is still going strong, attracting around 600,000 visitors a year and bringing in $21.6 million in annual ticket sales. According to Lollar, after the White House, it is the second most visited house in the United States. Visitors come to Graceland to tour Elvis's house, airplane, tour bus, and gravesite, which all lie on the attraction's property.[16]

## Reconfiguring an Existing Attraction

Another dimension of attraction development is to reconfigure, remodel, or rebrand an existing attraction in order to increase the value and public appeal of a tourism venue. This helps draw in new customers and, in the case of local and regional attractions, offers more options for regular patrons.

The Exploratorium science museum in San Francisco achieved both these goals when it relocated and expanded its facility. Originally situated at the Palace of Fine Arts near the Golden Gate Bridge, the museum was considered one of San Francisco's "hidden gems." Known for its hands-on, interactive exhibits and popular with local residents, the museum was off the beaten track from the heart of San Francisco's tourist district and restricted by limited space for growth.

A $300 million capital campaign and a new site on the Embarcadero in downtown San Francisco resulted in a facility that was much more centrally located and able to accommodate three times as many visitors. As reporter Jeremy Schoolfield notes, "The Exploratorium's big move across the city provided an opportunity to re-imagine not only its exhibit floor but its retail and dining facilities as well."[17]

Sometimes an attraction's remodel may be prompted by an unexpected crisis or event that forces the process. The devastation caused by 2012's Hurricane Sandy—also known as Superstorm Sandy—led to a number of changes to the amusement parks and piers dotting the New Jersey shoreline. One of the most haunting pictures from the storm was the image of the battered Jet Star Roller Coaster, partially submerged in ocean water. In the recovery and rebuilding effort from the Jersey store devastation, the owners of the Casino Pier park opted to create a new thrill ride to replace the Jet Star, which they aptly named the Super Storm. The ride opened in 2013, one year after Sandy.[18]

### Adding to an Existing Attraction

Adding features or services for visitors that build on existing strengths can sometimes enhance attractions. This can be accomplished by creating new features or exhibits, adding programs, expanding operating hours, etc.

The practice of adding on to an existing attraction to expand options for visitors has been increasingly evident in recent years in an unlikely segment of the attractions market—skyscrapers. For many years, high-rise buildings like the Empire State Building in New York City and the CN Tower in Toronto have been known for their spectacular views. These attractions have brought in those wanting to have a bird's eye view of the building's surroundings.

### Attraction Fun Fact
The Empire State Building has its own zip code: 10118.

In recent years, however, more and more of these municipal towers have begun adding attractions that go beyond the "magnificent view" experience. As reporter James Careless explains, "Great towers are all about great views. But smart tower managers know that other features matter, both for initially attracting visitors and then motivating them to come back."[19]

A remodel of the Empire State Building included the addition of an exhibit called "Dare to Dream," which depicts the story of the iconic landmark's construction and a restoration of the building's art deco lobby. One of the more popular attractions in Macau is the AJ Hackett Macau Tower, which now offers visitors the opportunity to try a 764-foot bungee jump from the tower's top. All of these efforts provide added value to existing attractions and expand their options for visitors.[20]

Educational attractions like zoos, aquariums, and museums are prime candidates for adding features to their existing repertoire of offerings. Zoos in particular are popular tourism attractions that can benefit from enhancements designed to encourage repeat business or offer unique experiences to visitors.

According to the Association of Zoos & Aquariums (AZA), more than 150 million people visit zoos each year.[21] While many of these visitors are families with children, zoos can reach out to those without children by creating experiences that give them an opportunity to go behind the scenes and learn about the inner-workings of a zoo. As an article in *Funworld* suggests, "Adding value to the experience will not only increase the appeal to adults with no children, it may also increase the appeal to those attractions visitors that currently are not visiting zoos at all."[22]

Some zoos have created backstage tours that enable visitors to interact with their animals. The Adelaide Zoo in Australia, for example, offers guests the opportunity to feed its two giant pandas as part of a VIP behind-the-scenes tour.[23]

Aquariums have also started incorporating programs that provide added value for customers. Florida Aquarium's "Dive with the Sharks" and Georgia Aquarium's "Journey with Gentle Giants" programs allow visitors who are certified scuba divers to swim with sharks and other marine life for a fee. Florida Aquarium also offers a companion program called "Swim with the Fishes" to non-certified divers who can snorkel in the aquarium's Coral Reef Gallery instead. The aquariums recruit participants by marketing their programs to local dive shops and clubs that have appropriate built-in audiences.[24]

## Turning the Unlikely or Unusual into an Attraction

With a bit of imagination and a good marketing plan, a creative idea can turn the unlikely or unusual into a successful attraction. Something that seems out of the ordinary can be just enough to pique visitor interest and bring in business.

Entrepreneur Colin Au transformed an airship hangar in Brandenburg, Germany into a water park called Tropical Islands. His successor, Ole Bested Hensig, added hotel rooms and developed the attraction into a resort featuring saunas, spas, and restaurants, as well as an indoor beach, rainforest, and campsite. As a business that operates year-round, the facility is marketed as a vacation destination to patrons outside Germany in places like Scandinavia, the United Kingdom, and Central Europe. The attraction draws up to 1.2 million visitors a year.[25]

## Replacing an Old Attraction with a New One

Although less typical, occasionally a new tourism venue can rise from the ashes of an old, outdated, or defunct attraction. A benefit of this approach is that existing infrastructure can be used as a blueprint to help guide development of the new attraction.

In 2011, Merlin Entertainment Group opened a Legoland theme park on the site of the former Cypress Gardens park in Winter Haven, Fla. Cypress Gardens was built in 1936, and in its heyday was one of the most popular attractions in Florida. Known for its beautiful gardens and water ski shows, it entertained generations of visitors before finally closing in 2008. According to Schoolfield, in transforming the site of the old Cypress Gardens into Legoland Florida:

> Merlin's crew rebuilt the park from the underground up, replacing or refurbishing much of the infrastructure. From the biggest tasks like upgrading sewer and power lines, to the smallest details of installing new pavers along the midways and painting everything in the bold Lego colors, Legoland Florida feels like an entirely new park.[26]

In creating a new attraction on the site of the old Cypress Gardens, however, designers were able to maintain a number of features that pay tribute to the original park. Regular water shows are held on the park's Lake Eloise, hearkening back to the water ski shows for which Cypress Gardens was once famous. The Cypress Gardens botanical park lies within Legoland Florida and contains an array of flowers and trees reminiscent of the original park. Schoolfield notes, "Perhaps the most appropriate nod of them all is a Lego-ized Southern Belle who reclines in the sunshine out in the gardens, a nod to the friendly greeters who used to roam the midways of this beloved Florida park."[27]

## Partnering for Successful Promotion

Regardless of the venue, an essential element for developing a successful attraction lies in knowing how to position it in the marketplace. One way to accomplish this is to partner with organizations that can help with promotion to create an awareness of the attraction. These might include local convention and visitor bureaus (CVBs), tourism boards, trade associations, and even nearby attractions.

Convention and visitor bureaus are in business to promote the regions they represent in order to encourage people to visit them. They reach out to external markets by emphasizing the reasons potential travelers should consider their regions as vacation destinations. In doing so, these organizations promote the resources and highlights of their regions—hotels, restaurants, retail venues, and local attractions.

In an article by Keith Miller, Maura Gest, executive director of Irving Conventions and Visitors Bureau in Irving, Tex., identified several ways attractions can make use of CVBs as part of their own promotional efforts. "Make us aware of some of the issues that affect you," she said. "If you're thinking about an expansion or a new ride, get us in on it, but give us time to do promotions."[28]

Trade associations are another resource for promotional opportunities. The International Association of Amusement Parks and Attractions (IAAPA) hosts an annual expo for the attractions industry each November, which brings in more than 25,000 attendees and more than 200 media representatives. As part of this expo, exhibitors are invited to schedule press conferences to unveil new exhibits or announce new attraction developments. As IAAPA media relations assistant Scott Cahoon explains, "IAAPA Attractions Expo is the largest annual gathering of attractions industry trade press and has the potential to expose exhibitors to media they may not reach otherwise."[29]

Attractions in the same locale may find value in forming their own associations. The Hong Kong Association of Amusement Parks and Attractions was established in 2012 to promote visitor attractions in Hong Kong. Members include theme parks such as Ocean Park and Hong Kong Disneyland, as well as standalone sites like the Peak Tram, Ngong Ping 360 cable car, and the Sky 100 observation tower. According to reporter Doug Meigs, founding members created the association as a means of promoting their individual businesses through a group effort.[30]

Partnering with other attractions can also be a good resource for promotion. A partnership between Ripley Entertainment, Inc., and the Science North museum in Ontario, Canada, led to the creation of a traveling exhibit called "The Science of Ripley's Believe It or Not." Reporter Sarah Wendorf called it "an adventure through the remarkable realms of scientific discoveries and genuine Ripley's artifacts."[31] The exhibit debuted in 2013 and was so successful for Ripley's that the organization took the show on the road, displaying it at multiple North American venues.

## Attraction Associations

American Alliance of Museums
http://www.aam-us.org

American Gaming Association
http://www.americangaming.org

American Public Gardens Association
http://www.publicgardens.org

Association of Academic Museums & Galleries
http://www.aamg-us.org/index.php

Association of Science-Technology Centers
http://www.astc.org/index.htm

Association of Tourist Railroads & Railway Museums
http://www.atrrm.org

Association of Zoos & Aquariums
https://www.aza.org

California Attractions and Parks Association
http://www.capalink.org

Event Planners Association
http://www.eventplannersassociation.com

Florida Attractions Association
http://www.floridaattractions.org

International Association of Amusement Parks and Attractions
http://www.iaapa.org

International Association of Fairs & Expositions
https://www.fairsandexpos.com/eweb/startpage.aspx

International Council of Museums
http://icom.museum

International Festivals & Events Association
http://www.floridaattractions.org

International Society of Travel and Tourism Educators
http://www.istte.org

International Zoo Educators Association
http://www.izea.net

National Amusement Park Historical Association
http://www.napha.org

National Association of Sports Commissions
https://www.sportscommissions.org

National Indian Gaming Association
http://www.indiangaming.org

National Park Service
http://www.nps.gov/index.htm

National Recreation and Park Association
http://www.nrpa.org

National Trust for Historic Preservation
http://www.preservationnation.org

New England Association of Amusement Parks and Attractions
http://www.neaapa.com

New Jersey Amusement Association
http://www.njamusements.com

Outdoor Amusement Business Association
http://www.oaba.org

Pennsylvania Amusement Parks Association
http://www.paamusementparks.com

Themed Entertainment Association
http://www.teaconnect.org

World Association of Zoos and Aquariums
http://www.waza.org/en/site/home

World Waterpark Association
http://www.waterparks.org

Zoological Association of America
http://zaa.org

## Conclusion

The first step in attraction promotion and marketing is to develop a tourism attraction that will appeal to customers and inspire them to want to see it first-hand. This involves coming up with an innovative idea and putting into place the resources needed to bring it to life. A feasibility study can help determine the extent of these resources. It can also be used to assess circumstances that could potentially affect the attraction, such as competition and industry trends.

Once an attraction has been given the go-ahead, the development phase begins. This includes design, construction, management, marketing, and promotion. Attraction development can encompass designing a new facility from the ground up. It might involve reconfiguring or expanding an existing attraction or even replacing an old attraction with a new one.

Partnering with other attractions or drawing on the resources of industry trade associations can help get the word out about an attraction. This sets the stage for the fine-tuning of the facility's promotional activities. The next chapter will provide an overview of these activities, with an emphasis on advertising and marketing.

## Notes

1. Nigel Evans, David Campbell, and George Stonehouse, *Strategic Management for Travel and Tourism* (Oxford, England: Butterworth Heinemann, 2003), 141.
2. Ibid.
3. See Deborah J. Barrett, *Leadership Communication* (Boston, MA: McGraw Hill/Irwin, 2006), 276.
4. Evans, Campbell, and Stonehouse, *Strategic Management for Travel and Tourism*, 15.
5. John Swarbrooke, *The Development and Management of Visitor Attractions, 2nd ed.* (Burlington, MA: Elsevier Butterworth-Heinemann, 2005), 124.
6. Evans, Campbell, and Stonehouse, *Strategic Management for Travel and Tourism*, 91.
7. "Frequently Asked Questions About Small Business," Small Business Administration, September 2012, 3.
8. Swarbrooke, *The Development and Management of Visitor Attractions, 2nd ed.*, 135.
9. See Evans, Campbell, and Stonehouse, *Strategic Management for Travel and Tourism*, 120.
10. Ibid., 173.
11. Swarbrooke, *The Development and Management of Visitor Attractions, 2nd ed.*, 107.
12. Roy A. Cook, Cathy H.C. Hsu, and Joseph J. Marqua, *Tourism: The Business of Hospitality and Travel* (Boston, MA: Pearson, 2014), 24.
13. Swarbrooke, *The Development and Management of Visitor Attractions, 2nd ed.*, 139.
14. See Brooks Barnes, "A Chance to Step into Disney's Childhood," *The New York Times*, December 3, 2013, C3.
15. Edward Rothstein, "A Monument to Star-dusted Las Vegas," *Honolulu Star-Advertiser*, February 2, 2013.
16. See Michael Lollar, "Still a Hot Ticket: Elvis' Drawing Power Proves a Safe Bet at Graceland," *McClatchy-Tribune Business News*, January 5, 2012.
17. Jeremy Schoolfield, "Exploratorium Metamorphosis," *Funworld*, January 2014, 37.
18. See Jennifer Weiss, "Ups, Downs for a Ride," *Wall Street Journal*, May 15, 2013, A17.
19. James Careless, "Come for the View, Stay for the Fun," *Funworld*, March 2013, 42.
20. Ibid.
21. See "Association of Zoos & Aquariums," Association of Zoos & Aquariums, http://www.aza.org.
22. PGAV Destinations, "Study: What All Attractions Can Learn from Zoogoers," *Funworld*, March 2012, 64.
23. See John Morell, "Wet & Wild," *Funworld*, November 2013, 187.
24. Ibid.
25. See Juliana Gilling, "Everything Under the Dome," *Funworld*, January 2013, 46.

26. Jeremy Schoolfield, "New Kid on the Block," *Funworld*, January 2012, 20.
27. Ibid., 23.
28. Maura Gest quoted in Keith Miller, "Mutually Beneficial," *Funworld*, May 2012, 61.
29. Scott Cahoon, "New Attractions Stand Out via Press Conferences at IAAPA Attractions Expo," *Funworld*, June 2013, 53.
30. See Doug Meigs, "Critical Mass: Hong Kong Attractions Join Forces to Create Association," *Funworld*, May 2012, 73.
31. Sarah Wendorf, "You Can Believe This," *Funworld*, November 2012, 145.

# CHAPTER FOUR

# Promotion, Advertising, and Marketing

## Introduction

Once the components of an attraction have been put into place, the process of promoting and marketing it begins. The primary role of promotion and marketing is to create awareness and stimulate interest in an attraction. This in turn can build anticipation and excitement on the part of consumers. Ultimately, this will lead them to take action and see what the attraction is all about.

The Communications Mix

Sales Promotions

Marketing

Merchandising

Advertising

Special Events

Public Relations

Communications Mix

Social Media

While the long-term goal of promotion and marketing may be to bring individuals into an attraction, the process of reaching these customers may involve other public groups as well. These include travel agents, tour operators, meeting planners, and members of the media who can help promote an attraction by telling others about it.

A number of promotional tactics can be used to generate interest in an attraction. Marketers often refer to them as the "communications mix."[1] They include advertising and marketing, public relations and publicity, and sales promotion and merchandising.

This chapter offers general information on developing effective promotional materials for attractions, with an emphasis on advertising and marketing. Subsequent chapters will address media relations, social media marketing, sales promotion and merchandising, and special events.

## Effective Promotional Materials

Regardless of the type of promotional materials used, there are certain steps to take to ensure they will reach their mark and generate positive results. These include setting clear objectives, developing a realistic budget, defining a target audience, preparing a focused message, choosing an appropriate medium, and timing material delivery.

### Set Objectives

The first step in the process is to develop clear objectives by determining the purpose of the promotional materials. Are they meant to bring in new business? Reach out to existing customers? Highlight an upcoming program or event? Promote a new attraction? As Terence Shimp explains, "Objectives provide the foundation for all remaining decisions."[2] Once objectives have been set, steps can be taken to determine the kinds of promotional materials to be used as well as what they should say and how they should look.

### Develop a Realistic Budget

When it comes to meeting an attraction's promotional objectives, the creative possibilities are limitless. No matter how grandiose the ideas may be, however, just as with attraction development, the bottom line can be a harsh reality check. Therefore, it's necessary to set a realistic budget for promotion before getting started with the creation of materials.

Authors Victor Middleton, et al. recommend:

> Experience suggests that allocating around 10% of admissions revenue for marketing purposes is a realistic guideline for most visitor attractions. There may well be a convincing argument for spending more than this, however, especially to promote awareness of new facilities and on seasonal sales promotion efforts if the evidence achieved through visitor research indicates that the promotional efforts are paying off in admission revenue.[3]

For nonprofit organizations such as museums and zoos, a realistic budget might be much less than 10%. A great deal will depend on the size of the attraction, existing donor base, available government grants, and potential fundraising activities planned to supplement the available spending of the organization.

## Define a Target Audience

The approach used in the promotional materials should be influenced by the audience for whom they are intended. Rather than creating generic materials and hoping they will appeal to a broad audience, a better strategy is to first identify the audience and tailor the materials to fit their needs. The target market for an attraction's promotional materials may be determined by age, geographic location, lifestyle, and expected length of stay, among other factors.

In some cases it may be apparent that a general approach is appropriate, depending on the nature of what is being promoted. However, in other instances, more concentrated target marketing may be needed to focus on a particular segment of an attraction's audience.

## Prepare an Effective Message

Developing an effective message involves formulating an idea and crafting it in a way that is readily communicated to the target audience. The message should be clear, concise, and easy to remember. From a creativity standpoint, different writing approaches can be incorporated into the message such as testimonials, slogans, analogies, humor, and plays on words. The more creative the message, the more likely the audience will be able to remember it.

Marketers for Colonial Williamsburg, a popular heritage attraction known for its historical reenactments, took a creative approach when they launched a pair of commercials called "Family Vacation" and "Romantic Vacation." One of the ads featured a woman having lunch with a friend and enthusiastically recounting her recent trip to Williamsburg.

"There were fights breaking out in the streets, angry mobs...the whole place was like a war zone," she says. As for the kids, she tells her friend, "We shackled them to a post in the middle of town. I don't know what they loved more—the shackling or the pool."[4] The ads used humor to show the "depth and breadth of the Colonial Williamsburg experience," according to a spokesperson for the Greater Williamsburg Chamber & Tourism Alliance.[5]

## Select an Appropriate Medium

Once the message has been crafted, an appropriate medium needs to be chosen to communicate it. Some messages may be best communicated briefly, as in the few lines of an advertisement, for instance. Other messages might be more appropriate for a longer, more in-depth piece like a brochure.

The selection of the medium will also have an impact on how much formatting and design effort is required to communicate the message. An attraction's website, for example, will make heavy use of design elements and images, whereas a press release used to promote something to the media will rely primarily on words.

## Consider Timing and Delivery

As the old saying goes, timing is everything. When developing promotional tools for an attraction, it's essential to ensure they are released to the public when they're likely to have the most impact. When preparing advertisements, for example, an important element of timing should include the development of a schedule for when to run ads. An organization may want to advertise at certain times of the year, for example, or in tandem with attraction events.

A schedule can also help when determining delivery dates for promotional pieces. When preparing marketing collateral materials such as brochures, for instance, it's necessary to build in sufficient preparation and production time. These materials may need to be scheduled far in advance of the date they are wanted to allow for on-time delivery. Regardless of the type of promotional tool used, putting some thought into the timing and delivery of its preparation and distribution can increase the chances of having it hit its mark and maximize public response.

## Role of Advertising

Advertising is one form of promotion within the communications mix that attractions can use to generate business. Its purpose is to "to inform, create awareness, attempt to persuade, and reinforce the buying behavior of present customers," according to Stowe Shoemaker et al.[6] In the attractions industry, it also serves as a way of bringing in new business by drawing the attention of potential customers.

As a promotional tool, advertising has advantages that make it a good investment for an attraction. It has the ability to reach a broad audience of prospective customers and communicate a consistent message. "Frequency is another advantage," says author G.P. Raju, as messages can be repeated often to increase their chances of being absorbed by consumers.[7]

Advertising can also be targeted to reach specific audiences, which works well in the attractions industry. John Swarbrooke explains, "As most attractions are not mass-market products, but rather are niche-market products, there is usually no need to utilize the expensive mass-market media. Highly targeted advertising strategies are usually more relevant."[8]

Strategies might include targeting customers in a particular market or geographic area, or advertising at a certain time of the year when the ads are likely to have a greater impact on an audience. An amusement park open only during summer months, for example, might launch a series of ads in late winter/early spring to promote new rides and get people excited about the upcoming season.

While there are many benefits to advertising, there are also downsides. One of the biggest deterrents, especially for smaller attractions, can be cost. Unlike publicity, which can be relatively inexpensive by comparison, advertising can eat up a large chunk of an attraction's promotional budget in order to have the desired reach. For some smaller attractions, these costs may be prohibitive. As a result, notes Swarbrooke, "advertising decisions are usually a trade-off between the available budget and what managers would ideally like to do."[9]

Another disadvantage is the information overload factor. According to Shoemaker, et al.:

> The consumer today is constantly bombarded with advertising messages from all directions (over 400 different messages each day by some estimates). The human mind is not capable of paying attention to all these messages. Instead, the mind will selectively perceive, attend to, comprehend, accept, and retain those to which it is most responsive. What the mind is most responsive to is those features, experiences, needs, and wants that solve a problem or fulfill a need or desire.[10]

If an attraction makes the decision to spend money on advertising, it is well worth the effort to put careful thought into what, where, and when to advertise in order to have the greatest impact on the audience.

---

### *Attraction Fun Fact*
Billboards promoting South Dakota roadside attraction Wall Drug adorn 300+ miles of I-90.

---

## Types of Advertisements

The advertising options for attractions are extensive and encompass a wide variety of media. Choosing the appropriate medium may depend on the message to be communicated and the target audience the attraction wants to reach. Here is a sampling of the possibilities.

### *Print Advertisements*

Newspapers, magazines, specialized directories, and trade publications are all examples of potential print ad sources. Even with the impact of online media on print readership in the last two decades, print publications are still a good bet when it comes to advertising reach. Newspapers, for example, have the ability to reach a mass market and can be good sources for general ads designed to appeal to a broad audience. They require only short lead times for ad placement and can be segmented by geographic markets.

Magazines can also be a good option for print advertising when trying to reach a wide-ranging audience, as some may have far-flung reach while others may be highly specialized and appeal to niche markets. As Alastair Morrison notes, "Magazines run the gamut from major national consumer publications such as *National Geographic*…to specialized travel trade intermediary periodicals such as *Travel Weekly* and *Travel Trade*."[11] Magazines generally have a greater shelf life and pass-along rate than newspapers. However, they also have longer lead times than newspapers, so more planning is needed when placing ads in these publications.

Other sources for print advertisements include specialized directories, industry trade publications, and auto club directories, among others. These publications are useful for reaching meeting planners, tour operators, travel agents, and others who work with groups of potential travelers.

### *Broadcast Advertisements*

Television and radio fall under the umbrella of broadcast media. Both have the ability to reach thousands of potential viewers and listeners. They offer attractions flexibility in the types of advertising packages that can be put together for them. Television is regarded as the most widespread option for advertisers. According to Morrison, "Television commercials can be highly persuasive because of their ability to employ all the creative formats and to make full use of emotions and humor to get viewers' attention and give added mood."[12]

Attractions with far-reaching audiences—casinos, large-scale theme parks, or iconic attractions, for example—may choose to advertise with national network or cable stations. Network affiliate stations reaching customers within a smaller service area may better serve attractions that cater primarily to local audiences. Although television advertising has many benefits, cost can be a determining factor in the decision to advertise on TV. Fees for both television commercial production and placement can be well beyond the advertising budgets of many attractions.

Radio, on the other hand, may be a more reasonable alternative. Radio advertising can be geared toward specific listening audiences by placing commercials or "spots" on stations with particular program formats. Attractions can pay to have their spots air at designated times in between programs. They can also sign on as sponsors of specific programs to foster name and brand recognition. Radio ads are generally more affordable than television ads. Like newspapers, they often have short lead times for ad placement.

## Outdoor Advertisements

An alternative to traditional print and broadcast advertising is the use of outdoor advertising sites. A typical example of an outdoor site is a billboard placed in the vicinity of an attraction or on a roadway leading to the attraction. More creative forms of outdoor advertising sites include transit shelters and stations, stadiums, shopping centers, and even modes of transport such as buses or taxis.

The country of Ecuador used outdoor advertising when it launched its "I Discovered" campaign in Washington, D.C., in 2013. City buses were wrapped with ads promoting some of the country's features such as the Galapagos Islands, Andes Mountains, and Amazon rainforest. The purpose was to promote consumer awareness of what the country had to offer U.S. visitors.[13]

*Figure 4.1: Buses and transit shelters offer promotional opportunities that are alternatives to traditional print and broadcast advertisements.*
(Photo Credit: Andi Stein)

The attention-grabbing novelty factor of outdoor advertising can help promote the reach of the ads. Outdoor advertising will also have a longer exposure time. A billboard ad, for instance, is likely to remain in place for several months, whereas an ad in a daily newspaper will offer one-day exposure.

## Online Advertisements

Although the medium has not yet been perfected, more and more companies have begun advertising online since that is where their customers are likely to be. Online ads continue to evolve, as marketers test out different formats to see what resonates with users and translates into results. The effectiveness of online advertising is determined by what's called a "click-through rate," when a user clicks on an advertisement and is taken to the advertiser's website.

A variety of formats are used in online advertising. Banner advertisements are static ads that appear on a website, usually along the side or at the top of a page. Pop-up ads do just as their name suggests—pop up suddenly while a web page is loading. Video ads are short videos that appear onscreen when a web page opens. In some cases, users aren't able to access the page without first viewing the video.

Another form of online advertising is paid search advertising. "Advertisers pay to have their ads displayed to users as they type queries into search engines. The ads usually appear as links in the search engine results pages."[14]

Compared to other forms of advertising, studies have shown that online advertisements lack the punch of more traditional media ads, largely because they "greatly annoy Internet users," says Shimp.[15] However, because of high customer reliance on technology, as this form of advertising continues to develop, attractions may eventually find it to be a worthwhile investment.

# Approaches to Advertising

Advertisements for tourism attractions may be packaged as part of an overall campaign, consisting of different components focused on a central theme and designed to work together to communicate this theme. In 2012, Atlantic City developed a marketing campaign called, "Do Anything. Do Everything. Do AC." The campaign emphasized the highlights of the seaside resort through a series of TV, print, radio, and online ads.

A year later, Atlantic City repeated the campaign but added several components to it, including a social media presence on Pinterest and Foursquare and a series of videos on YouTube. The second year the campaign also showcased Atlantic City's gaming industry as part of the ad mix, which had not been included the previous year.[16]

In anticipation of the 2014 World Cup, Brazil launched a worldwide marketing campaign a month before the event, which was intended to reach 1.3 billion people through ads on television, video billboards, and social networks in 113 countries. The president of Brazil's ministry of tourism explained the motivation behind the campaign:

> The hospitality of our country invites tourists from all continents to visit us. We prepared in a special way, knowing that Brazil will be the setting of the biggest sporting event, with an expected 600,000 international visitors in our country and more than 26.3 million viewers across the world. This new campaign aims to show a small preview of what Brazil has to offer.[17]

---

### *Attraction Fun Fact*

California's Hollywood sign was originally a real estate billboard
promoting "Hollywoodland."

---

## Internet Marketing Tools

In addition to online advertising, the Internet provides a host of marketing opportunities to reach existing and potential customers. Following are some online resources for attractions to consider when planning their marketing efforts.

### *Websites*

Today an attraction's website is likely to be its ultimate marketing tool, as many consumers start there when looking for basic information about an attraction. A website should be attractive, easy to navigate, and updated on a regular basis, so the material on it is always current.

The home page of an attraction's website can contain information about timely developments such as the opening of a new ride or exhibit. It might include teasers about upcoming special programs or events with clickable links to screens with more details. For families with small children, interactive games are good website draws.

The home page should also offer clear indications for where on the site to find details about opening hours, admission costs, and directions, as well as easily accessible contact information for the attraction, including an address and phone number.

According to the authors of *Guerrilla Tourism Marketing*, Carol Wain and Jay Conrad Levinson, every website should also have a call to action (CTA) such as "Click here to buy tickets." "CTAs have proven to help businesses convert more website visitors into actual, paying customers. Some people simply need to be told what to do when they reach your website, so ask them to take a specific action and they often will."[18]

Engaging copy and high-quality, attractive images are a must to encourage users to stay on an attraction's website as long as possible. Because websites are such heavily used marketing tools, it is well worth the time and expense for an attraction to have its website professionally designed or to recruit someone in-house with outstanding copywriting and web design skills.

Sometimes partnerships with outside organizations can help drive attraction traffic through the use of websites. In a unique tourism partnership arrangement, the National Geographic Society announced plans for a project designed to increase geotourism to 10 states bordering the Mississippi River. According to journalist Jim Anderson, geotourism "focuses on a destination's unique culture and history and intends to have visitors help enrich those qualities rather than turn the place into a typical tourist trap."[19]

The aim of the website project was to pull together information from tourism-related businesses along the Mississippi River, using the Society's website as a central location where visitors could access this information. The ultimate goal was to brand the river "as a unique world-class tourist destination, raise awareness of the river's cultural heritage and spark local tourism planning and growth."[20]

## Blogs

Another way for an attraction to reach out to audiences is by starting a blog. While a website is intended to provide essential information about the attraction, a blog is useful for keeping visitors up-to-date on what's going on at the attraction on a day-to-day basis. Ideally, this will inspire them to check it out for themselves.

Attractions can also use blogs to talk about new developments, industry trends, interesting or offbeat facts, and other nuggets of information that may be useful to customers. As Wain and Levinson explain, "One of the benefits of blogging is that it gives you a platform to brand yourself as an expert in your field. You can answer questions and provide valuable information about your industry, destination, business, products and services."[21]

The DisneyParks blog, for example, is part of the multitude of marketing tools used to promote the Disneyland and Walt Disney World resorts and the Disney Cruise Line. The blog is managed by one of the company's social media directors but features contributions from individuals who work in all different capacities of the parks and who write about their areas of expertise.[22]

An attraction can include a blog as part of its website or as a standalone feature. If the latter approach is taken, say Wain and Levinson, include a link to the website so readers can easily access it, as well as a mechanism for them to sign up to receive notifications about blog posts.[23]

## Email

Although some might argue that social media has replaced email as a way of reaching out to customers, the good news is that email is not dead yet. In fact, it can be a powerful marketing tool when used effectively because it offers many benefits. It costs less to use than other forms of marketing. It can also be targeted to reach out to individuals who most likely provided their email addresses to the attraction in the first place because they were interested in being informed about it.

Email is useful for notifying customers about upcoming events, promoting contests, and announcing breaking news that directs traffic to an attraction's website for more details. It can also be used to offer customers discounts and advertise on-site promotions. Attractions can use their websites to build an email database. "You can also build your list by using contests, sweepstakes [and] Facebook promotions," note Wain and Levinson. "You can have an email list or a mobile list but it is preferable to have a list that includes both the email and the mobile contact information."[24]

Emails should be concise, uncluttered, and easy-to-understand. They should also have an attention-grabbing subject line and an upbeat tone. An effective email will also include a definitive call to action such as "Click here to enter sweepstakes," or "Visit our website for more details," along with an accompanying link.

Attractions need to be judicious in the frequency of their emails, advises author Marsha Collier. "How important can your message be to your customer that you have to e-mail them every day? Instead of e-mailing your customers daily, why not reach out to them when you have an offer that stands out from the crowd?"[25]

Because of the vast number of companies using email for marketing, there are laws in place that regulate how to use it. Before launching an email marketing program, it's recommended to review the guidelines set by both the Federal Trade Commission (http://business.ftc.gov/documents/bus61-can-spam-act-compliance-guide-business) and the Federal Communications Commission (http://www.fcc.gov/guides/spam-unwanted-text-messages-and-email).

## Marketing Collateral Materials

Many organizations develop additional resources to supplement their ad campaigns and Internet marketing efforts. These are called collateral materials and may include brochures, direct mail, and DVDs.

### Brochures

Even in today's electronic-savvy world, brochures still have relevance for tourism attractions. They are great resources to place in travel agent offices, hotel lobbies, retail outlets, and visitor information centers. Potential customers can easily pick up a brochure and learn what an attraction has to offer from its engaging copy and eye-catching images. Brochures can also prompt spontaneous sales. For both leisure and business travelers, for example, a brochure picked up at a hotel may be the tool that makes a potential customer aware of a nearby attraction and prompts a visit to check it out.

Brochures can provide general information or promote special offers or exhibits. According to Swarbrooke, to maximize their effectiveness, brochure features should include an eye-catching design, informative content, and an easy-to-carry size. To extend the shelf life of a brochure, it's advisable to leave out information that is likely to become outdated, such as admission costs.[26]

A variety of channels are available for brochure distribution. As noted above, brochures can be distributed to outlets such as hotels and visitor centers where potential customers can easily pick them up. They can also be distributed to consumers as direct-mail pieces. Digital versions of brochures, or "e-brochures," may be sent electronically to previous customers who have provided email addresses. This can reduce production and distribution costs and can also help keep these visitors up-to-date on new developments at an attraction.

### Direct Mail

While direct mail has declined in popularity since the advent of Internet marketing, it still holds value for tourism attractions wanting to reach out to specific target markets. These markets might include past customers, customers within a specific geographic area, or individuals such as travel agents and meeting planners who have access to large groups of potential customers.

Print is generally the medium of choice for direct-mail pieces, which can include personalized letters, postcards, fliers, and brochures, among others. There are a number of ways to develop mailing lists for direct-mail distribution, according to Morrison. "The most powerful source of direct-mail marketing lists is an organization's own in-house records of past customers and inquirers," he says. "Many specialized lists can also be acquired from other organizations (e.g., membership directories) or from commercial mailing list brokers. These companies' lists can be rented for a fee."[27]

The downside of this type of marketing is that direct mail can be seen as "junk mail," and discarded without being read. In many cases, notes Shimp. "It is not the amount of mail that concerns most people but the fact that virtually any business or other organization can readily obtain their names and addresses."[28]

*Figure 4.2: Brochures remain useful marketing tools for attractions even in an online-driven environment.* (Photo Credit: Andi Stein)

## Audiovisual Materials

Audiovisual materials such as promotional DVDs are another form of collateral marketing tools. Large companies like Disney, for example, send out DVDs to customers and travel agents who request them as part of their marketing efforts for the company's theme parks and other properties. A promotional DVD might contain visuals of a tourism destination or attraction, as well as testimonials from people who have enjoyed their experiences there. The material should include explicit contact information, so interested potential customers can take the next step to arrange a visit.[29]

## On-Site Marketing Materials

Many of the advertising and marketing materials discussed above are designed to bring visitors into an attraction. However, an attraction can continue to promote itself through on-site marketing materials that guests can access once they walk through the entrance. These include maps and signage.

Maps, for example, should be designed to clearly indicate where to find and how to get to an attraction's offerings. Maps should also show the locations of an attraction's restaurants as well as retail outlets for guests who might want to stop and have a bite to eat or take a souvenir of their visit home with them.

The way an attraction presents its signage can affect how customers make decisions when purchasing tickets, merchandise, or food. Creating attractive, easy-to-read signs that highlight special deals and don't overwhelm customers with choices can eliminate purchase anxiety. Adding technology with the use of LCD screens showing guests enjoying different aspects of an attraction can also help stimulate sales, explains Jeanine Jones of Georgia's Stone Mountain Park. "The concept is that guests see what we have to offer and can make a more informed decision when they reach the counter."[30]

## Advertising and Marketing Effectiveness

"Advertising is an investment and like all investment should produce measurable results," says Raju.[31] The process of measuring advertising and marketing success, however, can be a complex one. According to allBusiness.com:

> Advertising is not an exact science. There's no precise way to measure the success of an ad campaign. You can't, for example, determine how many sales dollars are generated by each advertising dollar you spend. But there are methods that will give you a rough idea of whether your ads are hitting the mark.[32]

A number of criteria have been developed over the years for the assessment of advertising effectiveness, particularly with traditional media. Some of these include exposure, processing, comprehension, response, conversion, and action.[33]

Assessing the impact of Internet marketing can be less daunting than determining the effectiveness of traditional media, says Morrison, because the technology allows for what he calls a "'track record' of interactions."[34] Attraction analysts can collect data on website traffic, for example, including the number of users and the amount of time they spend on each page.

Likewise, counting the number of pieces distributed and comparing it to the number of responses generated can measure the effects of direct mail. Because of the complex nature of measuring advertising and marketing effectiveness, especially with traditional media, attractions may choose to subscribe to market research firms that will collect and analyze data for them.

## Working with Outside Agencies

When it comes to developing advertising and marketing campaigns, tourism attractions have several options. They can do the work in house, hire a full-service agency, or do some work themselves and hire out the rest. While nonprofit and small attractions may need to do all of their work in house to keep costs down, larger attractions may choose to hire an agency, or several agencies, to develop their advertising and marketing programs.

Advertising and marketing agencies provide a full range of services, which include conducting research, developing concepts, preparing copy and visuals, and scheduling media placement. Because agencies often buy advertising space in bulk, they also have the ability to negotiate better placement rates with the media than organizations might be able to secure on their own. Attractions can also engage agencies to oversee public relations and publicity campaigns and to develop sales promotions.

There are both pros and cons of relying on an outside agency for advertising and marketing services. "The primary advantages include acquiring the services of specialists with in-depth knowledge…and obtaining negotiating leverage with the media," says Shimp. "The major disadvantage is that some control…is lost when it is performed by an agency rather than in house."[35]

When selecting an agency, it is advisable to be deliberate, take time to do sufficient research, and ask questions to ensure a good fit between the attraction and the agency. Keep in mind that "the choice of an advertising agency will depend on the size of a promotional budget, the range of services required and above all the objective assessment of the professional qualities of the agency," says Raju.[36]

---

### Tips for Hiring Outside Agencies

1. Identify your advertising/marketing needs.
2. Consider potential costs and existing budget.
3. Implement request for proposal (RFP) process.
4. Select short list of candidates.
5. Request client lists and references from potential agencies.
6. Evaluate past work of agency candidates.
7. Compare your goals to the agencies' goals.
8. Choose a finalist, and make an offer.
9. Agree upon specific terms and conditions of service.
10. Appoint in-house liaison to work with selected agency.

---

## Conclusion

Promotion and marketing can help build awareness of an attraction and generate customer excitement and interest. The combination of elements used to create this awareness is known as the communications mix. It includes advertising and marketing, public relations and publicity, and sales promotion and merchandising.

Developing effective marketing materials can contribute to the success of an organization's promotional efforts. This involves setting objectives, defining a target audience, preparing an effective message, and selecting the right medium for message delivery. All of this should be accomplished in a manner that fits within the attraction's budget.

Advertising and marketing are key elements of the communications mix. Attractions often rely on a variety of print, broadcast, and online advertisements to communicate their messages to ensure they reach diverse audiences.

Likewise, the right mix of marketing tools can be extremely important in getting the word out about an attraction. These tools can range from online materials like websites and blogs to more traditional media such as brochures and direct mail. Attraction marketers may choose to prepare promotional materials in-house or contract with an outside agency, depending upon the nature and scope of the job.

While advertising and marketing are only a piece of the communications mix, when combined with other factors, they can play an essential role in an attraction's promotion and marketing efforts. The next chapter will discuss the role of media relations and the options it offers in expanding an attraction's reach with its publics.

## Notes

1. See Stowe Shoemaker, Robert C. Lewis, and Peter C. Yesawich, *Marketing Leadership in Hospitality and Tourism, 4th ed.* (Upper Saddle River, NJ: Pearson, 2007), 628.
2. Terence A. Shimp, *Advertising, Promotion, and Other Aspects of Integrated Marketing Communications, 8th ed.* (Mason, OH: South-Western Cengage Learning, 2010), 156.
3. Victor Middleton, Alan Fyall, Michael Morgan, and Ashok Ranchhod, *Marketing in Travel and Tourism, 4th ed.* (Burlington, MA: Butterworth-Heinemann, 2009), 421.
4. "Colonial Williamsburg TV Commercial: Family Vacation," http://www.youtube.com/watch?v=VfM6E6c-vZbk.
5. Steve Vaughan, "New Ads Use Humor," *McClatchy-Tribune Business News*, May 16, 2014.
6. Shoemaker et al., *Marketing Leadership in Hospitality and Tourism, 4th ed.*, 424.
7. G.P. Raju, *Tourism Marketing and Management* (Delhi, India: Manglam Publications, 2009), 147.
8. John Swarbrooke, *The Development and Management of Visitor Attractions, 2nd ed.* (Burlington, MA: Elsevier Butterworth-Heinemann, 2005), 228.
9. Ibid., 229.
10. Shoemaker et al., *Marketing Leadership in Hospitality and Tourism, 4th ed.*, 427.
11. Alastair M. Morrison, *Hospitality & Travel Marketing, 4th ed.* (Clifton Park, NY: Delmar, 2010), 512.
12. Ibid., 519.
13. "Washington D.C. Is Next Stop for Ecuador's Tourism & Commerce Advertising Campaign," *Marketing Weekly News*, August 17, 2013, 216.
14. "Online Advertising Basics," Digital Publishing 101, http://digitalpublishing101.com/digital-marketing-101/digital-marketing-toolbox/part-3-email-and-online-advertising/online-advertising-basics.
15. Shimp, *Advertising, Promotion, and Other Aspects of Integrated Marketing Communications*, 400.
16. See "Atlantic City's $20 Million Tourism Campaign Starts April 15," *PR Newswire*, April 9, 2013.
17. Vicente Neto quoted in "Brazil Launches New International Advertising Campaign in Advance of the 2014 FIFA World Cup," *AroundtheRings.com*, May 14, 2014, http://www.aroundtherings.com/site/A__46975/Title__Brazil-launches-new-international-advertising-campaign-in-advance-of-the-2014-FIFA-World-Cup/292/Articles.

18. Carol Wain and Jay Conrad Levinson, *Guerrilla Tourism Marketing* (Lexington, KY: WINning Entrepreneur Press, 2012), 91.

19. Jim Anderson, "A New Tourism Model Touted for Mississippi River," *McClatchy-Tribune Business News*, April 4, 2014.

20. Ibid.

21. Wain and Levinson, *Guerrilla Tourism Marketing*, 91.

22. See "DisneyParks Blog," *Disney.com*, http://disneyparks.disney.go.com/blog.

23. Wain and Levinson, *Guerrilla Tourism Marketing*, 91.

24. Ibid., 97.

25. Marsha Collier, *Social Media Commerce for Dummies* (Hoboken, NJ: John Wiley & Sons, Inc., 2013), 240.

26. Swarbrooke, *The Development and Management of Visitor Attractions, 2nd ed.*, 224.

27. Morrison, *Hospitality & Travel Marketing, 4th ed.*, 524.

28. Shimp, *Advertising, Promotion, and Other Aspects of Integrated Marketing Communications*, 426.

29. Ibid., 428.

30. Jeanine Jones as quoted in John Morell, "Desirable Design," *Funworld*, November 2012, 179.

31. Raju, *Tourism Marketing and Management*, 145.

32. "Metrics for Measuring Ad Campaign Effectiveness," *allBusiness.com*, http://www.allbusiness.com/marketing/advertising/1415-1.html.

33. See Morrison, *Hospitality & Travel Marketing, 4th ed.*, 508.

34. Ibid., 340.

35. Shimp, *Advertising, Promotion, and Other Aspects of Integrated Marketing Communications, 8th ed.*, 193.

36. Raju, *Tourism Marketing and Management*, 152.

# CHAPTER FIVE

# Media Relations

## Introduction

Generating media coverage for a tourism attraction can be an effective way to bring in customers. Although the advent of social media has changed the landscape for promotion and marketing in recent years, traditional media are still valued as essential partners for spreading the word about attractions. Media professionals have the ability to communicate with potential customers through print, electronic, and online sources.

Understanding the needs of media can facilitate the development of good working relationships with the press. This can ultimately help generate publicity for an attraction. This chapter discusses steps attractions can take to build effective working relationships with media professionals. It offers examples of stories that are likely to appeal to reporters and editors as well as suggestions for how to pitch them.

## Roles of Public Relations and Journalism

In working with the media to obtain publicity for an attraction, it's important to understand that public relations practitioners and journalists have different job responsibilities. The primary purpose of public relations (PR) is to communicate information about a company's activities to different public groups that may have an interest in the organization or could benefit from having this information. These include external publics like consumers, stockholders, community members, government agencies, and the news media. They also include internal publics such as employees who have responsibility for maintaining the daily operations of an organization.

Individuals working in a public relations capacity serve as advocates for their organizations. Their goal is to make their different public groups aware of what their organization is doing in order to pique the interest of these publics and gain their support. In the attractions industry this might encompass keeping the public informed about a new ride, exhibit, or event. Ideally, providing this information will result in people wanting to see or experience it for themselves.

The role of journalism is to inform the public about newsworthy events and activities. A journalist's overall goal is to present information as objectively as possible and let readers and viewers draw their own conclusions about the information. Journalists gather information from a variety of sources in order to produce their stories. They conduct interviews, gather data, and research facts. Journalists also use information provided to them by public relations practitioners as part of their source material when preparing stories. They expect this information to be newsworthy, timely, and truthful.

Although they serve different functions, journalists and public relations practitioners depend on each other to get their jobs done. PR practitioners know they have the potential to reach a mass audience if the media cover something their attraction is doing. They can raise public awareness beyond what they can do themselves with community outreach and social media.

At the same time, media often seek out public relations practitioners for story suggestions about newsworthy events and activities they can report on. Some stories might never be brought to light if not for public relations practitioners who make the media aware of these stories. PR practitioners can also connect reporters with individuals in their organizations who can provide quotes and background information pertaining to these stories.

Journalists look to members of an attraction's PR staff when they are working on stories related to the company's business. In addition, in cases of unexpected events or crises, journalists may contact an organization's PR staff for information that can help explain or clarify a situation.

## Tips for Successful Media Relations

Because of this interdependent relationship, it is beneficial to have an understanding of what journalists do and what they need from PR staff in order to get their jobs done. In turn, working cooperatively with the media can help an attraction's PR staff build a sense of trust on the part of reporters and editors. This can lead to a positive, professional relationship that will ultimately help cultivate media interest in the attraction's activities.

### Forge Relationships with Reporters

"Working with the press is all about the relationships you build and manage," according to an article in *PR News*. "Remember that no two journalists are alike, and it is to your advantage to get to know the writer or editor, working with each in the way he or she prefers."[1] There are a number of ways public relations staff can establish relationships with journalists that will be mutually beneficial to both groups. One of the key roles of an attraction's PR staff is to come up with interesting, newsworthy story ideas to pitch to the media that will generate news coverage for the attraction.

Some media outlets employ reporters who have specific "beats" or topics they cover on a routine basis. These beats may include local news, crime, business, education, or entertainment and tourism. This means that an attraction's PR staff member could end up working with the same individuals on a regular basis when pitching story ideas or responding to media inquiries.

One of the first steps public relations staff can take to develop a good working relationship with the media is to learn who the reporters are that regularly cover their business. This can be accomplished by reaching out with a phone call or email to the reporters. Journalist Kim Button offers some pointers for establishing this contact.

> There is a method to developing relationships with journalists. Reach out to local media personalities, such as TV reporters, newspaper editors, radio DJs, and area bloggers. Expand beyond local media by searching for bloggers and reporters that specialize in a certain field, such as family travel, educational travel, etc.[2]

When contacting reporters, Button suggests, PR practitioners should offer some brief background information about their attractions and invite journalists to learn more.

In establishing this contact, a PR person can become more than just a name to a reporter. Instead, he or she can begin to establish a professional relationship that will serve both of them well in the long run. As Button explains, "Many journalists will be simply too busy to respond, but they will likely remember you when they are developing a story."[3]

Once initial contact is made, a public relations practitioner can find out more about the preferences of individual reporters. This might include the types of stories a journalist is interested in covering, the best method to use when contacting the reporter, and the reporter's deadlines.

## Develop a Media Contact List

After identifying who has the potential to cover an attraction, it is helpful to compile a media contact list that can be easily accessed and updated. The contact list should include media outlets that will be a good fit for the attraction. Reporter Jackie Clark suggests, "The idea is to first think of different traits characterizing your potential customers, and second, to identify media outlets that will reach these potential [customers]."[4]

The list should include the names and contact information of journalists who are likely to be interested in reporting what an attraction can offer their readers or viewers. The contact list can include brief background information about different media outlets as well as the names of reporters from each outlet and the types of stories they cover. This can help identify specific individuals who specialize in reporting on particular topics. A media contact list can also include information about how each reporter prefers to receive information from an organization. If a reporter states up front that he or she prefers to be pitched by email rather than by phone, for example, this can be noted on the contact list.

## Cooperate with Media Inquiries

Journalists are often on deadline and may need information in a hurry, so it's essential to respond in a timely manner. As Button explains, "Media requests can be as mundane as fact checking ticket prices to as complicated as requesting an interview or special access to the attraction…. Acknowledging receipt of the request lets the media know you are willing to work with them."[5]

It's never advisable to refuse to speak with a reporter, even if an inquiry relates to a story that could possibly be unflattering. If a reporter can't obtain what is needed from an official source, he or she may go looking for it from unofficial sources. This could potentially cause more harm than simply providing what the reporter is requesting. A better approach is to give as much information as possible under the circumstances and offer to provide follow-up as soon as the organization is able to release more information.

### Avoid Micromanaging Reporters

It's important to understand that a public relations practitioner does not have the authority to dictate the direction of a story to a reporter. While he or she can offer suggestions and provide information to try and influence what gets covered, it is ultimately up to the journalist to determine the angle of the coverage.

Additionally, while a reporter may contact a PR staff member to clarify something within a story, it is highly unlikely the reporter will allow that person to review the story before it airs or goes to press. Requesting prior review of a piece may be met with resistance and often outright rejection on the part of the journalist.

An article in *PR News* suggests that attempting to micromanage a reporter can cause problems in the relationship with the reporter. "Overstepping your bounds is the worst thing you can do; it produces an 'us versus you' mentality. Your objective needs to be the creation of allies, not enemies."[6]

### Provide Complimentary Admission

Some reporters may be interested in covering an attraction but may be restricted by limited company budgets and unable to pay the cost of admission out of pocket. One way to accommodate this is to provide press passes or complimentary admission. Depending on the nature of the attraction, this could include a ticket for the reporter and a guest or, in some instances, a limited number of tickets for family members as well.

Be aware that some media outlets have policies that prohibit their reporters from accepting comps. These journalists may still be interested in covering an attraction but be required to pay for it themselves or have it paid for by their employers. Depending on the situation, it might be possible instead to offer discounted tickets that help defray the cost of admission.

## Challenges of Media Relations

In the last 20 years, the media landscape has changed drastically as the increase of online media has resulted in the decline of traditional media outlets. This has led to a reduction in force of reporters, editors, and photographers who are available to cover attraction-related stories. Fewer media outlets and smaller staffs mean increased competition for space.

Additionally, today's print reporters are no longer just expected to be able to tell a good story using the power of their words. They may be responsible for taking photographs, shooting and editing video, and posting stories to their media outlets' Facebook pages. TV reporters have higher demands placed on them as well, according to author Dave Armon. "Every successful broadcast news operation is engaging with viewers using Twitter and the station's Web site,"[7] he says.

"Everyone is doing more than one job," explains Kathy Burrows, public relations manager for Hershey Entertainment & Resorts. Because of this, she adds, "The easier you can make someone's job, the more effective you're going to be."[8]

---

### Attraction Fun Fact
ABC covered the opening day of Disneyland, July 17, 1955, with a live television broadcast.

---

## What Reporters Want

One way to make reporters' jobs easier is to have a good understanding of the types of stories that are likely to be of interest to the media. Making an effort to pitch these kinds of stories can increase the chances of having an attraction covered by the press.

### News Stories

A new development or turn of events is always of interest to reporters. For an attraction, this could be the opening of a new ride or exhibit, announcement of a leadership change, or visit by a celebrity or dignitary. When something like this occurs, it's advisable to reach out to the media to let them know what's happening. It's also a good idea to provide reporters access to those within the organization who have the most information about the story, such as the CEO or someone with extensive knowledge of the situation.

Keep in mind that not all news stories may be positive. If something unexpected happens at an attraction such as an accident or crisis, the media will want to cover that as well. While stories like this might not necessarily shed the best light on an attraction, how those within the organization respond to the media can make a big difference in how a story is covered. If a reporter calls and wants information during a crisis situation, it's in the best interest of the organization to respond quickly and provide as much information as possible under the circumstances. More details about crisis communications will be provided in Chapter 11.

### Behind-the-Scenes Stories

Taking reporters behind the scenes of an attraction can offer them a chance to see what the general public cannot. This enables them to be the ones to reveal this information to their audiences. A behind-the-scenes story might involve a glimpse into the inner-workings of an attraction or the roles of the people who keep the attraction running.

At Legoland Florida, for example, many of the park's Lego creations are designed and assembled by master model builders in a small building hidden behind trees near the entrance to the park. Park patrons willing to shell out an additional fee can take a tour of the "Lego factory" where the models are built, but most Legoland visitors never get to see what goes on behind the scenes. In an article called "Brick by Brick: How Legoland's Famous Models Are Built," reporter Jeremy Schoolfield was able to reveal to his readers some of the tricks of the trade that go into building the Legoland creations. This offered insights about the Lego factory to his audience that might otherwise have remained unknown.[9]

*Figure 5.1: Behind-the-scenes stories provide reporters a chance to get a close-up look at an attraction's facilities and share it with their audiences.*
(Photo Credit: Andi Stein)

## Unusual Features

Stories about the weird and wonderful may also be of interest to reporters. These can include features at an attraction that are one of a kind or out of the ordinary. In 2013, for example, the San Antonio Zoo celebrated the birth of a two-headed turtle, which zoo officials aptly named "Thelma and Louise." Local, national, and international media took a shine to the unusual amphibian story, resulting in worldwide media coverage for the turtle and the zoo.[10] Staff members at the zoo also created a Facebook page for Thelma and Louise and used it to update the media and the public about the turtle and the zoo's conservation efforts.[11]

## Milestone Events

Birthdays, anniversaries, and other milestone events make for good stories to promote to the media. Some of these may be ongoing celebrations while others might be one-shot deals that have the potential to generate big crowds. In March of 2014, for instance, SeaWorld Orlando announced the start of an 18-month celebration of the park's 50th birthday called "Sea of Surprises." This was followed by kick-off promotional events at the company's three parks in Florida, Texas, and California. The *Orlando Sentinel* and other media outlets around the country picked up the announcement of the celebration.[12] These media organizations continued to follow the anniversary events as the celebration unfolded.

While the SeaWorld campaign was designed as an ongoing event, the Walt Disney Company staged a 24-hour celebration on April 10, 2014, to signify the 50th anniversary of the "it's a small world" theme park attraction. The event included a sing-along and an appearance at Disneyland by Richard Sherman, who co-wrote the ride's signature song with his brother Robert.[13] As the "small world" attraction is featured in five Disney parks, and its accompanying song is recognized all over the world, the one-day event brought thousands of fans into the parks and garnered extensive media coverage, including live coverage of the sing-along on Good Morning America.[14]

### Local Angles on National News

One of the main characteristics reporters look for when covering stories is proximity. While national and international media may be interested in stories that have global appeal, local media are likely to want to cover news that happens in their own backyards. Under the right set of circumstances, sometimes a national story can be transformed into a local one with a little ingenuity on the part of an attraction's PR person. In addition, finding a way to link something happening at your attraction to something that's already in the news may be worthwhile, says Clark.

> Inserting yourself into existing media coverage is one of the easiest ways to generate media coverage, so if there's a story in the local paper, on the local television news program or even circulating in a national debate that applies somehow to you, tying yourself to the story could deliver exceptional results.[15]

## Appropriate Story Pitches

When pitching potential stories to the media, there are certain guidelines to follow that can help increase the chances of grabbing the attention of reporters and editors. Here are some tips to keep in mind.

### Ensure Newsworthiness

The first step is to make sure a potential story is newsworthy. Reporters want to cover stories that are new, different, and timely. They are generally not interested in reporting on topics that have been covered before or that don't offer anything new to their audiences. Sending out information about last year's hot item is not likely to make an impression this year unless there is a new angle to the story. Additionally, as Lee Davies explains, "Be honest about the 'importance' of the news. Truly important news will 'sell' itself on its own merits, so watch out for hyperbole and overstatement."[16]

## Be Relevant

Reporters also want to hear about stories that are going to appeal to their specific audiences. Bombarding media outlets with information that doesn't relate to their readers or viewers will not increase the chance of coverage. Brian Parrish explains, "Guard against wasting a journalist's time with a story that does not fit the publication's domain. Pitching inappropriate story ideas causes you to lose credibility, eroding the chances that future pitches will be viewed seriously."[17]

Pitching a story about a new baby zebra at the local zoo, for example, is not likely to be of interest to the editor of a newspaper in a town 2,000 miles away. There can be exceptions, of course. If the baby zebra's daddy happens to be on loan from the zoo in that town, it could make for a potential story. In most cases, however, it's worthwhile to be discriminating about where to send promotional materials when getting ready to pitch a story.

## Gather Background Information

Taking time to get the facts straight before pitching a story can add to the overall credibility of the pitch. When Burrows is promoting a new roller coaster at Hersheypark, for example, she will first educate herself on the background of the coaster before releasing information to the media. This might include talking to the appropriate engineer to find out about the technology of the ride.

When she pitches the roller coaster to the media, Burrows is then able to answer technical questions for them as well as provide basic information about the ride's debut. "You really need to do your homework," she explains. "Knowledge is power. The more you know, the more effective you're going to be."[18]

## Be Prepared for Anything

Despite all the assistance provided to a reporter in the preparation of a story, sometimes the resulting coverage may not be exactly what the PR person had hoped for. If something in a story is inaccurate, it's perfectly acceptable to let the reporter or editor know and request that clarification be provided.

However, if a story is simply different from what was expected—in its angle, depiction, or content—complaining is not likely to result in a better story. Instead, it might alienate the reporter, leading to a damaged relationship between the attraction and the media outlet. In this case it might be more prudent for an attraction to try to tell its own version of the story using social media.

## Respect Time Constraints

With journalists wearing multiple hats these days, they have little time to waste on PR staff that don't understand the demands of their jobs. That's why it's essential to be mindful of a reporter's time constraints. Be aware and respectful of deadlines. Don't hound a reporter with endless follow-up emails or phone calls about a press release or story pitch. While it's acceptable to check on the status of a story, making unreasonable demands will simply annoy a reporter and is not likely to result in better coverage for an attraction. In general, when working with the media, take a lesson from the Golden Rule: "Do unto others as you would have them do unto you."[19]

## Useful Media Resources

In addition to pitching appropriate stories to the media, public relations staff can facilitate coverage by providing journalists with relevant materials that can help them tell these stories.

### Press Releases

Press releases, also known as news releases, are documents used to announce an organization's newsworthy activities or events. Reporters and editors review them to determine if what the releases are promoting might be of interest to their audiences. A well-written press release should be written like a news story, with pertinent information—who, what, when, where, why, and how—in the release's opening paragraphs. Using this format makes it easy for journalists to instantly absorb the key message of a press release.

A press release should also include a few sentences of brief background about the attraction. It should contain contact information for someone associated with the attraction who can answer questions and provide additional details about the subject of the release if needed.

Press releases can be sent through traditional mail or, more commonly, distributed electronically in the body of an email or as an email attachment. The advantage of sending a press release electronically is that it can include embedded links to the attraction's website or other online resources such as audio or video. Some reporters prefer to receive press releases in the body of an email rather than as a separate attachment as a precaution against computer viruses.

### High-Quality Images

A typical press release may be accompanied by high-quality images. These can help reporters tell a story about an attraction using pictures as well as words. Button offers tips on what to consider when submitting images to help promote an attraction.

> A supply of high-resolution images is a must. Photos taken on a phone might be OK for a blog but will not work for a print magazine or on TV. Hire a professional photographer to take commercial images. If cost is an issue, run a contest seeking great guest images, with the agreement that the copyright transfer to the attraction for professional use.[20]

## What to Include in a Media Kit

✓ Introduction letter
✓ Press releases
✓ Fact sheets
✓ Backgrounders
✓ Frequently asked questions (FAQs)
✓ Bios of key executives
✓ Testimonials
✓ Brochures and other collateral material
✓ High-quality images
✓ DVDs or CDs
✓ Contact information

## Media Kits

Preparing a media kit, or press kit, is a way of bundling publicity materials into a single package to help promote an attraction. Reporter Al Lautenslager says:

> A press kit is like a résumé for your company. In it is a collection of company information and articles put together to address questions from the media, investors, potential clients and others. The goal of the press kit is the same as all other marketing that a company does. It should grab the reader's attention, make a lasting impression and create enough interest that they will contact you for more information.[21]

In addition to press releases and images, a typical media kit might include a fact sheet about the attraction, list of frequently asked questions (FAQs), bios of key personnel, media clippings, and testimonials, among other items.

## Online Pressrooms

An online pressroom on an attraction's website specifically earmarked for journalists is a useful resource to provide to the media. It offers journalists a handy way to access information on their own and at their convenience. As Button notes, "This is especially important for tight deadlines and after-hours work."[22]

An online pressroom can include electronic versions of an organization's media kit contents such as recent press releases, fact sheets, downloadable images and videos, and a list of media contacts. It can also contain links to social media and background information about an attraction such as copies of annual reports, company history, personnel bios, and media policies.

*Social Media Platforms*

An attraction's social media platforms may be of interest to the press as well as the public. Some reporters will opt to contact PR staff via Facebook or Twitter rather than by phone, text, or email. For this reason, PR staff need to make sure material posted on social media platforms is regularly updated and contains information that keeps users informed about new developments and happenings at the attraction. Additional information about the use of social media for promotional purposes will be provided in Chapter 6.

*Interview Contacts*

Another way to help reporters tell a story is to provide them access to individuals who may have the most knowledge about the story being pitched. These can include key administrators or personnel who are closely involved with the subject of a story. When a new exhibit is set to open at a museum, for example, arranging an interview between a reporter and the curator of the exhibit can give the reporter a chance to ask specific questions about the exhibit's backstory or significance. This could result in a longer piece about the exhibit itself, one that goes beyond a one- or two-line calendar announcement of the exhibit's opening.

---

### *Attraction Fun Fact*

The Metropolitan Museum of Art in New York owns the oldest piano in existence, made by Bartolomeo Cristofori in 1720.

---

## Media Training Programs

Sometimes the best sources for a story might not necessarily be the best spokespeople for the company. They may be anxious and uneasy about talking to reporters or unfamiliar with how to behave on camera. One way to help employees learn how to be successful in an interview is to provide them with media training.

As part of her public relations activities at Hershey Entertainment, Burrows offers a class called "Media Training 101." She works with employees to teach them how to do interviews, appear on camera, and feel at ease when dealing with the press. Her goal is to make Hershey employees "feel better about themselves and their ability to communicate." As part of the training, Burrows uses role-playing exercises and has her students videotaped, so they can see how they appear on camera.

The training is ultimately beneficial to both journalists and employees and makes for a successful interview experience. "At the end of the day, both the interviewer and interviewee want it to be good because they look better," Burrows explains. Media Training 101 "helps them be their most effective self."[23]

# Media Training 101

❖ Prepare! Don't treat the interview like a conversation.

❖ Try to work in the organization's message: there's something for everyone, there are things to do year round, and Hershey is "The Sweetest Place on Earth."

❖ Doing a television interview IS like public speaking.

❖ It's OK to ask questions before the interview starts if you need to clarify the subject.

❖ Keep answers short, simple, and understandable.

❖ Approach the interview with a sense of purpose—positive, eager, and enthusiastic.

❖ Know something about WHO is interviewing you—if possible, watch the interviewer on television prior to the interview.

❖ Speak to the reporter. Try to be relaxed.

❖ You can't control the interviewer; you can only control yourself and your response.

❖ Think about the audience you are speaking to. Why do THEY care about what you are saying in the interview?

❖ Try to deliver a good "sound bite" during the interview. A sound bite is one or two sentences that capture attention and deliver a message in a witty or dramatic way.

❖ Speak in complete sentences during the interview.

❖ Lead off with your "strongest stuff."

❖ Keep it short and simple.

❖ Don't use industry jargon. Be concise and specific.

❖ Use the name of the company whenever possible, not the word "we."

❖ Always be calm and never say anything that is "off the record."

❖ Never answer "no comment." If you can't answer the question, try to bridge to something positive.

❖ If you don't understand the question, rephrase it.

❖ Use facts to support your interview.

❖ When you respond, answer the question and try to include your "message."

❖ End the interview by asking if the reporter would like any additional materials from you.

Source: Kathy Burrows, Public Relations Manager, Hershey Entertainment & Resorts.

# Conclusion

Media coverage can contribute to the public's awareness of an attraction. Although journalists and public relations practitioners have different roles, they rely on each other to disseminate information to the public. Fostering good working relationships with journalists can increase an attraction's chances of reaching audiences through the media.

Those working in a public relations capacity for an attraction can build these relationships by reaching out to reporters who cover their business. They should respond to media inquiries in a timely manner and cooperate with reporter requests whenever possible. Pitching ideas for stories that are newsworthy and timely can also generate media interest. These stories may encompass new developments, behind-the-scenes views, unusual features, and milestone events.

Public relations staff can provide journalists with materials to help them prepare their stories. These include press releases, fact sheets, and high-quality images. Providing access to individuals within the attraction who are subject matter experts is also beneficial to media.

In recent years, social media platforms have provided additional options for getting the word out about an attraction. The next chapter will discuss the role social media marketing now plays in helping attractions reach their audiences.

# Notes

1. Brian Parrish, "Back to Basics: Pitch-Perfect Media Relations Gives PR a Head Start in Tough Economy," *PR News*, February 16, 2009.
2. Kim Button, "10 Tips to Help You Become Media Savvy," *Funworld*, November 2013, 208.
3. Ibid.
4. Jackie Clark, "Media Relations: A Proven Tool," *Automatic Merchandiser*, April 2010, 22.
5. Button, "10 Tips to Help You Become Media Savvy," 207.
6. Leslie Yeransian, "Message Control Without Micromanaging: Changing the PR-Journalist Dynamic," *PR News*, July 12, 2010.
7. Dave Armon, "Make the Changing Media Paradigm Work for You," *PR News*, April 30, 2012.
8. Kathy Burrows, personal interview, December 31, 2013.
9. See Jeremy Schoolfield, "Brick By Brick: How Legoland's Famous Models are Built," *Funworld*, January 2012, 21.
10. Presentation by Debbie Rios-Vanskike, IAAPA Attractions Expo, November 20, 2013.
11. See San Antonio Zoo, *A Year of Adventure: San Antonio Zoo Annual Report, Fiscal Year 2012-2013*, https://sazoo.org/media-room/annual_report.
12. See Jason Garcia, "SeaWorld Kicks Off 50th Anniversary Campaign," *Orlando Sentinel*, March 21, 2014, http://www.orlandosentinel.com.
13. See Sarah Tully, "Disneyland's 'It's a Small World' Turns 50," *Orange County Register*, April 21, 2014, http://www.ocregister.com/articles/world-610750-disney-sherman.html.
14. See Jennifer Fickley-Baker, "Disney Parks Celebrates 'it's a small world' Live on 'Good Morning America,'" DisneyParks Blog, April 10, 2014, http://disneyparks.disney.go.com/blog/2014/04/disney-parks-celebrates-its-a-small-world-live-on-good-morning-america.
15. Clark, "Media Relations: A Proven Tool," 22.
16. Lee Davies, "The 'Did You Get My Email' Phone Call to Reporters Has Little Ring Left," *PR News*, December 16, 2013.
17. Parrish, "Back to Basics: Pitch-Perfect Media Relations Gives PR a Head Start in Tough Economy."

18. Burrows, personal interview, December 31, 2013.
19. "The Golden Rule," *Internet Encyclopedia of Philosophy*, http://www.iep.utm.edu/goldrule.
20. Button, "10 Tips to Help You Become Media Savvy," 208.
21. Al Lautenslager, "The Ingredients of a Press Kit," *Entrepreneur.com*, November 18, 2002, http://www.entrepreneur.com/article/57260.
22. Button, "10 Tips to Help You Become Media Savvy," 208.
23. Burrows, personal interview, December 31, 2013.

# CHAPTER SIX

# Social Media Marketing

## Introduction

In the last two decades, the use of technology has completely transformed the process of communication. Laptop computers, smart phones, tablets, and other electronic devices have had an astounding impact on how people consume, process, and share information. Not surprisingly, businesses have scrambled to adapt to this constantly changing landscape by trying to figure out ways to reach out to consumers through technology. For the attractions industry, this has resulted in new strategies for public relations and marketing that make the consumer an active part of the promotion process.

This chapter takes a look at the role technology plays in the promotion of tourism attractions. It discusses how the proliferation of social media has resulted in the need for new strategies in communicating with an attraction's audiences. As is typical with the changing nature of technology, some of what is covered here will continue to evolve as new products and developments influence the market.

## Role of Social Media Marketing

Although social media marketing is a relatively new phenomenon, the increasing number of social media platforms has made it an essential part of doing business today. This is only likely to increase as new platforms emerge, and the creation of additional devices for communication continues to explode.

Social media marketing is a form of outreach intended to fuel consumer interest by engaging consumers in the communication process. As reporter Suzy Knauf explains, "The ultimate goal with social media is to increase brand awareness, drive fan/follow acquisition and maintain customer loyalty, whilst stimulating revenue growth."[1] From an attractions perspective, the use of social media is now regarded as a requirement of running a successful operation. Attractions are using social media to promote their offerings by engaging their customers as advocates. This offers an added bonus of what reporter Richard Palmer calls social proof.

"Regardless of the data that supports it, common sense tells us that we're far more likely to trust a brand, buy a product or visit an attraction if it's recommended by a friend," he notes.[2] Tina Hatcher, CEO of 3i Advertising/Public Relations, adds, "You have to look at social media as word-of-mouth exposure," which has always been part of the marketing process. "With social media, it's more apparent and much quicker."[3]

## Social Media Platforms

Some social media platforms such as Facebook and Twitter have enjoyed success for a number of years. Others have burst onto the scene with great fanfare, generating brief excitement and buzz before dying a slow, quiet death.

Because of the quixotic nature of social media, it's not advisable to rely on a single social media platform when trying to connect with customers. A better approach is to be open to change, willing to explore different options and see what sticks. Knauf explains, "It is critical to develop an engaging, multi-channel social media campaign plan of action for your attraction and, with an abundance of social networks available, it's also important to determine which sites will be most effective for your brand."[4]

Following is a description of some of the more popular social media platforms used by tourism attractions at the time of publication. Some of these may be likely to change over time, as new tools come onto the market and less popular ones fade away.

---

### Explaining Social Media with Ice Cream

| | |
|---|---|
| Facebook: | I like ice cream. |
| Twitter: | I am eating ice cream. |
| Instagram: | Here's a picture of me eating ice cream. |
| Foursquare: | This is where I eat ice cream. |
| YouTube: | Watch me eat ice cream. |
| Pinterest: | Here's a recipe for making ice cream. |
| Linkedin: | My experience includes eating ice cream. |
| Yelp: | This is a great place to eat ice cream. |
| Tumblr: | See my photos of ice cream. |
| Wordpress: | Read my blog about ice cream. |

Source: Compiled and adapted from a variety of Internet sources. Variations have included donuts, cupcakes, coffee, and cookies.

## Facebook

Launched in 2004, Facebook has evolved into the number one social networking site. From a tourism perspective, Facebook is regarded as an ideal platform for community building and customer engagement. Travel marketing consultant Frederic Gonzalo points out, "Studies have shown that 80–85% of people who like a brand on Facebook are past and present customers, so the network represents an opportunity to foster a strong community of loyal fans."[5]

*Figure 6.1: Social media sites such as Facebook, Instagram, and Pinterest allow users to post scenic images they've captured at attractions and share them with others.*
(Photo Credit: Andi Stein)

Many Facebook users post photos on their personal sites, and attractions benefit from this when they become part of the scenic backdrop for these photos. Attractions can use their own Facebook pages to post news and information about current happenings and generate buzz about upcoming events. They can also publicize promotions or contests, answer customer questions, and solicit user feedback.

Facebook offers businesses options to expand their reach through paid advertising and marketing, notes Gonzalo, which helps increase traffic to their sites. "At the end of the day, though, Facebook is mostly about people interacting with other people, brands or celebrities. In this context, travel brands should grasp this opportunity."[6]

## Twitter

While Facebook has wide-reaching potential as a communications tool for attractions, Twitter's strength lies in its ability to ensure communication is short and to the point. At the same time, brevity can pack a powerful punch, explains Nic Ray, managing director of Quirk London.

The shorter format of tweets (140 characters) means that relationship building is not Twitter's primary aim. Rather, it's the ideal medium to keep people up to date with news and special offers and share blog content. Twitter was designed for sharing and people will naturally spread your content for you—as long as it's worth sharing.[7]

Gonzalo notes that in 2014, there were 255 million people actively using Twitter, 78% of them on mobile platforms. That allowed them handy access to news and other information tweeted by attractions. Additionally, he says, "Twitter has embraced the potential of photo and video sharing…allowing for multiple photo-sharing [and] tagging people in pictures."[8] Twitter also offers attractions a handy means of communicating information quickly during times of crisis when an immediate response is warranted.

While some attractions may use Twitter to send out multiple tweets each day to keep in touch with followers, author Bruce Martin advises using Twitter judiciously. "No-one likes to be sold all the time and so it's important to avoid direct sales messages and concentrate on building relationships."[9]

## Instagram

When Instagram was acquired by Facebook in 2012, it had 25 million users. Two years later, it boasted upwards of 150 million users, according to research analyst Cooper Smith, with 90% of these users under the age of 35.[10] Instagram is designed for sharing photos and videos, which can be identified with specific hashtags. From a tourism perspective, notes Gonzalo, "destinations have embraced this trend by promoting a given hashtag, inviting travelers to share pictures and monitoring them through various social media tools."[11]

Instagram is ideal for attraction photo contests and promotions. It is also useful for cross-platform marketing efforts, explains blogger Margaret Murphy.

> Its combination of aesthetics and social networking allows photos and ads to be shared across multiple platforms. Posts can be synchronized among networks such as Twitter, Facebook and the blogging platform Tumblr using Instagram's "share" tool, making it easier to market yourself in creative ways.[12]

## Pinterest

Pinterest serves as an electronic bulletin board or scrapbooking site, allowing users to "pin" images onto online "boards." Building on the adage, "a picture is worth 1,000 words," it works nicely as a recruitment tool for travelers who are in the planning stages of their attraction visits. Pinterest users can view pinned images of potential destinations during their trip-planning process. This can help them decide where to go and what to do once they get there.

A feature called "Place Pins" gives tourism attractions the ability to attach information about a location to a pin. This can potentially inspire customers in the fact-gathering stages of their travels to seek out more information from an attraction's website, Facebook page, or other marketing platform. "Pinterest can play an interesting role within a brand's online ecosystem…. Many destinations…have embraced the potential for visual storytelling that comes from a dynamic presence on Pinterest,"[13] says Gonzalo.

*YouTube*

According to Kelly Wheeler of Quirk London, "YouTube has always toed the line between a content platform and a social network."[14] Attractions can use YouTube to showcase their offerings and activities through self-created or user-created video. YouTube videos have great versatility and potential for directing people to additional social platforms managed by an attraction, explain Carol Wain and Jay Conrad Levinson, authors of *Guerrilla Tourism Marketing*.

> The video itself can be footage that you shoot, a slide-show with music, a slide-show with a voice over or a person sitting in front of a web cam. The best part about video is that you can embed it on your website, show it on your Facebook page, pin it to Pinterest and, if it strikes a chord with viewers, you may just find that it gets plenty of shares.[15]

*Other Options*

The platforms listed above are just a few of the numerous social media marketing tools available to attractions for promotional purposes. Others that may be of interest are Google+ for customer networking; Vine for video posting; Snapchat for photo sharing; Tumblr for blogging; Linkedin for reaching business travelers; and TripAdvisor for customer reviews.

## Role of an Organization's Website

The use of websites as a marketing tool was discussed in Chapter 4. However, websites are worth a second mention in this chapter because of their relationship with social media platforms. According to Hatcher, "Social should be directing everybody to your website. That's the goal."[16] The website is what provides potential customers with in-depth information about an attraction.

As previously noted, customers frequently start with an organization's website when seeking out information. To that end, a company's website should contain essential details about opening hours, admission costs, location and directions, and other basic information that will steer users toward the attraction. Websites are also useful for promoting new attractions, advertising upcoming events, and posting images that emphasize some of the highlights of the attraction.

Websites have the ability to go beyond simply being repositories of static information. They can serve as a means of actively engaging customers with an attraction's brand by offering them extra incentives to stay linked to a site. Because of this, it's worthwhile to invest effort into creating an interactive website that makes it an automatic go-to resource for consumers.

Websites are a natural place to showcase the different social networking tools an attraction uses, offering customers additional reasons to stay engaged with the attraction electronically. This can be accomplished by strategically placing clickable social media platform logos on the home page, which link directly to the social networking sites.

Some attraction websites are designed to promote tourism through the use of social media. Visit Tallahassee launched "Trailahassee.com" to provide outdoor enthusiasts with a one-stop resource to help them plan vacations to the region. "With a user-friendly design suitable for laptops, smartphones and tablets, users explore rotating featured trails through videos, blog entries and Instagram feed photographs," according to *Leisure & Travel Week*. "The site also links directly to the county's consumer tourism site (www.VisitTallahassee.com) for information about upcoming events, hotels, restaurants and attractions."[17]

---

### Attraction Fun Fact

Approximately 76% of social media users post their vacation photos during or after their trips.

---

## Guidelines for Using Social Media

Once an attraction determines which social media marketing tools to use, the next stage in the process is to figure out what to do with them and how to make the most of their use. Following are some guidelines to help maximize an attraction's social media marketing strategy.

### Do Research, Start Slowly

Before launching into a social media marketing program, it's important for attractions to select platforms that will work most effectively with their audiences. According to Ray, "The first step is to clearly define your aims—what do you want to achieve by having a social media presence?…. Next, you need to assess what each social platform can offer you, along with its strengths and weaknesses," he says. "Whichever platform best matches your business objectives is the place to start."[18]

---

### How to Generate Buzz with Social Media

- ☑ Find out what customers want.
- ☑ Use a variety of social media platforms.
- ☑ Provide engaging content.
- ☑ Update content regularly.
- ☑ Post in a timely manner.
- ☑ Use attention-grabbing images and graphics.
- ☑ Promote on-site events through social media sites.
- ☑ Engage users with contests and sweepstakes.
- ☑ Use social media to drive traffic to website.
- ☑ Respond to user comments.
- ☑ Promote across social media platforms.

One approach is to begin by researching the competition, advises reporter Jennifer Salopek. "Do all of the attractions in your area have Facebook pages? Is the content fresh and current? Are they streaming video on their web site or linking to YouTube?"[19] At the same time, she says, take a good, hard look at the demographics of the attraction's audiences to determine what is likely to resonate with them. By assessing their media consumption habits and responding in kind, "You can really generate passion among your visitors and become part of their daily lives."[20]

It doesn't hurt to ask customers their preferences directly, says Hatcher. Use the attraction's website or Facebook page, or ask visitors when they arrive, "What social platform do you use the most? What do you want from social media?"[21] Additionally, while an attraction may ultimately want to implement several social media platforms to communicate with customers, these platforms don't necessarily all need to be launched at the same time. It's better to start slowly, test out a medium, see how people respond to it, and gradually add more. This will help build a following by showing users the attraction is serious about doing it right.

## Engage Customers with Content

One principle to keep at the forefront of all social media marketing decisions is that effective content is crucial for engaging and maintaining users. Regardless of the platform, content should be timely, interesting, relevant, and designed to entice users and keep them coming back for more. A starting place comes from Palmer who advises, "keep it easy, keep it fun."[22]

Create content to include a mix of text, images, videos, and other material designed to promote interactivity. This will provide customers with sufficient variety, so they don't lose interest in an attraction's activities. "The key is to create a strategy that allows you to post content in line with your [attraction's] voice and that is relevant to your audience," suggests Knauf.[23]

## Post in a Timely Manner

The types of social media used will impact the frequency of an attraction's posts. Overall, however, it's a good idea to try and post something new on social media sites at least once a day, recommends Knauf.[24] When using Facebook, Gonzalo says, "the average life expectancy of a post is 2.5 hours."[25] Given that, he believes posting 1–3 times a day will work for most tourism attractions.

Since messages posted on Twitter are so short, Gonzalo says, tweeting multiple times a day at regular intervals is not likely to oversaturate the audience. "The key thing is to be consistent. [There's] nothing worse than brands who stay silent for a couple of days or weeks, and then wake-up with a string of drive-by tweeting or posting like there's no tomorrow."[26]

In addition, advises Martin, "Post your tweets at times when your followers are online—during the commute, lunchtimes, evenings and weekends."[27] This can increase users' chances of noticing and absorbing the tweets. Regardless of the frequency of posts, Knauf advises those in charge of posting to regularly remind users to share content with others. "Relying on your fans and followers to 'like,' retweet, share, repin or comment on your posts without asking them to do so can lead to less than favourable results."[28]

## Monitor User Responses

Although attractions may only post to their social media platforms at pre-determined intervals, they need to be constantly monitoring user activity to see what their customers and potential customers are saying and doing. For example, it used to be that looking at Facebook three times a day was enough, explains Hatcher. However, she says, people tend to use Facebook early in the morning and after work from 5 p.m. to midnight.

"The golden hour of complaints is during that time period," she says. In addition, "You're going to have more questions on a weekend," when people have time to ask them. "You want to have answers to them right away."[29] Having someone available to monitor social media sites after regular business hours enables attractions to keep on top of any customer issues that could become potential problems before the start of the next business day.

## Manage Online Reputation

Not only do attractions need to monitor their own social media platforms, they also need to be aware of what's being said about them outside their realm of control.

As noted earlier, social media has become a new form of word-of-mouth advertising for businesses. One aspect of this new approach comes through the use of customer review sites such as TripAdvisor, Yelp, and Foursquare, where users can post comments that may influence future customers. For this reason, it's imperative that attractions stay on top of what's being said about them online. Wain and Levinson explain:

> For many businesses, one of the biggest hurdles to leaping onto the Internet is realizing that people will be talking about your company whether you like it or not. Mistakes are bound to happen in any business, but when they do it is quite possible that the story will wind up on the Internet—forever—where anyone searching for your business can find it.[30]

To prevent this from happening, attractions need to be proactive in managing their online reputations. This can be accomplished by regularly monitoring posts on customer review sites and responding quickly to comments, both positive and negative. "Because of the impact good (and bad) reviews can have on the bottom line, online reputation is usually handled by general managers, PR specialists and owners," says Gonzalo. "But the most important thing is to make sure there are dedicated resources to handle this key responsibility within your organization."[31]

## Measure Results

No matter how many social media platforms an attraction uses, unless they are regularly tracked, their effectiveness might never be known. The million-dollar question is, how? "Every company will (and should) have different goals for their social media campaigns," says RapidAdvance's Mark Cerminaro.

"It's not enough to track and report on simple numbers. Likes, follows, shares and even clicks all mean different things. So once you've got your goals set, you need to categorize their numbers to determine what kind of impact you are really having."[32] Some of these categories might include the degree of user awareness, level of engagement, and conversion to a brand as customers.

Awareness goes beyond numbers of fans. "It's not just reaching your fans, it's reaching the friends of those fans," says Hatcher. As for engagement, "If customers don't engage, it's almost like dead weight."[33] To determine the level of engagement, Cerminaro recommends tracking elements such as number of shares, retweets, and contest entries, among others.[34]

Conversion is the ultimate goal, explains Hatcher. Attractions need to assess whether users are satisfied enough with an attraction's brand to take the next step—clicking on "like," going to a website, making a purchase. "It's not that if you build it they will come," Hatcher notes. "You have to build it, post it, monitor it. You've got to be on it at all times."[35]

Some attractions may find that the analytics programs built into various social media platforms are sufficient to help them track their users. "Sometimes, though, these aren't sufficient for your needs, and you may have to turn to third party tools," says Cerminaro.[36]

### Get the Word Out

Regardless of the social media marketing platforms an attraction uses, what's most important is to let customers know about them, say Wain and Levinson. "Communicate to your customers and prospects that this is where they can find you by putting social media icons on your website and by listing your account names on print materials."[37] Hatcher adds, "Make sure you're cross-promoting. In your emails, include logos to social with links. Use Facebook to promote contests on other platforms." The bottom line, she stresses, is to "promote across the board."[38]

## What to Do with Social Media

Given all the different social media platforms, attractions have a great deal of flexibility in what they can do with them to reach their audiences. Following are some examples of different approaches attractions have taken with their use of social media.

### Develop a Strategy

While an attraction may rely on several channels to communicate with audiences, it may want to use different strategies with each social media platform. Reporter Juliana Gilling explains the approach taken by Paolo Viarengo, marketing manager at the Gardaland theme park in Verona, Italy.

> The park is developing distinct strategies for each of its social media channels. With Facebook, Viarengo recommends customizing the page with creative images, regularly uploading new photos and videos, and encouraging fans by posting original messages. For YouTube, his tips include creating short videos, using immersive music, optimizing tags, and inserting the park's logo into videos.[39]

Approaches taken by attractions may vary from one to the next. While many businesses use Twitter as a means of promoting on-site happenings, Gilling notes that Alton Towers in Staffordshire, United Kingdom, takes a different approach. "Alton Towers treats Twitter as a customer service tool rather than a selling channel," she explains. The attraction's policy is to try and answer customer questions within 30 minutes.[40]

## Create Contests and Promotions

Contests and promotions are easy ways for attractions to engage customers using social media. The San Diego Zoo Safari Park used Instagram to promote the opening of its Tiger Trail exhibit in 2014. Visitors entering the trail were greeted by a sign advertising the contest. The contest encouraged visitors to tag pictures taken along the Tiger Trail on Instagram, using the hashtag #TigerTrail. First prize was a park safari for four with a $400 value.[41]

When Disney launched a Vine account in 2013, the company ran a promotion called "Vine Your Disney Side" to run in conjunction with the company's advertising campaign, "Find Your Disney Side." Users were invited to submit six-second films to "celebrate their unique interest in Disney theme parks, characters, and more."[42] Winning videos were then posted on the Disney Parks' Vine account, with selected winners each receiving $1,000.

Knauf explains the value of online contests and promotions.

> Depending on the setup of your promotion, many of these campaigns allow you to increase conversions and sales, track your return on investment and build brand awareness. These types of social campaigns can help drive traffic to your website as well as your social media pages and boost the amount of time users spend on those sites.[43]

## Integrate Platforms

Many attractions try to blend their use of social media platforms to create brand awareness and get customers actively involved with the brand. According to Salopek, "'Integration' is a key word in digital marketing strategy and can mean several things. First, it means to link all of the pieces of your online presence. If you post a video on your web site, post it also on YouTube. Post a link to it on your Facebook page, and send out a link on Twitter."[44]

The Andy Warhol Museum in Pittsburgh, Pa., relies on multiple channels to promote the museum and the Warhol brand. The museum uses Twitter to tweet out quotes from Warhol and promote monthly events. In 2013, according to reporter Mackenzie Carpenter, the Warhol Museum was deemed the "seventh most 'followed' museum in the world on Twitter, right after New York's Metropolitan Museum of Art and just ahead of the J. Paul Getty Museum in Los Angeles."[45] The museum also maintains a presence on Facebook and Google+.

In addition, notes reporter Abby Mathieu:

> The museum encourages social-media engagement by setting up several iPads that link back to these sites for guests to use during their visit. The museum offers an app for smartphones called "D.I.Y. Pop" that allows users to create a silkscreen-style image, just like Warhol, and then post it to social media, tagging the museum.[46]

## Impact of Mobile on Social Media Marketing

One element that is having a dramatic effect on social media marketing is the ever-increasing use of mobile technology. Smartphones, tablets, and other portable electronic devices provide users easy access to information on a 24/7 basis, as reporter Craig Hanna explains.

Even as visitors make their way through…gates into lands of make-believe, they still engage in the outside world constantly, maintaining their connection to family, friends and co-workers with email, Facebook, Twitter, Instagram, Vine and everything else that vies for attention on that supercomputer nestled in their handbags, backpacks and pockets.[47]

This increased reliance on on-the-go technology may be perceived as a hindrance to fully enjoying the experience an attraction has to offer. At a theme park, for example, "It's not unusual to see visitors completely bypassing massive multiple inversion coasters, colourful parades or night-time spectaculars because, head bowed, they're more compelled to check in on Facebook about riding the coaster, seeing the parade or watching the fireworks than actually experiencing them," says Hanna.[48]

While this might seem disappointing to those who invested countless hours into creating and developing an attraction, from a marketing perspective, it presents new opportunities for growth. As the old saying goes, "If you can't beat 'em, join 'em." A number of attractions are devising ways to engage customers through mobile technology, using what reporter Jason McManus calls the "B.Y.O.D." approach—Bring Your Own Device.[49] This might involve encouraging customers to use their devices to post their locations on Facebook, check for on-site tips through an attraction's Twitter feed, use their smartphones to take photos of themselves at the attraction, and immediately post the pictures to Instagram.

## Mobile Apps

Many attractions now offer users apps that enable them to do a variety of tasks while on-site. These apps provide customers the ability to access maps, check wait times, make restaurant reservations, keep abreast of animal feedings or show times, and see what features are within easy reach of their locations.

Dreamworld, an amusement park in Queensland, Australia, has even gone so far as to develop a parking app that has a feature for "those who are always so excited to race into parks and jump on big rides that they forget where they parked," says reporter Keith Miller.[50] The app helps guests locate their vehicles when they emerge from the park at the end of the day.

---

### *Attraction Fun Fact*

The Google Art Project supports virtual tours of artwork from museums around the world.

---

## Virtual Tours

Some attractions actually provide guests with handheld devices to help them make the most of their experiences through virtual tours. Visitors to the Jasper Tramway in Alberta, Canada's Rocky Mountains, for example, receive a smartphone device called a vGuide, which has both visual and audio capabilities. Icons on the device provide links to the names and backgrounds of the peaks seen from the tram as it rises 7,472 feet through the mountains, explains reporter James Careless.

When the users click on a link, audio, video and graphics related to the specific icon are played back on their vGuides. At the same time, they can look over the devices at the real thing, and then back again, allowing a smooth flow between automated tour and actual sightseeing.[51]

## Augmented Reality

Another way to allow visitors to use their mobile devices to combine the real with the virtual is through augmented reality. A company called Zoo-AR has developed a program that uses technology to enhance the attraction experience. Miller explains, "Visitors use a smartphone or tablet camera to scan markers at exhibits, which then generate 3-D augmented reality displays based on those markers."[52]

## Interactive Exhibits

Museums, zoos, and other attractions can tailor their exhibits so patrons can interact with them while using their mobile devices. At the Spielzeug Welten Museum in Basel, Switzerland, visitors can use their tablets and smartphones to access background information, images, and videos as they go through the museum's vast collection of toys and teddy bears.

Another way for attractions to encourage interaction is to empower visitors to have a say in an attraction's entertainment offerings. During one season at the Isla Magica amusement park in Sevilla, Spain, guests were able to use their smartphones to choose the ending of the park's nightly show, "Indigenas Contras Alienigenas." The show featured a battle between Spanish conquistadores and invading aliens.

"All day in the park, Isla Magica's guests voted on who would win by using their cellphones to send an SMS message to a phone number, and the ending of the show would be based on this vote," says Miller. "Isla Magica also held a raffle using the votes of the 'winning option' each evening. The winner of the raffle was announced over the sound system and received a free admission ticket to the park."[53]

# Conclusion

Social media marketing has become an integral part of the communications mix for attractions. The variety of available social media platforms provides an abundance of options for reaching audiences and informing them about an attraction's offerings. Among these platforms are Facebook, Twitter, Instagram, and Pinterest, to name just a few. All of these should ultimately drive traffic to an attraction's website.

A successful social media program requires the selection of platforms that are best suited for an attraction's audiences. These should be designed to draw in customers with engaging and timely content. Social media is ideal for keeping audiences updated about current events and happenings. It can also be used to generate interest through attraction-sponsored contests and promotions. Attraction marketers need to regularly monitor these sites to see how customers are using and responding to them.

In addition to social media, the increasing use of mobile technology now offers attractions new ways to reach audiences. This can be accomplished through the creation of mobile apps, virtual tours, and interactive exhibits that encourage customers to engage with an attraction by using their mobile devices.

Social media and mobile technology applications are among the many different promotion and marketing techniques that can be used to attract and engage visitors. The next chapter will look at ways attractions can bring in customers through the use of sales promotions and merchandising.

# Notes

1. Suzy Knauf, "#SocialMedia," *Park World*, March 2013, 36.
2. Richard Palmer, "Face Value," *Attractions Management*, 2013, 56.
3. Tina Hatcher, personal interview, July 1, 2014.
4. Knauf, "#SocialMedia," 36.
5. Frederic Gonzalo, "Social Media Best Practices in Travel: Facebook," *Socialmediatoday.com*, June 16, 2014, http://socialmediatoday.com/gonzogonzo/2517836/social-media-best-practices-travel-facebook.
6. Ibid.
7. Nic Ray, "Social Gathering," *Attractions Management*, 2013, 58.
8. Frederic Gonzalo, "Social Media Best Practices in Travel: Twitter," *Socialmediatoday.com*, May 17, 2014, http://socialmediatoday.com/gonzogonzo/2436311/social-media-best-practices-travel-twitter.
9. Bruce Martin, "Six Steps to More Effective Tweeting," *TTG Digital*, February 17, 2014, http://www.ttgdigital.com/toolkit/six-steps-to-more-effective-tweeting/4690463.article.
10. Cooper Smith, "Here's Why Instagram's Demographics Are So Attractive to Brands," *Businessinsider.com*, March 13, 2014, http://www.businessinsider.com/instagram-demographics-2013-12.
11. Frederic Gonzalo, "Social Media Best Practices in Travel: Instagram," *Socialmediatoday.com*, June 1, 2014, http://socialmediatoday.com/gonzogonzo/2479236/social-media-best-practices-travel-instagram.
12. Margaret Murphy, "How to Sell and Market Your Business on Instagram," *Socialmediatoday.com*, May 2, 2014, http://socialmediatoday.com/margaretmurphydidit/2390021/how-sell-and-market-your-business-instagram.
13. Frederic Gonzalo, "Social Media Best Practices in Travel: Pinterest," *Socialmediatoday.com*, May 10, 2014, http://socialmediatoday.com/gonzogonzo/2413466/social-media-best-practices-travel-pinterest.
14. Kelly Wheeler, "Social Update," *Attractions Management*, 2013, 74.
15. Carol Wain and Jay Conrad Levinson, *Guerrilla Tourism Marketing* (Lexington, KY: WINning Entrepreneur Press, 2012), 128.
16. Hatcher, personal interview, July 1, 2014.
17. "Visit Tallahassee Launches Innovative Website Featuring Area Trails," *Leisure & Travel Week*, November 16, 2013, 41.
18. Ray, "Social Gathering," 58.
19. Jennifer J. Salopek, "10 Lessons in Digital Marketing," *Funworld*, February 2010, http://www.iaapa.org/news/newsroom/news-articles/10-lessons-in-digital-marketing-funworld-february-2010.
20. Ibid.
21. Hatcher, personal interview, July 1, 2014.
22. Palmer, "Face Value," 56.
23. Knauf, "#SocialMedia," 36.
24. Ibid.
25. Frederic Gonzalo, "8 FAQ About Social Media in Travel," *Socialmediatoday.com*, December 7, 2013, http://www.socialmediatoday.com/content/8-faq-about-social-media-travel.
26. Ibid.
27. Martin, "Six Steps to More Effective Tweeting," http://www.ttgdigital.com/toolkit/six-steps-to-more-effective-tweeting/4690463.article.

28. Knauf, "#SocialMedia," 36.
29. Hatcher, personal interview, July 1, 2014.
30. Wain and Levinson, *Guerilla Tourism Marketing*, 73.
31. Frederic Gonzalo, "Best Practices in Travel: Online Reputation," *Socialmediatoday.com*, June 26, 2014, http://www.socialmediatoday.com/content/best-practices-travel-online-reputation-0.
32. Mark Cerminaro, "How to Measure the Impact of Your Social Media Efforts," *Socialmediatoday.com*, June 26, 2014, http://www.socialmediatoday.com/content/how-measure-impact-your-social-media-efforts.
33. Hatcher, personal interview, July 1, 2014.
34. Cerminaro, "How to Measure the Impact of Your Social Media Efforts," http://www.socialmediatoday.com/content/how-measure-impact-your-social-media-efforts.
35. Hatcher, personal interview, July 1, 2014.
36. Cerminaro, "How to Measure the Impact of Your Social Media Efforts," http://www.socialmediatoday.com/content/how-measure-impact-your-social-media-efforts.
37. Wain and Levinson, *Guerilla Tourism Marketing*, 129.
38. Hatcher, personal interview, July 1, 2014.
39. Juliana Gilling, "Engagement Party," *Funworld*, November 2011, 124.
40. Ibid.
41. See Stephanie Frasco, "Social Media Contest—San Diego Zoo Safari Park & #TigerTrail," *Convert With Content*, https://www.convertwithcontent.com/social-media-contest-san-diego-zoo-safari-park-tigertrail.
42. "Disney Parks Launch New User-Generated Video Contest," *Amusement Today*, November 2013, 24.
43. Knauf, "#SocialMedia," 36.
44. Salopek, "10 Lessons in Digital Marketing," http://www.iaapa.org/news/newsroom/news-articles/10-lessons-in-digital-marketing-funworld-february-2010.
45. Mackenzie Carpenter, "Andy Warhol Museum Uses Strong Twitter Following to Broaden Art," *McClatchy-Tribune Business News*, January 4, 2013.
46. Abby Mathieu, "Warhol Museum Uses Social Media to Give Fans Their Moment," *Pittsburgh Tribune-Review*, February 11, 2014, 12.
47. Craig Hanna, "Heads Up," *Attractions Management*, 18:4, 2013, 48.
48. Ibid.
49. See Jason McManus, "b.y.o.d.: The Personal Device and Its Changing Role in Themed Entertainment," *InPark Magazine*, 9:5, 2013, 22.
50. Keith Miller, "Make Way for the Mobile Revolution," *Funworld*, June 2013, 36.
51. James Careless, "Virtual Tours," *Funworld*, March 2013, 67.
52. Miller, "Make Way for the Mobile Revolution," 38. See also Keith Miller, "A New Breed," *Funworld*, March 2013, 52.
53. Keith Miller, "The Power of the Vote," *Funworld*, May 2014, 83.

# CHAPTER SEVEN

# Sales Promotions and Merchandising

## Introduction

Sales promotions and merchandising are additional segments of the communications mix that can be used to generate attraction customers. Sales promotions rely on incentives and other short-term practices to stimulate business. They can give attractions a boost during off-peak periods or during tight economic times when business may be lagging.

Merchandising involves the sale of attraction-related products that bring in added revenue. Customers often want to take a souvenir of an attraction home with them as a reminder of their positive experiences. Attractions can cater to this interest by providing visitors with a wide range of merchandise options.

This chapter looks at different kinds of sales promotions and how they can be implemented by tourism attractions. It also examines the role merchandising plays in helping to promote attractions.

## Sales Promotions

Sales promotions are a way of enhancing business and generating new customers through the use of short-term incentives. These incentives might include coupons, discounts, contests, and sweepstakes, to name just a few. According to author Alastair Morrison, "The potential of sales promotions is in creating almost immediate sales increases, which are especially helpful during off-peak periods."[1]

Sales promotions are ideal for stimulating sales, getting customers to try new products and services, bringing in new customers, and encouraging repeat business from previous visitors.

They can be geared toward individual consumers or toward third parties like travel agents or tour operators who have access to potential customers. While they may prove immediately popular with consumers, sales promotions should not be thought of as a means of compensating for otherwise lackluster advertising efforts. They should also not be interpreted as a way to completely reverse declining sales trends, advise authors Stowe Shoemaker et al. "Promotions tied to negative features—for instance, lack of business when it is expected to be good—tend to backfire."[2]

## How They Work

An important factor to remember is that sales promotions should be short-term incentives used on an as-needed basis to stimulate sales. They may change a brand's perceived value temporarily, but they should not be designed to do so for long periods of time, or they lose their impact, advise authors Victor Middleton and Jackie Clarke. "If they are sustained for too long, they become perceived as part of the standard product, price or terms of trade. They erode profitability as well as lose their effectiveness to secure vital additional sales."[3]

To be effective, sales promotions should be in tune with other elements of an attraction's promotional efforts, such as advertising and public relations, so they complement rather than contradict them.[4] In some ways sales promotions serve as a means of prompting customers to respond to other promotional efforts, explains Terence Shimp.

> Consumers often need to be induced to buy now rather than later, to buy your brand rather than a competitor's, to buy more rather than less, and to buy more frequently. Sales promotions are uniquely suited to achieving these imperatives. Whereas advertising can make consumers aware of your brand and shape a positive image, promotions serve to consummate the transaction.[5]

## Developing Sales Promotions

The first step in developing an effective sales promotions program is to identify a need and set an objective, according to authors Philip Kotler et al. "The objective may be to entice customers to try a new product, lure customers away from competitors, or hold and reward loyal customers."[6] It may be to increase traffic flow at times when attendance is usually light by bringing in new visitors. After setting an objective, the next step is to assess what kinds of sales promotions would be appropriate and likely to resonate with customers. While there are many different types of promotions, some will be better suited for certain organizations than others.

It's essential for attractions to determine a promotion's break-even point, say Shoemaker et. al. Although some ideas may sound like winners from a consumer perspective, if they end up costing the attraction more in revenues than they make up for in volume, they defeat the purpose. "Break-even analysis should be conducted early in the sales promotion planning.... It is imperative to understand the economic consequences of the sales promotion before its execution."[7]

Once the promotion has been set, attraction marketers should communicate it using as many channels as possible—advertisements, social media, press releases, in-house signage, email, direct mail, word-of-mouth, etc. "All parts of the communication mix should be evaluated for their ability to bring customers to a promotion," advise Shoemaker et al. "No sales promotion will be successful if customers are unaware of the activity."[8]

As part of this communication process, it's important to keep employees in the loop about any attraction sales promotions as well, so they can both support and publicize them, advise Shoemaker et al.

> Make sure all of your employees know about the product or service you are promoting, what it is, how it works, how you get it, what you do with it, and so forth. The key to the success of any in-house promotion is the knowledgeable employees who publicize it to the customers.[9]

Finally, once a sales promotion has concluded, attractions should make an effort to evaluate the results. This can be accomplished by comparing sales before, during, and after a promotion, advise Kotler et al.[10] Attractions can also survey customers to see what they thought of a promotion, how it affected their actions, and if they would be likely to respond to similar promotions. This can help in the planning of future promotions.

## Types of Sales Promotions

Attractions can use a variety of sales promotions as customer incentives. According to Morrison, these can be grouped into two categories—sales offers and sales communication. "Offers are short-term inducements given to customers, travel trade intermediaries, and sales representatives to take action," he says.[11] These might include coupons or discounts that reduce the price of admission to an attraction. Sales communication might come in the form of a specialty advertising product or through in-person interaction at a trade show. It "gives the promoter additional options for communicating with present and potential customers, and travel trade intermediaries."[12] Following are examples of both types of sales promotions.

---

### Types of Sales Promotions

| Sales Offers | Sales Communication |
|---|---|
| Discounts | Trade shows and expos |
| Coupons | Specialty advertising |
| Contests | Familiarization tours |
| Season passes | Personal selling |
| Premiums | Point of sale displays |

Source: Adapted from Alastair M. Morrison, *Marketing and Managing Tourism Destinations*, and "Sales Promotion," Inc.com, http://www.inc.com/encyclopedia/sales-promotion.html.

---

### Coupons and Price-Off Discounts

Coupons typically offer customers savings on their purchases. They may reduce the price of an item, such as a retail purchase. They can also be used to boost sales by making something a good deal for consumers, as with a two-for-one admission coupon.

Morrison describes different ways companies can configure coupons. "A time-fused coupon offer includes several individual coupons that can be used during specified days, weeks, or months during the offer period. Coupons should all have a clearly indicated expiry date."[13] On the other hand, he explains, a bounce-back coupon encourages repeat business. These are point-of-sale items given to attraction customers in person as an incentive to return in the future.

Coupon distribution can be done through traditional means such as newspaper inserts or direct mail. Coupons can be sent electronically as emails, text messages, or downloads for mobile devices. Outside vendors such as supermarkets may also be authorized to distribute attraction coupons. Some attractions find online coupon services like Groupon to be useful in reaching potential customers.[14]

Price-off discounts reduce the regular price of an item such as the cost of admission. They do not require coupons but may have certain criteria that need to be met in order for them to be used. An example would be an admission discount that is only valid during specified hours or on certain days of the week. Attractions might offer discounts to specific target markets such as military personnel on Veteran's Day or moms on Mother's Day. They might also use them to reward customer loyalty or repeat business. Some attraction discounts are available to members of certain groups such as the American Association of Retired Persons (AARP) or the American Automobile Association (AAA).

Discounts can also be offered in conjunction with charitable causes. Knott's Berry Farm, in Buena Park, Calif., for example, runs a price-off promotion that benefits the Orange County Food Bank. Anyone who brings two or more canned food items to the park receives discounted admission.[15]

## Contests and Sweepstakes

Offering customers the chance to win prizes and recognition through contests and sweepstakes is another type of sales promotion. Contests invite customers to compete using some sort of skill. Sweepstakes give them a chance to win by submitting their names and contact information into a drawing. While contests are generally decided based on aptitude, sweepstakes are determined by chance.

Animal naming contests are routine promotions for zoos when new animals are born or acquired, says reporter John Morell. "The public is asked to suggest or vote on names for a new arrival."[16] This can be done on-site or using an organization's website or social media platforms. When Cleveland Metroparks Zoo acquired four grizzly bear cubs, for example, the zoo held a naming contest, which was appropriately called "Dub the Cubs."[17]

To commemorate the 100th anniversary of the *Titanic* in 2012, the Titanic Museum Attractions in Branson, Mo., and Pigeon Forge, Tenn., held a "Back to Titanic 100th Year 'Tour Ireland'" sweepstakes. Six winners received airfare for two to Belfast, where the *Titanic* was built, as well as guided tours of Dublin, Cobh, and Kilkenny.[18]

Social media platforms are ideal for contests and sweepstakes, notes marketing professional Dimitris Zotos. "Social media contests…enable brands, products or services to gain visibility in social media channels, increase audience and the interaction with them, [and] reinforce brand awareness."[19]

Contests and sweepstakes not only get customers tuned into an attraction but are also an effective way to generate media interest.

## Season Passes and Memberships

Season passes allow guests to pay one set price for a pass that is good throughout the length of an attraction's season. For year-round attractions, these passes are sometimes called annual passes or memberships. Passes generally include unlimited admission for the duration of the pass and often come with additional benefits such as retail discounts or invitations to special events and programs.

The Georgia Aquarium in Atlanta, for example, "rewards annual pass holders with perks that include faster entry via its members' lane; the first chance to experience new offerings like the 'Journey with Giants' swimming and scuba diving programs; free admission to its 4-D theater show; plus discounts on tickets for guests, parking, behind-the-scenes tours, and café and gift shop purchases," says reporter Juliana Gilling.[20]

Season passes are especially helpful to attractions during times of recession when business may slow down. They pull people into an attraction who might not otherwise visit but who, once inside, are then likely to spend money on additional items like food and merchandise. They also reinforce the appeal of the attraction for customers, explains John Robinett, senior vice president of Economics Research Associates. "By getting people to return, you're refreshing the visitor experience in their minds and reinforcing the value of your product in their decision-making process. You're building your brand and keeping it in front of people."[21]

Even with the perceived value of a season pass, some customers may be reluctant to purchase them because of high costs. Whereas a one-day attraction ticket might be reasonable and affordable to customers—depending on the attraction—an annual pass could cost several hundred dollars, which might seem cost-prohibitive. Some attractions have solved this dilemma by offering customers payment plans. "Allowing guests to spread the payments for season passes over several months is becoming more popular as [attractions] look for opportunities to increase sales and offer additional benefits to guests," says reporter Jodi Helmer.[22]

When business is booming, attractions offering season or annual passes may need to adjust the terms or costs of their passes. "There's always a balance to be struck between maximizing attendance versus optimizing admissions yield," says Gilling.[23] "You've got to do some math to figure out where that balance is, and it's different for every attraction," explains Robinett.[24]

---

### Attraction Fun Fact

The first Ferris wheel debuted at the World's Columbian Exposition in 1893. It was named after its creator, George Ferris.

---

## Specialty Advertising Products

Specialty advertising is a type of sales communication that involves giving away free products to customers or third-party agents who have contact with potential customers. They are used to promote an attraction by prominently displaying the organization's name, logo, and/or contact information. According to Morrison, "These items normally are either office products or unique or unusual gifts. They include pens, pencils, cups, glasses, paperweights, calendars, mouse pads, stationery, key rings, tote bags, balloons, T-shirts, and many other items."[25]

To be effective, specialty advertising products should be durable, tasteful, and something recipients will either want to use or keep as souvenirs. Every time the product is used or viewed, the organization's brand is reinforced in the user's mind. Some products such as pens and pencils may also be appropriate to distribute to employees who come into direct contact with attraction visitors. This enables customers to see the products being used, offering another means of brand exposure and reinforcement.

### Trade Shows and Expos

Another form of sales promotion that falls within the sales communication category is the trade show or expo. According to journalist Robert Morello, "Trade shows bring together every aspect of the travel industry in one place and allow time for meetings, interaction and new deals. They also draw media attention, public attendees, and, if they are large enough, national travel agencies."[26]

*Figure 7.1: Trade shows like the IAAPA Expo provide an excellent opportunity for attraction promotion.* (Photo Credit: Andi Stein)

Trade shows offer attraction personnel opportunities to attend seminars, network with other industry professionals, check out new products and services, and promote their own facilities to others. Within the tourism industry there are a number of professional organizations that sponsor annual trade shows and expos where attractions can promote themselves. These include the International Association of Amusement Parks and Attractions; American Alliance of Museums; Association of Zoos and Aquariums; and Association of Science-Technology Centers to name just a few.

### Familiarization Tours

Although less popular with attractions than other segments of the tourism industry, familiarization or "fam" tours are another option within the communication sector of sales promotion. Fam tours are low-cost trips to an attraction's facilities offered to travel agents, tour operators, and members of the media. Their purpose is to show off an attraction's facilities to these groups in hopes they will then promote them to their customers or audiences.

Familiarization tours are useful when launching a brand new attraction or unveiling a new or remodeled area within an existing attraction. In 2013, for instance, Legoland Florida offered a fam tour for U.S. and Canadian travel agents, which included representatives from the American Automobile Association (AAA) and Canadian Automobile Association (CAA). According to Jessica Roberts of Visit Central Florida, "Following the FAM tour, Legoland Florida reported an increase in online sales of their tickets—via AAA and CAA agents," which the attraction attributed to the tour.[27]

# Merchandising

Attraction visitors often want to take home a reminder of their experiences at the end of their stay. This has prompted the sales promotion practice known as merchandising. Shoemaker et al. believe, "Merchandising is marketing to the 'captive customer'…. The goal of merchandising is to provide opportunities for customers to purchase related or auxiliary products and services."[28] Among these are T-shirts, photos, hats, plush toys, and any number of items bearing an attraction's logo.

However, note the authors, "The goal of merchandising…should not be just to stimulate sales; it also has a more long-term goal of increasing customer satisfaction."[29] Many customers purchase merchandise toward the end of their visits, leaving satisfied both with their purchases and their day at the attraction. These purchases serve as a long-term reminder of the good times they had there. Products such as T-shirts and coffee mugs containing attraction logos subtly remind guests of the attraction's brand every time they are used.

## *Advantages of Merchandising*

Merchandising offers many advantages for attractions. For theme parks alone, retail sales can comprise 10–20 percent of revenue.[30] According to authors David Weaver and Laura Lawton, "Unlike other forms of promotion, merchandising also generates direct income, and all the more so since logo products often sell at a premium."[31] Eye-catching product displays in retail venues help stimulate customer impulse purchases. "Merchandising excites the visual senses at the point of purchase and also results in increased sales," says Morrison.[32]

For some attractions, merchandising has become so profitable that it has taken on a life of its own. This trend began with the opening of the Wizarding World of Harry Potter—Hogsmeade at Universal's Islands of Adventure in Orlando, Fla., explains reporter Jason Garcia.

> In addition to the obligatory rides and shows, Universal built a collection of intricately detailed shops and eateries, all based on locations from the Potter books and movies—and all selling custom-designed items based on the same material, from chocolate frogs to golden snitches. The results stunned the industry. When Wizarding World opened in June 2010, the lines to get into the stores often surpassed the queues for the rides. Per-visitor spending on food and souvenirs at Universal Orlando jumped nearly 30 percent in just the first year, from less than $20 to almost $26.[33]

## Attraction Merchandise

**Apparel**
T-shirts
Sweatshirts
Jackets
Shorts
Hats
Pajamas
Aprons
Socks
Costumes

**Accessories**
Handbags
Backpacks
Tote bags
Phone cases
Luggage

**Toys**
Plush animals
Dolls
Games
Puzzles
Puppets
Models

**Media**
Books
Posters
DVDs
CDs

**Housewares**
Mugs
Dishes and glasses
Flatware
Salt and pepper shakers
Pillows and blankets
Tea towels

**Jewelry**
Watches
Earrings
Necklaces
Pins
Rings

**Specialty Items**
Snow Globes
Photographs
Picture frames
Holiday ornaments
Locally made products
Gift cards
Magnets
Keychains
Bumper stickers
Lanyards

**Food Items**
Candy
Cookies
Gourmet popcorn
Coffee and tea

*Types of Merchandise*

Attraction merchandise should offer intrinsic value to customers with diverse backgrounds and interests, notes reporter Marion Hixon. "Putting their money down means taking home a piece of the attraction—their experience; so while classic logo souvenirs will always sell, it's important to offer a variety of options. Retail managers and manufacturers know this and are stocking the shelves accordingly."[34] Following are examples of different kinds of merchandise that have proven to be effective for attractions.

## Apparel

T-shirts, sweatshirts, baseball caps, and even pajamas are among the many items of clothing purchased by attraction visitors. These products are popular because they have practical value, which helps customers justify their purchase. Often apparel items bear the logo of an attraction or an image pertaining to a ride, exhibit, program, or event sponsored by the organization. When customers wear these items, they can feel a sense of pride in having experienced first-hand whatever their clothing items depict.

Not only are logo-bearing clothing popular sales items, they also serve an important marketing function, note Weaver and Lawton. "The purchasers of these products are likely to spend time acting as walking billboards for the company or destination."[35] Therefore, apparel plays a valuable role in an organization's merchandising efforts.

## Novelty Hats

One apparel item that has gained in popularity at theme parks in recent years, according to journalist Jeremy Schoolfield, is the novelty hat. On a typical day, park patrons can be spotted walking around with everything from crowns to wizard hats to traffic cones perched atop their heads. While they may wear these products only within the confines of the attraction, they wear them with pride.

"Novelty hats are a way for guests to become part of the experience, not just an observer," Schoolfield explains. "Surrounded by bright colors, fun costumes, exciting attractions, and larger-than-life characters, guests can use the hats like their own costume and become a part of the fabric of that attraction."[36]

From a merchandising standpoint, novelty hats can be developed to help market new features at an attraction. When Disney's California Adventure in Anaheim, Calif., opened its Cars Land area in 2012, for example, one of the products sold at the park was a hat shaped like a giant tire representing a ride called "Luigi's Flying Tires." From the start, product sales took off like one of Cars Land's racecars.

Although novelty hats may have limited lifespans as clothing items, says Schoolfield, "When the fun is over, the hat becomes a way to access that memory—and, in turn, the hat becomes a strong marketing piece for the attraction from whence it came."[37]

## Locally Made Products

Although a great deal of merchandise may be fairly generic, manufactured in bulk, and often produced overseas, some attractions find handcrafted products produced by local artisans and vendors to be a big hit with visitors. Seattle's Woodland Park Zoo, for instance, sells toys, clothing, and artwork produced by Washington-based artists.

At the Monterey Bay Aquarium, glass products produced by an artist in a nearby town have proven popular. In order to sell products at the aquarium, artisans must meet certain organizational guidelines, notes Hixon. "The aquarium's merchandise must reflect the marine life and conservation at the facility and, when possible, represent the marine habitat present in the surrounding Monterey Bay."[38]

Products made by local vendors are in high demand during times of recession. "People want to help their neighbors," explains Molly Harty, retail manager for The Orchard Shop at

Minnetrista, the museum honoring the Ball Brothers in Muncie, Ind.[39] The shop sells locally handcrafted items as well as books by local authors.

**Mission-Based and Sustainable Products**

In addition to locally made products, merchandise that supports an attraction's mission is also greatly appreciated by customers. The Luther Burbank Home & Gardens in Santa Rosa, Calif., serves to educate the public about the famed horticulturalist and his contributions to agriculture. In keeping with this focus:

> Best-selling souvenirs include seed packets, self-published books and booklets about Burbank, and unique T-shirts with garden themes as well as garden caps, garden aprons and hand towels. Matted reproduction prints and beautiful photos of plants also sell well.[40]

Growing interest in the environment has also deepened customer appreciation for attractions that make an effort to incorporate sustainable products into their retail mix. The San Diego Zoo, for example, sells a plush panda toy made entirely of organic fibers produced by the Aurora World toy company, notes Schoolfield. "The San Diego Zoo panda is one of several custom jobs Aurora creates for zoos across the United States, made from soybean and kapok (a sustainable silky fiber found in rainforests); even the tag is made from recycled cardboard."[41] The product is popular with zoo customers despite the fact that it costs twice as much as a regular stuffed toy.

**Photographs**

Attractions with roller coasters and other thrill rides have found ride photos to be lucrative merchandising options. "Capturing hilarious faces as a log flume is about to splash down, or squeamish looks as a coaster enters a daredevil element, can be priceless for guests," explains reporter Keith Miller.[42] Attraction managers advise the best way to market these products is to keep prices reasonable, which in turn will generate volume sales.

If possible, it's also worthwhile to make electronic photo purchases an option for guests. Park Xplor in Quintana Roo, Mexico, "is full of ziplines and rafting tours and has 34 or 35 different photo ops," says Miller. "As people go on these tours, they wear helmets with RFIDs that track them, and their movement sets off cameras that take their picture. A photo library of their tour is built up, and, at the end, guests can purchase the photos on USB flash drives."[43]

**Gift Cards**

As part of their merchandising strategies, some attractions have found it profitable to sell gift cards that can be used to pay for admission to the attraction or on-site purchases. The cards are an effective means of getting people in the door, notes Miller. "If a person receives cash as a gift, they can go spend it anywhere. But an attraction gift card pulls a recipient to the facility, and that person may be a new guest who's never been there before."[44] The Walt Disney Company, for example, offers a generic gift card that can be used "for all things Disney—theme park tickets and vacations, food and beverage, merchandise—just about any Disney business you could name, including Adventures by Disney, Disney Cruise Lines, and Disneystore.com."[45]

---

### *Attraction Fun Fact*
The Walt Disney Family Museum in San Francisco has 26 of Walt Disney's 32 Academy Awards on display.

---

Gift cards can be sold on-site, online, or at outside retail outlets, says Miller. In the case of the Disney cards, for example, "They don't have to be bought at the parks, but can now be purchased online 24/7, as well as at 8,000 grocery stores and at all Walgreen's stores—15,000 outlets in all."[46]

*Figure 7.2: Gift cards can be effective tools for bringing new customers into an attraction.* (Photo Credit: Andi Stein)

## Merchandising Venues

When it comes to merchandising venues, location and accessibility are key factors for success. Some attractions like museums and national parks may have one central gift shop where patrons can purchase souvenirs of their visits. Others may have stores and kiosks scattered throughout their facilities.

Some patrons leave their shopping to the end of their attraction visits to avoid carrying merchandise around with them all day. Retail venues located near attraction exits are ideal for catering to customers who want to make their purchases the culmination of their visits. On the other hand, for some customers, merchandise is an impulse purchase, often related to something a customer saw or experienced at an attraction, explains reporter Ed Avis.

"The impulse to buy a themed item—such as a sword that looks like the swords used by characters in your pirate boat ride—is most likely to happen immediately after an attraction."[47] This also applies to special exhibits at museums and displays of popular zoo animals like pandas or koalas. Kiosks or stores adjacent to these areas can offer specialized merchandise that directly pertains to them.

Regardless of their locations, merchandise venues should be attractive, well lit, and easy to navigate. Shelves should be sufficiently stocked and designed so merchandise is within handy reach. In addition, staff need to be knowledgeable, enthusiastic, and customer focused. "You'll sell more souvenirs, and provide a more enjoyable shopping experience for patrons, if your retail staff members are excited about what they're selling," says Avis.[48]

## Online Merchandising

As an increasing number of people turn to online shopping, attractions have found ways to continue their merchandising efforts after the fact. Online stores built into an attraction's website can promote merchandise sales after customers have gone home and resumed their regular lives, says James Careless.

> By joining the digital marketplace, they have expanded their sales reach beyond their physical premises and the limits of their operating hours. More important, these attractions have found a vehicle that not only makes them extra money, but can be used to entice visitors to their physical attractions.[49]

To ensure customers are aware of these expanded shopping options, attractions need to promote their online stores using as many forms of media as possible—brochures, advertisements, on-site signage, etc. The International Spy Museum in Washington, D.C., for example, sells a variety of spy-related merchandise through its online store, including games, apparel, spy toys, and other products developed for the museum, he says. According to the museum's retail director:

> In our brick-and-mortar store locations in downtown D.C. and Washington's Union Station, we cross-promote the online store to facilitate the growing trend toward multichannel or omni-channel shopping. In our 5,000 square-foot flagship store, we have deployed QR codes on in-store signage and on window graphics where we provide content and an online shopping offer.[50]

This principle works in reverse as well. Since online shoppers are also potential attraction customers, the online store can be used to promote the attraction itself.

## Conclusion

Sales promotions are a way of stimulating business during off-peak periods and in times of economic recession. They provide short-term incentives designed to drive traffic to an attraction. These might consist of coupons, off-price discounts, contests and sweepstakes, or season passes and memberships.

Promotions can also come in the form of sales communication. Specialty advertising products communicate an attraction's brand through giveaways imprinted with an attraction's name or logo. Trade shows and familiarization tours are a way of reaching out to travel agents and tour operators to promote an attraction.

Merchandising builds on customers' desires to take a piece of their attraction experience home with them. Merchandise includes a variety of products such as apparel, locally made items, photographs, and gift cards. Customers can purchase these products during their stay at an attraction or online after their visit is over.

Another way to stimulate sales and bring people into an attraction is to offer them something of added value to enhance their visits such as a special event or program. The next chapter will focus on the role special events play as promotion and marketing tools for attractions.

## Notes

1. Alastair M. Morrison, *Hospitality & Travel Marketing, 4th ed.* (Clifton Park, NY: Delmar, 2010), 482.
2. Stowe Shoemaker, Robert C. Lewis, and Peter C. Yesawich, *Marketing Leadership in Hospitality and Tourism, 4th ed.* (Upper Saddle River, NJ: Pearson, 2007), 437.
3. Victor T.C. Middleton and Jackie Clarke, *Marketing in Travel and Tourism, 3rd ed.* (Oxford, England: Butterworth-Heinemann, 2001), 263.
4. See Shoemaker, Lewis, and Yesawich, *Marketing Leadership in Hospitality and Tourism, 4th ed.*, 436; and Morrison, *Hospitality & Travel Marketing, 4th ed.*, 549.
5. Terence A. Shimp, *Advertising, Promotion, and Other Aspects of Integrated Marketing Communications, 8th ed.* (Mason, OH: South-Western Cengage Learning, 2010), 482.
6. Philip Kotler, John T. Bowen, and James C. Makens, *Marketing for Hospitality and Tourism, 5th ed.* (Boston, MA: Pearson, 2010), 411.
7. Shoemaker, Lewis, and Yesawich, *Marketing Leadership in Hospitality and Tourism, 4th ed.*, 443.
8. Ibid.
9. Ibid., 450.
10. Kotler, Bowen, and Makens, *Marketing for Hospitality and Tourism, 5th ed.*, 418.
11. Morrison, *Hospitality & Travel Marketing, 4th ed.*, 551-2.
12. Ibid.
13. Ibid., 566.
14. See, for example, James Careless, "West Edmonton Mall Still Drawing Crowds After Thirty Years," International Association of Amusement Parks and Attractions, http://www.iaapa.org/news/newsroom/news-articles/west-edmonton-mall-still-draws-crowds-after-three-decades.
15. See "Knott's Berry Farm's 12th Annual Canned Food Drive," *Theme Park Adventure Magazine*, December 19, 2013, http://themeparkadventure.com/knotts-berry-farms-12th-annual-canned-food-drive.

16. John Morell, "Fringe Fame," *Funworld*, March 2013, 65.

17. Ibid.

18. See "Back to Titanic 100th Year 'Tour Ireland' Sweepstakes," Titanic Museum Attractions, http://www.titanicattraction.com/ireland/about.php.

19. Dimitris Zotos, "6 Tips for Designing and Running Social Media Contests," Webseo Analytics, http://www.webseoanalytics.com/blog/6-tips-for-designing-and-running-social-media-contests.

20. Juliana Gilling, "Pass It On," *Funworld*, May 2009, http://www.iaapa.org/news/newsroom/news-articles/pass-it-on-funworld-may-2009.

21. John Robinett quoted in Gilling, "Pass It On," http://www.iaapa.org/news/newsroom/news-articles/pass-it-on-funworld-may-2009.

22. Jodi Helmer, "Pass It On," *Funworld*, September 2013, 77.

23. Gilling, "Pass It On," http://www.iaapa.org/news/newsroom/news-articles/pass-it-on-funworld-may-2009.

24. Robinett quoted in Gilling, "Pass It On," http://www.iaapa.org/news/newsroom/news-articles/pass-it-on-funworld-may-2009.

25. Morrison, *Hospitality & Travel Marketing, 4th ed.*, 553.

26. Robert Morello, "Tourism Promotion and Marketing," *Houston Chronicle.com*, http://smallbusiness.chron.com/tourism-promotion-marketing-57157.html.

27. Jessica Roberts, "PCTSM Educational Tour Results in Increased Sales of Legoland Florida Tickets by AAA and CAA Travel Agents," *SunnyCentralFlorida.com*, November 14, 2013, http://sunnycentralflorida.com/2013/11/14/pctsm-educational-tour-results-in-increased-sales-of-legoland-florida-tickets-by-aaa-and-caa-travel-agents.

28. Shoemaker, Lewis, and Yesawich, *Marketing Leadership in Hospitality and Tourism, 4th ed.*, 445.

29. Ibid.

30. See Michael Switow, "Let's Go Shopping!" *Funworld*, April 2013, 51.

31. David Weaver and Laura Lawton, *Tourism Management*, 2nd ed. (Milton, Queensland: John Wiley & Sons, Australia, 2002), 228.

32. Morrison, *Hospitality & Travel Marketing, 4th ed.*, 482.

33. Jason Garcia, "Theme Parks Seize on Potter's Success to Peddle New Must Have Items," *Orlando Sentinel.com*, June 16, 2013, http://articles.orlandosentinel.com/2013-06-15/news/os-theme-park-spending-battle-20130614_1_wizarding-world-universal-orlando-harry-potter.

34. Marion Hixon, "Fly Off the Shelves," *Funworld*, September 2010, http://www.iaapa.org/news/newsroom/news-articles/fly-off-the-shelves-funworld-september-2010.

35. Weaver and Lawton, *Tourism Management, 2nd ed.*, 228.

36. Jeremy Schoolfield, "Tip of the Cap," *Funworld*, April 2013, 59.

37. Ibid.

38. Marion Hixon, "In Their Own Backyards," *Funworld*, September 2010, http://www.iaapa.org/news/newsroom/news-articles/in-their-own-backyards-funworld-september-2010.

39. Molly Harty quoted in "Museum Shop Retail: Tips to Stock the Right Souvenirs," *Tourist Attractions & Parks*, November 2013, 150.

40. "Museum Shop Retail: Tips to Stock the Right Souvenirs," 151.

41. Jeremy Schoolfield, "From the Runway to the Midway," *Funworld*, June 2009, http://www.iaapa.org/news/newsroom/news-articles/runway-to-the-midway-funworld-june-2009.

42. Keith Miller, "Picture Perfect: Ride Photo Systems Bring a Great ROI When Done Right," *Funworld*, November 2010, http://www.iaapa.org/news/newsroom/news-articles/picture-perfect-funworld-november-2010.

43. Ibid.

44. Keith Miller, "Plastic Gold," *Funworld*, November 2010, http://www.iaapa.org/news/newsroom/news-articles/plastic-gold-funworld-november-2010.

45. Jill Thomas quoted in Miller, "Plastic Gold," http://www.iaapa.org/news/newsroom/news-articles/plastic-gold-funworld-november-2010.

46. Miller, "Plastic Gold," http://www.iaapa.org/news/newsroom/news-articles/plastic-gold-funworld-november-2010.
47. Ed Avis, "Better Buying: 7 Ways to Improve Your Guest Shopping Experience," *Funworld*, May 2013, http://www.iaapa.org/news/newsroom/news-articles/7-ways-to-improve-your-guests%27-shopping-experience-funworld-may-2013.
48. Ibid.
49. James Careless, "Go Where Your Customers Are: Tips for Effective Online Merchandising," International Association of Amusement Parks and Attractions, http://www.iaapa.org/news/newsroom/news-articles/strategies-for-successfully-selling-attraction-merchandise-online.
50. Jodi Zeppelin quoted in Careless, "Go Where Your Customers Are: Tips for Effective Online Merchandising," http://www.iaapa.org/news/newsroom/news-articles/strategies-for-successfully-selling-attraction-merchandise-online.

# CHAPTER EIGHT

# Special Events

## Introduction

With proper planning and execution, special events can be powerful promotional and marketing tools for attractions. Events bring people together for a specific purpose and provide them with a reason to celebrate, interact with others, and be entertained. Author C.A. Preston explains, "Events are about excitement, creativity, and enthusiasm and the generation of experiences and memories."[1]

A special event can be a form of brand marketing. It serves as a way of making people aware of an attraction and bringing them into the venue. An event provides an opportunity to shine a spotlight on the attraction itself and what it has to offer customers in the way of entertainment, leisure, education, and fun. A well-developed event may also appeal to journalists interested in bringing it to the attention of readers and viewers. As Preston notes, "In creating a well-received event, it is possible for an organization to target a number of important audiences with positive public relations."[2]

Special events can vary in size and scope, depending on the nature of an attraction. They may be something as small as a wine-and-cheese reception held before the opening of a museum exhibit or as large as a city-sponsored festival designed to bring tourists to a specific locale. Some events are seasonal, marking an occasion like Halloween or Christmas. Others might be a routine part of an attraction's operations, such as a monthly speaker series.

Whatever the purpose, events have the potential to entice large numbers of people to an attraction. For this reason, they require a certain degree of planning, strategy, and promotion to ensure their success. If executed correctly, a special event can be a big draw for a tourism venue, something attendees are likely to remember. This chapter discusses different types of special events that have proven successful for attractions. It offers guidelines on how to develop, organize, and promote an event that will generate buzz and bring customers to an attraction.

## Types of Events

Attractions use a variety of special events to complement their regular offerings. These range from one-time happenings that commemorate something specific to annual celebrations that bring back visitors year after year. Following are examples of special events that have proven effective for different kinds of tourism attractions.

### Milestone Events

Milestone events like anniversaries or birthdays offer attractions a reason to celebrate. As noted in Chapter 5, they can also attract media attention, helping to increase awareness of a tourism venue. Milestone events pay homage to an attraction's existence. For longstanding customers, they may evoke pleasant memories associated with childhood or with turning points in their own lives that pertain to the attraction. This can encourage return visits by customers who may not have been to the attraction for a long time and want to re-live these memories.

Planning a milestone event can take months or years, depending on the venue and the resources available for the event. Decisions need to be made about how the event will be commemorated and communicated to the public. A milestone event such as a 50th anniversary, for example, might be an ongoing process that spans a certain length of time. It could include special promotional opportunities such as gimmicks designed to bring people to the attraction. "Many attractions raffle off vacations or give away new cars. Others roll prices back to decades-ago levels," says journalist Dan Rafter.[3]

When the Mall of America in Minneapolis celebrated its 20th birthday, for instance, the venue gave away prizes every day for 20 days prior to the mall's actual birthdate. On the birthday itself, noted Rafter, "Buddy Valastro, star of the TLC show 'Cake Boss,' created a 3-D birthday cake to mark the milestone."[4] Mall patrons gobbled up 2,000 pieces of the cake.

Milestone events also provide great opportunities to encourage the use of social media through online contests and promotions. Social media platforms such as Facebook or Twitter, for example, can help spread the word about the event to potential customers ahead of time or be incorporated into the event itself.

---

### *Attraction Fun Fact*
More than 400 events are held at the Mall of America every year.

---

### Seasonal/Holiday Events

Holidays provide ideal opportunities for attractions to sponsor events. Traditional holidays such as Halloween, Christmas, and Easter hold widespread appeal for families looking for activities to do together. These events can be spread out over a period of time leading up to a holiday. They can also be one-time activities held on a specific day, as with an Easter Egg Hunt or a Valentine's Day Ball.

*Figure 8.1: The Holiday Lights festival at Kennywood is an annual event for the Pittsburgh, Pa., amusement park.* (Photo Credit: Photo courtesy of Kennywood Amusement Park.)

In recent years, Halloween has emerged as a major holiday for attractions when it comes to generating excitement among patrons. As a result, many attractions have found Halloween-related events to be profitable for them. Knott's Berry Farm in Buena Park, Calif., was the first theme park to recognize the holiday's potential. The park launched a Halloween event in 1972, which has since become an annual tradition. In the month preceding Halloween, the theme park closes early and then re-opens at night as "Knott's Scary Farm," with a separate admission fee.

The annual Halloween Haunt features "scare zones" populated by goblins, ghosts, and zombies, as well as live shows featuring entertainers such as Elvira, Mistress of the Dark.[5] Given the success of this event, other attractions such as Ocean Park in Hong Kong, Busch Gardens in Tampa, Fla., and Kings Island in Cincinnati, Ohio, have followed suit with similar Halloween-related events.

Christmas light displays are another form of seasonal events used by venues such as theme parks and zoos. After many years of a successful Halloween event, the Kennywood amusement park in Pittsburgh, Pa., decided to extend its holiday season into December. In 2011, the park launched a "Holiday Lights" festival, explains Jim Futrell, historian for the National Amusement Park Historical Association.

> Kennywood looked at Christmas traditions and how they would fit in the park. At the heart of the event was a light show in the trees and structures surrounding the lagoon. Other activities included photos with the park mascots...letters to Santa, and holiday craft vendors.[6]

The event also featured ice carving, cookie decorating, nightly performances by local choral groups, and the transformation of the park's train into the "Gingerbread Express complete with its own Christmas decorations and soundtrack," says Futrell.[7]

While seasonal events may be good for business, they pose certain challenges for venues in cold-weather locales. These include the ability to provide heat and running water for food venues. The costs involved in addressing these issues need to be taken into account when planning events in these types of venues.

Even periodic holidays can offer opportunities for events. The Oregon Zoo celebrated the Year of the Snake during the 2013 Chinese New Year. Free admission and a chance for visitors to get an up-close look at Bubba, a 15-foot Burma python, were among the event's offerings.[8]

## Partnership Events

One way to use events for bringing in new business is by forming partnerships with local organizations that can supply an attraction with potential customers. A partnership between the Ohio State University (OSU) Alumni Association and the Cedar Point amusement park in Sandusky, Ohio, was the driving force behind OSU Day at Cedar Point in May 2013. The park opened its gates the day before the official opening day of the summer season and invited OSU alums to be the first to ride its newest roller coaster, the Gatekeeper.

While at Cedar Point, OSU alumni had access to the park's rides, shows, and vendors. Alumni also held a pep rally and brought in the school's band to kick off the event. The partnership was a way to build goodwill between the amusement park and the University. It enabled Cedar Point to reach out to the OSU alumni community and show them what the park has to offer.[9]

## Charity Events

Attractions can also reach out and partner with local organizations by sponsoring charity events. Hosting a charity event on-site at an attraction helps support the partner organization's fundraising efforts and simultaneously offers visitors exposure to the attraction. Dollywood in Pigeon Forge, Tenn., hosts an annual food drive to raise money for a local food ministry, according to reporter Keith Miller. "Dollywood allows people who live or work in Sevier County, where Dollywood is located, to get into the park for just $5, and then the money is donated to the food ministry."[10]

## Mega and Hallmark Events

Mega events are those that become tourism attractions unto themselves just by taking place. They bring thousands of people together from all over the world to a specific location for a particular purpose. According to author Donald Getz, "Mega-events, by way of their size or significance, are those that yield extraordinarily high levels of tourism, media coverage, prestige, or economic impact for the host community, venue or organization."[11]

Mega-events include the Olympics, World Cup, and World's Fairs and International Expositions. Because of the large-scale nature of a mega-event, the planning process may take place over a period of years. A mega-event will involve multiple stakeholders who contribute to the planning and execution of the event. These stakeholders might include the city hosting the event, organization sponsoring it, and local civic groups.

Hallmark events are large-scale happenings associated with a specific host locale. They, too, can attract international crowds and make the event's host an attraction in its own right, as authors Johnny Allen et al. explain.

> Hallmark events may even relate to whole countries rather than just cities or regions, with some examples being the Tour de France and Mexico's Day of the Dead celebrations. Such events, which are identified with the very character of these places and their citizens, bring huge tourist dollars, a strong sense of local pride and international recognition.[12]

Other popular hallmark events include the Boston Marathon, Kentucky Derby, Munich's Oktoberfest, Pamplona's Running of the Bulls, and New Orleans' Mardi Gras celebration.

---

### *Attraction Fun Fact*
The first Olympic Games were held in Olympia, Greece, in 776 B.C.

---

## Cultural Celebrations and Festivals

Events created to celebrate different cultures work well to bring diverse groups of people together. According to Getz, "Festivals are one of the most common forms of cultural celebration."[13] They may be designed to commemorate specific holidays such as Cinco de Mayo or Chinese New Year. They can also celebrate a particular heritage or ethnic group.

According to Norman Kahn of Utopia Entertainment, "Bringing in celebrations from other cultures and other parts of the world…can allow you to reach a new audience you may not be currently serving."[14] Parades, rituals, and costumes reflecting a particular culture or heritage can be incorporated into cultural celebrations. These events can also include the sale of ethnic foods and live entertainment programs that pay tribute to the culture being celebrated.

Festivals can also be organized around a universal theme such as music, art, dance, or food. These types of events are a way of drawing people to an attraction because they are especially interested in the chosen theme. According to Allen, et al., "Regional festivals, too, are a growing phenomenon, with many large and small towns expressing their unique character and distinctiveness through well-honed festival and community celebrations."[15] Examples include the Eugene Celebration in Eugene, Ore., and the Heritage Festival in Placentia, Calif.

## Offbeat or Unusual Events

Just as tourism venues themselves can be offbeat or unusual, this same one-of-a-kind concept can be incorporated into a special event at a more traditional attraction. An offbeat event is likely to generate interest from regular patrons who are eager to experience something new and different in a tried-and-true venue. It can also bring first-time visitors to a venue for the event itself, providing them an introduction to the attraction and ideally inspiring them to make return visits.

Coney Island Park in Cincinnati, Ohio, used this approach when it hosted "Fire Up the Night," the first fireworks competition ever staged in the United States. Modeled after a similar event in Montreal, the contest "pitted the United States, Canada, and Mexico against one another in an international competition for bragging rights…. The result was a solid hour of dueling pops, blasts, and streamers that lit up the night sky."[16] The park charged a flat fee per carload for those who attended. During the competition, visitors had access to the park's rides and food vendors. "Fire Up the Night" was so popular that it became an annual event for the park.

## Developing a Successful Event

From the outside, a well-run special event may appear effortless to the audience. In reality, many factors contribute to the success of a special event. These include planning and organization, budgeting, staffing, communication, operations, promotion and marketing, and evaluation.

### Planning and Organization

Putting on a special event requires a keen eye for detail and a commitment to planning and organization. According to authors Anton Shone and Bryn Parry:

> It can be argued that the planning process itself is the real key to what will happen. In having to sit down and prepare a plan, you have to think about the event you are going to undertake, and therefore to identify the elements and issues that need to be sorted out. For this to work well, there has to be a systematic approach, because unless you break the plan down into smaller component parts, something important could easily be missed.[17]

---

### Types of Special Events

- Holiday celebrations
- Cultural and heritage festivals
- Educational programs
- Birthday/anniversary celebrations
- Sporting events and games
- VIP events
- Grad nights
- Member appreciation events
- Fundraisers
- Community events
- Donor recognitions
- Concerts and performances
- Theme parties
- Food festivals
- Grand openings

## Establish a Purpose

A good starting point for an attraction in the planning of an event is to determine its purpose. Is the event intended to attract new customers? Provide added value to existing ones? Expand the local community's awareness of the organization? All of these may guide the direction of the event in terms of how it is planned and organized. As Getz explains, "A good statement of purpose will provide event organizers and managers with a firm foundation upon which vision and strategies can be built."[18]

## Determine Scope and Feasibility

Once the purpose has been established, the details of the event can begin to unfold. A key factor in getting the planning process started is to determine the scope of the event and the resources available to support it. Events require a great deal of effort, and conceiving something that is too unwieldy can cause subsequent problems.

Organizers need to make decisions early on about the length of the event. It might be a one- or two-day happening held on specific dates, or a seasonal event such as a Halloween promotion or anniversary celebration that goes on for an extended period of time. The length of the event can potentially affect a number of other planning-related issues such as activities, staffing, advertising and marketing, and budget.

Doing preliminary research can assist in determining the scope and feasibility of an event. Research can help identify the target audience, their interests, and the best way to reach them. It can also provide insights into what the competition might be doing in the way of similar events that could potentially influence this target audience.

## Assign Responsibility

Another early step in the planning process is to determine who will be responsible for putting on the event. For most attractions, special events are generally team efforts. Although one person may be in charge of the overall execution of the event, many brains and hands are likely to be involved in pulling it all together.

Some attractions have dedicated staff members whose jobs entail organizing events on a regular basis. Others may fold event planning into the realm of public relations or marketing. For nonprofit attractions such as museums or zoos, the event planner may be someone responsible for the organization's fundraising efforts. Some organizations may opt to hire an event-planning consultant to organize their events while maintaining a point person within the company to serve as a liaison with the outside consultant.

## Prepare a Budget

A realistic budget is especially important when planning a special event. An event budget will include fixed costs for items such as equipment rental, salaries, fees for entertainers, etc. "Fixed costs must be paid regardless of attendance at the event, and regardless of revenue," explains Getz[19]

The event will also include variable costs that may fluctuate, depending on actual attendance figures and the impact attendance may have on operations. Consequently, when budgeting for an event, it is better to overestimate costs than to find at its conclusion that the event ended up costing the organization more financially than it gained in long-term benefits with the public.

Potential sources of income for an event may come from food, beverage, and merchandise sales generated during the event. While this revenue stream can potentially be quite lucrative, it may not always be a dependable source of income since it comes after the fact. If event attendance is hampered by bad weather or crisis, for example, the expected revenue from these sources may be directly affected.

### Find a Potential Sponsor

Some tourism attractions routinely designate monetary resources for special events when planning their annual budgets. Others may need to raise funds for an event from outside donors or sponsors. According to Getz, "A sponsor is any individual, agency, or group that provides resources in exchange for specific benefits or performance."[20] In the case of an event, the benefits may include the use of a sponsor's name in marketing and promotional materials. It might even involve attaching the sponsor's name to the event.

The Quassy Amusement Park in Middlebury, Conn., for example, put on an annual Fourth of July celebration, which doubled as a charity event for a local food bank. According to reporter Lisa Anderson Mann, the park solicited "corporate sponsors for both the fireworks show and the "Magic in the Sky" laser show…. Sponsors [received] advertising publicity, press release mentions, signage, and courtesy passes."[21]

When choosing a sponsor to help finance an event, Getz recommends that organizations look for those that seem to be an appropriate match. "Sponsorship has to fit the event and its culture, goals and strategies…. The best sponsors are not just those that provide the most resources but those that ensure harmony, or a close fit between the goals, images, and programs of each."[22]

## Recruitment and Staffing

When organizing a special event, an attraction needs to ensure there are sufficient individuals on-site to accommodate attendees. Events sometimes require that an attraction be open beyond normal operating hours. This means additional help may be needed to supplement the attraction's regular employee base.

### Hire Paid Staff

Using current employees to staff an event is ideal, of course, because they are already familiar with the attraction and its regular customers. However, some staff members may be better suited than others to handle the volumes of traffic a special event can potentially draw to a tourism attraction.

Hiring outside paid staff with experience in running events can ease the burden of staffing, as their expertise can complement the knowledge of in-house staff. Outside staff can be recruited through local tourism associations, industry trade publications, employment agencies, and job websites like Craigslist.

### Recruit Volunteers

Nonprofit attractions such as museums and zoos are often heavily dependent on volunteers to staff their events. These individuals may be part of the organization's regular core of volunteers or recruited specifically for a particular event. Volunteers bring their own set of challenges since they are donating their time and may have different needs and expectations than those of paid staff. It's advisable to recognize this and ensure the expectations of the attraction are clearly delineated and communicated, as authors Maureen Connolly, et al. explain.

> Volunteers need to know specifically what their duties and responsibilities will be and what skills they need for a particular task…. Volunteers should also be made aware of where their job begins and where their responsibilities end. This is not to curtail the enthusiasm of the individual; rather, the fact that the volunteer understands the specific boundaries of a task prevents… communication problems and potential conflict.[23]

Organizations can recruit volunteers by reaching out to local schools and universities, senior centers, youth groups, clubs and organizations, and by contacting attraction patrons through social media.

## Training and Communication

Regardless of who may be staffing an event, building a coherent staff team or small groups of teams can make a world of difference in how prepared workers are for the event. A key element in building successful event teams is providing sufficient training to all staff, whether they are from inside or outside the attraction.

As Allen, et al. note, "It is unrealistic to expect teams to perform effectively without appropriate training. Training should include the team's role in the activity and how the role contributes to the activity's overall success."[24] Training should also instill staff with an understanding of any relevant policies and procedures set up for the event, the procedural chain of command, and clear guidelines on what to do in the case of an accident or emergency during the event.

Regular and consistent communication with those working the event should be incorporated into the event planning process. Staff should be kept in the loop about any last-minute changes that might affect their roles in the event. They also need to be provided with a means of communicating with each other and with higher-ups who can answer questions and provide assistance if needed. These might include two-way radios, cell phones, or other electronic devices that allow them easy access to others.

## Operations and Logistics

Every event offers a variety of logistical decisions and challenges. Some of these will need to be addressed ahead of time, while others may occur as the event unfolds.

### Admission and Ticketing

An early decision to be made relates to how people will be able to get into the event. Will entry be included in the cost of regular admission to the attraction, or will tickets be sold separately? If separately, will they be sold on-site, online, over the phone, or through third-party distributors such as travel agents or local merchants?

Shone and Parry advise:

> Do not exclude part of your potential target market by making it difficult, or impossible, for them to get the tickets or make the booking they want to. Ideally, you should have as many ways of selling tickets and as many outlets as you can imaginatively think of and can reasonably service.[25]

## Site Planning and Management

Site management encompasses the elements involved in preparing the venue for the event. This includes traffic flow, crowd control, accessibility, and safety. It can also include placement and arrangement of concessions, entertainment stages, restroom facilities, signage, etc. According to Getz, "Site planning is as important to the event as programming, with customer reactions to the site being critical in determining success."[26]

Attractions should ensure equipment is up-to-date and in good working order. Measures need to be put into place for crowd control to avoid fire or accident hazards and ensure a safe environment. In addition, sufficient parking, seating, and restroom accommodations are essential for the comfort of event guests. Proper signage will allow customers to find their way around with ease and will ideally reduce the number of people asking for directions. Strategically placed information booths on-site at the event can be beneficial for guests needing assistance as well. Attractions may also want to designate special areas for media covering the event.

## Event Programming

The essence of any special event is its program, as Allen et al. explain.

> The program of the event is the flow of the performers, speakers, catering and the other elements of the event over time. It is the 'what's on' of the event. The program creates the core event experience for the attendee. Ultimately, the event experience for the attendee and the sponsors rests on the success of the program.[27]

Those orchestrating an attraction event, therefore, will naturally want to do everything possible to ensure the program will appeal to those in attendance.

Event programs can include a myriad of activities, depending on the attraction itself. A theme park event, for instance, might feature parades, live performances, and fireworks. An event at a museum or gallery such as an exhibit opening could include speeches or educational presentations.

Regardless of the nature of the attraction, every event program should be prepared to offer value to attendees. Activities need to be well organized and scheduled at times when they are likely to draw crowds. If there are multiple programming activities happening simultaneously, they should be situated in different areas of the attraction, so they don't interfere with each other.

An event program schedule should be provided to attendees to help them plan their day. The schedule should also be listed on an attraction's website, so potential visitors can see it ahead of time. It can be printed and given to each attendee who comes through the attraction's gate. It should also be prominently posted in multiple locations throughout the attraction to make it easy for attendees to know when and where activities are happening.

No matter what an event program includes, it should be designed to engage the audience and highlight the best of the attraction to customers. "People expect to have fun at most special events," says Getz. "It is part of the social meaning of public festivities."[28]

## Promotion and Marketing

A marketing plan developed specifically for a special event is useful when strategizing how to reach potential customers and which communication channels to use to get their attention. "Marketing strategy for an event sets it on a road, with a specific destination," explains Preston. "This means that you need clear objectives and an understanding that there are different ways of fulfilling them."[29]

### Target Audience

The target audience should be the driving force behind an event's marketing and promotional materials. Some events may be intended for the general public while others will be geared toward specific populations of attraction visitors. Event promoters need to assess the best way to reach their audiences—advertisements, printed materials, electronic or online media, social media, direct mail, word-of-mouth, or a combination of all of the above.

It's helpful to have a sense of what kinds of event promotions are likely to resonate with different audiences. These might include discount coupons, special admission deals such as two-for-one ticket sales, interactive activities that incorporate mobile media, or event packages that bundle admission with food, beverage, and merchandise promotions. Surveys done on-site or through an attraction's social media sites well in advance of the event can help gather data that can be used to develop promotions aimed at specific target markets.

### Promotion Strategies

Much of an event's marketing and promotion may initially be done using social media channels and the organization's website. Both the website and an attraction's Facebook page are ideal for providing advance notice about an event. This information should be updated regularly, especially as the event date draws near. This will help keep potential attendees interested in the event, notes Preston. "The website is part of the event, and if visitors to your site are not getting what they are looking for in a sense, how will they know whether the live event will give them what they are looking for?"[30]

A planned media campaign should be set in motion well before an event. Depending on the nature and scope of the event, paid advertising campaigns that include print, TV, and radio may be implemented. To increase opportunities for press coverage, promoters should alert the media of event happenings through press releases and story pitches. On the day of the event, personnel need to be available to assist any media representatives who show up to cover it.

### Promotion Schedules

One factor to remember when developing promotional and marketing materials is to leave enough time before the event to do things right, as Shone and Parry explain. "Of all the marketing planning activities, the marketing schedule is the one most likely to surprise people new to the job. The lead times for preparing some marketing activities can be shockingly long."[31]

Because of this, it's advisable to develop a marketing and promotion schedule that includes specific activities and their deadlines. This schedule should include lead times for producing print publications, distributing promotional materials to the media, and launching social media.

## Post-Event Evaluation

A step in the event management process that is sometimes overlooked is post-event evaluation. After the crowds have gone home, the grounds cleaned up, and the remnants of the event packed away until next year, it's worthwhile to take a good, hard look at what went right with the event and what can be improved upon for next time. Authors Scott Forrester and Lorne Adams explain, "The purpose of evaluating the event is to measure the effectiveness of the event in terms of meeting its stated goals and objectives and to measure the quality of the performance of the event such as whether or not the event was profitable."[32]

## Evaluating an Event

Event evaluation provides valuable information that can be used to plan future programs and events. Here are some sample questions to consider when evaluating the success of a special event.

### Event Objectives
What were the objectives of the event?
How well did we meet these objectives?
What more could have been done to meet the event's objectives?

### Budget
Did event planning and execution fall within budget?
Did the event meet or exceed projected financial goals? If not, why?
What other financial resources might be needed to offer this event in the future?

### Event Set-Up and Facilities
Was the space allotted appropriate for the event?
How streamlined was the admission/registration process?
How convenient was the location of event activities, vendors, etc.?

### Event Staff
Did we have sufficient staff and volunteers to manage the event?
Were these individuals properly trained to do their jobs?
What more could be provided in the way of training for future events?

### Marketing and Publicity
What kind of promotion and publicity did we do for the event?
Was this sufficient in attracting the intended audience?
What additional promotion could be done for future events?

**Event Attendance**
How many people attended this event?
Did actual attendance reach projected numbers?
What factors might have affected attendance figures?

**Event Programming**
Did we have a sufficient mix of event programs and activities?
Were the event's programs well attended?
Were the programs well received by the public?

**Event Issues**
Were there any unexpected problems or crises that arose during the event?
How were these issues resolved?
Were customers and staff satisfied with the resolution of these issues?

**Future Events**
Should we plan this event again in the future?
What activities should be retained and repeated for future events?
What changes could make the event more successful?

A starting point for evaluation is to refer back to the purpose of the event and ask questions. Did the event achieve what it was designed to do? Were the costs of the event within budget? Were the marketing and promotional activities sufficient to bring the desired audience to the attraction? Determining the answers to these and other questions and keeping a record of the answers will be useful to those involved in planning the same or similar events in the future.

Event organizers can use surveys to gather data from attendees to find out what they liked and didn't like about an event. These can be distributed on-site at the event or sent electronically if email addresses or other contact information is available. Attractions can use survey data to make adjustments to elements such as the event's hours of operation, activities, staffing, food and drink options, and facilities such as restrooms and seating areas. From a marketing perspective, open-ended questions on a post-event survey may yield comments that can be used as testimonials in the promotion of future events.

Surveys are also useful for gathering demographic information about attendees. This is helpful in the planning of future events, as it can guide the types of activities or programming different populations might desire. As noted by Allen, et al., "Establishing an accurate demographic profile of the audience will enable marketing strategies to be refined and the spending of marketing funds to be better targeted."[33]

## Conclusion

Special events can add to an attraction's regular promotion and marketing activities. They offer customers something to enrich their visitor experience and provide them with a different perspective on the attraction. They can also appeal to journalists looking for new ways to cover an attraction.

There are many different types of events that are likely to appeal to visitors. Events can commemorate holidays or milestones like birthdays or anniversaries. They can help an attraction raise money for local charities. They can also celebrate different cultures or highlight specific themes such as art or music.

Planning and developing an event requires great attention to detail. Organizers need to determine the event's purpose, set a budget, and recruit and train staff. They also need to address logistics such as site management, programming, and publicity. Post-event evaluation can help organizers determine what went well with an event and what can be improved upon for next time to ensure an ideal visitor experience.

An important part of this visitor experience depends on customer perceptions of how well their needs are met during their attraction visits. The next chapter will discuss the roles guest relations and customer service play as marketing tools in the successful management of an attraction.

## Notes

1. C.A. Preston, *Event Marketing: How to Successfully Promote Events, Festivals, Conventions, and Expositions* (Hoboken, NJ: Wiley & Sons, 2012), 2.
2. Ibid., 8.
3. Dan Rafter, "Make Your Mark," *Funworld*, November 2012, 200.
4. Ibid., 202.
5. See Michelle Mills, "Halloween Comes to Area Theme Parks," *San Gabriel Valley Tribune.com*, September 17, 2013, http://www.sgvtribune.com/lifestyle/20130917/halloween-comes-to-area-theme-parks-knotts-scary-farm-halloween-horror-nights-and-more.
6. Jim Futrell, "Kennywood Lights Up the Holidays," *Funworld*, June 2012, 43.
7. Ibid.
8. See Katy Muldoon, "Oregon Zoo celebrates Year of the Snake on Sunday with Free Admission," *OregonLive.com*, http://www.oregonlive.com/portland/index.ssf/2013/02/oregon_zoo_celebrates_year_of.html.
9. See Alice Bacani, "Ohio State Day at Cedar Point Gives Alumni a Head-Start on Amusement Park Season," *The Lantern*, April 30, 2013, http://thelantern.com/2013/04/ohio-state-day-at-cedar-point-gives-alumni-a-head-start-on-amusement-park-season.
10. Keith Miller, "The Season of Giving," *Funworld*, May 2010, http://www.iaapa.org/news/newsroom/news-articles/the-season-of-giving-funworld-may-2010.
11. Donald Getz, *Event Management & Event Tourism, 2nd ed.* (New York: Cognizant Communication Corporation, 2005), 18.
12. Johnny Allen, William O'Toole, Robert Harris, and Ian McDonnell, *Festival & Special Event Management* (Milton, Queensland: John Wiley & Sons Australia Ltd., 2011), 13.
13. Getz, *Event Management & Event Tourism, 2nd ed.*, 21.
14. Norman Kahn, "In Any Event...Event Planning in Today's Theme Park Environment," *InPark Magazine*, November 2013, 19.
15. Allen, O'Toole, Harris, and McDonnell, *Festival & Special Event Management*, 15.
16. "Cincinnati's Coney Island Hosts First Fireworks Competition," *Funworld*, November 2012, 26.
17. Anton Shone and Bryn Parry, *Successful Event Management: A Practical Handbook, 3rd ed.* (Hampshire, United Kingdom: Cengage, 2010), 72.
18. Getz, *Event Management & Event Tourism, 2nd ed.*, 81.

19. Ibid., 274.
20. Ibid., 256.
21. Lisa Anderson Mann, "Two-Way Street: How to Make the Most of a Nonprofit Partnership," *Funworld*, April 2009, http://www.iaapa.org/news/newsroom/news-articles/two-way-street-funworld-april-2009.
22. Getz, *Event Management & Event Tourism, 2nd ed.*, 260.
23. Maureen Connolly, Lorne J. Adams, and Cheri Bradish, "The Event Planning Model: The Event Development Phase, Part II," in Cheryl Mallen and Lorne J. Adams, eds., *Event Management in Sport, Recreation and Tourism, 2nd ed.* (New York: Routledge, 2013), 60 and 62.
24. Allen, O'Toole, Harris, and McDonnell, *Festival & Special Event Management*, 247.
25. Shone and Parry, *Successful Event Management: A Practical Handbook, 3rd ed.*, 191.
26. Getz, *Event Management & Event Tourism, 2nd ed.*, 106.
27. Allen, O'Toole, Harris, and McDonnell, *Festival & Special Event Management*, 423.
28. Getz, *Event Management & Event Tourism, 2nd ed.*, 169.
29. Preston, *Event Marketing: How to Successfully Promote Events, Festivals, Conventions, and Expositions*, 50.
30. Ibid., 119.
31. Shone and Parry, *Successful Event Management: A Practical Handbook, 3rd ed.*, 152.
32. Scott Forrester and Lorne J. Adams, "The Event Planning Model: The Event Evaluation and Renewal Phase," in Cheryl Mallen and Lorne J. Adams, eds., *Event Management in Sport, Recreation and Tourism, 2nd ed.* (New York: Routledge), 149.
33. Allen, O'Toole, Harris, and McDonnell, *Festival & Special Event Management*, 494.

# CHAPTER NINE

# Guest Relations and Customer Service

## Introduction

Despite the number of advertisements, press releases, or sales promotions an attraction produces, if people don't have a good experience during their visit, all that effort is lost. A big part of an organization's promotion and marketing strategy also depends on the relationships it builds with both its external and internal publics.

Up to this point, this book has focused on what's involved in making audiences aware of and bringing them into a tourism attraction. Once they're there, however, attraction personnel need to work equally hard to make people happy and keep them coming back. This can be accomplished by gaining an understanding of what guests want and need from an attraction and by creating a culture of service to meet these needs.

This chapter addresses the important roles guest relations and customer service play in the success of a tourism attraction. It also offers suggestions on what attractions can do to ensure their customers' experiences are memorable ones.

## Understanding What Guests Want

"When someone is engaged with your business, they have invested their heart in your business," explain authors Carol Wain and Jay Conrad Levinson.[1] From a guest relations perspective, there are many things attractions can do to reassure visitors that their investment was a smart one.

A first step in developing a solid relationship with guests is to understand what they want, explains Matt Heller of Performance Optimist Consulting. When customers plan a vacation, he says, they have certain expectations. "On some level they're looking for a way to get away from what their everyday life is. They're looking for the experience to take them out of their normal day-to-day routine."[2]

*Figure 9.1: Most customers anticipate their attraction experiences will take them out of their normal routines.* (Photo Credit: Photo courtesy of Kennywood Amusement Park.)

Part of the desire to get away from this routine includes not wanting to deal with the stress and obligations that accompany their regular lives. Consequently, when they visit an attraction, they have high expectations that everything will be perfect or near perfect. At the same time, Heller says, attraction visitors want to feel like they're getting value for their time and money. They want to feel as though their time is well spent, and their money isn't wasted.[3]

Part of these expectations come from an attraction itself and the claims it makes to customers in its promotional materials, explain authors Ron Zemke and Kristin Anderson. "Organizations make direct promises to customers through advertising and marketing materials, in company correspondence and contracts, and in service guarantees and policies published for everyone to see."[4] These materials generally communicate to customers how exciting their experience is going to be. However, says Heller, a company needs to back up these claims once guests arrive. If an attraction promises the "best day ever," he says, customers will be disappointed if their day turns out to be less than that.[5]

## Creating a Culture of Service

In today's volatile work environment, developing a top-quality guest relations program can sometimes be a challenge, notes Heller. In recent years, the trend has been to try and do more with less. Whereas in the past there might have been two people to take care of the needs of 50 customers, now there is only one. This puts a strain on employees and may be woefully apparent to guests. "I think that has hurt customer experiences a little bit," he says.[6] To fulfill guest expectations, tourism attractions need to make it a priority to create a culture of service, one where addressing the needs and wants of customers is first and foremost.

## Tips for Outstanding Customer Service

→ Adopt an attitude of excellence.
→ Anticipate customer needs.
→ Show enthusiasm and interest in customers.
→ Go the extra mile for customers.
→ Thank customers for their business.
→ Listen to customer complaints.
→ Handle dissatisfied customers with care.
→ Resolve issues in a timely manner.
→ Apologize when things go wrong.
→ Follow up with customers.
→ Ask for and encourage feedback.

### Start at the Top

The key to establishing this culture of service is to begin with the CEO and upper-level management, says Lee Cockerell, author of *The Customer Rules* and former executive vice president of operations at Walt Disney World Resort.

> Unless the people at the top of an organization, division, or department are dedicated to developing and maintaining superior service, it won't happen. They have to create the right agenda, allocate the necessary resources, establish the appropriate priorities, and set the proper tone. The best of those leaders also serve as role models, demonstrating the attributes of great service with every word, action and communication.[7]

### Train and Empower Employees

If an attraction's CEO is committed to a culture of service, it should follow that everyone in the organization needs to be indoctrinated into this business approach. "Every employee in your organization needs to know how their role impacts the experience of their customers. Tell them why their performance is important," advise Wain and Levinson. "It is not just the front-line customer service reps or sales people that impact the experience it is everyone…from the front line staff to the janitor to the executives to the back-office staff. Each person makes an impact in one way or another."[8]

This can be accomplished by providing employees with customer service training. When employees are first hired, they are generally given basic information about an organization's expectations, procedures, and policies, as well as the company's mission and organizational culture. Much of this will be discussed in Chapter 10. Part of this training, however, should also address the organization's commitment to customer service and what that means to guests, as Cockerell explains.

> Some customers just want to be served quickly and efficiently. Others care mostly about convenience. Still others just want the best possible deal. And for some, the quality of human interaction ranks highest; they want to be treated with warmth, friendliness, and respect. Being able to ferret out and deliver what each customer wants most will go a long way toward winning you their repeat business and their loyalty.[9]

Additionally, customer service training needs to be an ongoing process, not simply a brief synopsis of information that employees receive on their first day of work. It should encompass learning opportunities, feedback from supervisors, and ongoing discussions about what more can be done to satisfy customers. Management consultant Shaun McKeogh says this is part of what's involved in creating a coaching culture, "when team members of all levels engage in respectful and productive conversations about work performance. Regular feedback is an expectation from everyone as the entire business strives to continually improve."[10]

Cockerell recommends bringing employees together from time to time for a conversation about some of the customer service issues they regularly encounter on the job. This conversation can include a discussion of some of the challenges employees might face in dealing with different customer situations, as well as role-playing exercises to reinforce how to effectively resolve them. Using this approach ensures that "employees have more mental capacity for problem solving, so that if a truly novel situation arises, they'll be able to come up with a better solution faster," he says.[11]

Part of preparing employees to address customer needs includes empowering them to make decisions. According to Alastair Morrison, "Empowerment means giving employees the authority to identify and solve guest problems or complaints on the spot, and to make improvements in work processes when necessary."[12] In some situations this may involve granting front-line employees the ability to make decisions that might normally be made higher up the organizational ladder. It also means upper-level management must be willing to trust the judgment of front-line employees to do the right thing in difficult situations.

## Aim for One-Stop Service

Although it may not always be feasible, empowering employees also helps promote the concept of one-stop service for customers. This prevents customers from having to go through multiple layers in an attraction's chain of command when an issue arises.

"There will be times when you have to 'call in the cavalry' to solve difficult customer problems or requests," explain Zemke and Anderson. "But your chief goal should be to address customer issues in 'one-stop.' Nothing pleases customers like having their questions answered or problems resolved with one easy, hassle-free contact."[13] If one-stop service is not realistic, note the authors, employees should be familiar enough with the attraction's organizational chart to know where to direct guests.

## Accommodate Special Needs

Some attraction guests may have needs that necessitate special accommodations. These include guests with disabilities and those with food allergies or other dietary restrictions. The Americans with Disabilities Act (ADA) provides attractions with a legal benchmark for what is required to accommodate individuals with various types of disabilities. However, attractions can garner customer appreciation by providing services that go well beyond what is required by law.

A place to start is by making sure employees are fully aware of their responsibilities to guests with disabilities. According to McKeogh, this can be accomplished by providing them with "policies, standard operating procedures, communication tools, and training to provide consistent quality service to guests with disabilities."[14]

Attractions may find it advantageous to consult with local organizations that provide services to people with disabilities. They can solicit advice from these organizations on how to best serve visitors who may need special assistance, says McKeogh.[15] Attractions should also post information on their websites to let visitors know ahead of time what services and accommodations they can expect when they arrive.

Another issue that may be of concern for some visitors is special dietary needs such as food allergies. Guests with allergies or other dietary issues may be interested in purchasing food at an attraction's restaurant or concession stand, but they need to know that what they eat won't hurt them.

Attractions can address these concerns by taking steps to accommodate visitors with special dietary needs, explains reporter Jodi Helmer. In the theme park industry, for example, "To ensure the safety and enjoyment of guests, a growing number of parks have added allergen-friendly items to their menus, serving gluten-free caramel corn, nut-free ice cream, and dairy-free cookies."[16]

Providing special dietary accommodations may require doing some initial research. The chefs at the Silver Dollar City theme park near Branson, Mo., for example, went through all the park's recipes to determine what modifications needed to be made in order to serve guests with food allergies. They also made arrangements to have all special meals prepared in a centralized kitchen to prevent cross-contamination with other foods.[17] While making adjustments to meet the needs of a relatively small percentage of visitors might initially seem both time consuming and expensive, from a guest relations perspective, it can go a long way to build goodwill with customers, says Helmer.[18]

---

### Attraction Fun Fact

The oldest operating amusement park in the world is Bakken, near Copenhagen, Denmark. It opened in 1583.

---

## Thank and Reward Customers

A big part of creating a culture of service is knowing how to say thank you. Taking time to thank customers makes them feel their business is genuinely appreciated, explain Zemke and Anderson. "In your job, you need to say thanks to your customers every day. You need to sincerely value the gift of business they bring you."[19]

Attraction staff can thank customers verbally, in writing, or with a gift, the authors say. A verbal thank you should be offered after every interaction or transaction. A written thank you might come in the form of a post-visit email. A gift could consist of a pen or a sticker imprinted with the attraction's logo.

Some attractions offer loyalty programs to acknowledge and reward repeat customers. Many casinos, for example, issue players' cards to their patrons, which they can insert into slot machines to earn points for play. When enough points are accumulated, customers can redeem them for discounts on food or accommodations.[20]

*Figure 9.2: Many casinos offer patrons loyalty reward programs as a way of thanking them for their business.* (Photo Credit: Andi Stein)

## Providing Added Value to Customers

In striving to make outstanding customer service a routine part of business, some attractions are discovering the benefits of offering added value features to their guests. They are accomplishing this by improving customer wait times, providing VIP experiences to customers, and making provisions for pets.

### Improve Customer Wait Times

Even at the most popular attractions, waiting in line can take some of the fun out of the visitor experience. Some attractions are finding ways to use technology to incorporate entertaining, interactive activities into their queues, making wait times less burdensome. At Disneyland, Universal Studios Hollywood, and Six Flags Magic Mountain in Southern California, for example, "The queues feature videos, interactive games and animatronic characters to entertain waiting riders," says *Los Angeles Times* reporter Hugo Martin.[21]

In addition, Martin says, in the Magic Kingdom in Florida's Walt Disney World, guests waiting to ride the Dumbo the Flying Elephant attraction no longer have to stand in line until it's their turn to board. Instead, they are "ushered into an air-conditioned tent, where kids can play on slides, a climbing tower and a toy fire engine while parents wait for the buzz of a pager telling them it's time to ride the attraction."[22]

Attractions are also allowing guests to use their mobile and other electronic devices to cut down on wait times to get into attractions, says reporter Juliana Gilling. "Consumers are changing the way they buy tickets. The days of people standing in a ticket line at the front gate are disappearing; the majority of guests are arranging their admission in advance, either at home or on their smartphones."[23]

## Offer VIP Tours

In recent years, VIP tours have become another way to provide added value to guests, as an increasing number of customers are willing to spend a little more money for an added level of attention. Zoos, museums, aquariums, theme parks, and other attractions have created programs that offer guests enhanced services for additional fees.

"Upgraded packages can be a big source of extra revenue from those well-heeled visitors who want to be treated like VIPs," explains Martin. Attractions have come up with a variety of specialty programs that "offer the velvet-rope exclusivity that high rollers get at restaurants, nightclubs and hotels."[24]

While the cost of a VIP tour can be a deal-breaker for some, those who are willing to pay receive five-star service. According to Helmer, VIP packages might include behind-the-scenes tours, parking upgrades, and personalized character meet-and-greets.[25] Other perks are "upscale food served in a private lounge," notes Martin.[26] Visitors to Disneyland in southern California, for example, pay upwards of $300 for the Disneyland VIP tour, Martin says. "The price includes a tour guide, a customized itinerary, front-row seating at shows and parades, front-of-the-line access to rides and valet parking. The price does not include admission."[27]

Cedar Point in Sandusky, Ohio, initially offered VIP tours only to celebrities who came through the park, says Helmer. "When noncelebrity guests started calling to inquire about exclusive park experiences, operators decided to make their VIP package available to all guests who were willing to invest in the experience."[28]

To ensure guests receive the level of service they are paying for, some attractions provide their staff with specialized training to make certain they are properly prepared to treat guests like VIPs. "Experienced and knowledgeable VIP tour guides are priceless," explains Helmer.[29]

---

### Attraction Fun Fact

Route 66 was commissioned in 1926. It ran through 8 states and 3 time zones.

---

## Make Provisions for Pets

According to Keith Miller, in recent years there's been a growing trend of people wanting to bring their pets along with them when they travel. Consequently, some attractions offer pet-sitting and boarding services, where pets are cared for while their owners enjoy their day out at an attraction.

Dollywood in Pigeon Forge, Tenn., for example, offers an on-site kennel called "Doggywood," where visitors can leave their four-footed loved ones for the day for a fee. Efteling theme park in the Netherlands offers a similar service but doesn't charge for it, says Miller. "Guests are so pleased with the free kennel they regard it as a park amenity, and even locals often choose to bring their dogs rather than leave them home alone."[30]

The growing number of on-site pet services has been a byproduct of the increased number of pet-friendly hotels, which has prompted more people to travel with their pets rather than leave them home. An on-site pet service also means guests are less likely to leave their pets in their vehicles, which can be dangerous, especially during hot summer months. Instead, the animals can be cared for in air-conditioned comfort while their owners enjoy their day without worrying about their pets.

## Addressing the Needs of Unhappy Customers

Despite the effort an attraction puts into establishing a culture of service, there will be times when things don't go exactly as planned. The result can be unhappy, frustrated, upset, and even angry customers. As part of developing a culture of service, attractions need to incorporate procedures for addressing and resolving any unexpected customer issues that may arise to ensure they don't become even bigger problems. "If something goes wrong, you have to have somebody who can fix it," says Heller. "You have to have someone who can work with the guests to make it right. That is part of your customer service experience, too."[31]

### Address Customer Complaints

In today's age of multi-platform, instantaneous communication, a small problem can escalate into a huge one in a matter of minutes, as Lee Cockerell notes.

> In the age of social media, you can easily lose customers a thousand—even a million—at a time. With a few keystrokes, one unhappy, frustrated, ticked-off customer can now tell her whole e-mail list, all her Facebook friends, and everyone who reads her blog or follows her on Twitter why they should not do business with you. She can voice her outrage into a smartphone and put it up on YouTube with clever graphics. With a little creativity, she can even…shoot a mini-documentary, complete with music and special effects, and generate enough viral buzz to do serious damage to your business.[32]

Customer dissatisfaction can be the result of any number of factors. As noted earlier, some of the expectations visitors have about an attraction come from the organization's own marketing materials. When reality fails to live up to these expectations, people may be disappointed, frustrated, or angry, says Heller.[33]

Even the most well-managed attractions may occasionally give rise to situations that prompt customers to complain. A customer may be upset by an unpleasant encounter with an employee, for example. Having to wait longer than expected to get into an attraction, or having the attraction malfunction midstream may produce customer frustration and annoyance. No matter the cause of unhappy or dissatisfied customers, it's essential to take customers' complaints seriously, says Heller, "to be able to fix the situation to make sure they leave happy."[34]

### Listen Carefully

Before an issue can be resolved, it first needs to be fully understood. Part of comprehending a situation comes from listening to customers as they articulate their issues or air their grievances, say Zemke and Anderson. "It's important to listen actively, almost aggressively…. When you listen well, you figure out what your customer wants and needs, prevent misunderstandings and errors, gather clues about ways to improve the service you provide, build long-term customer relationships," they explain. "Customers are ready, willing and able to tell you everything (or almost everything) you need to know."[35]

It's also important to watch for nonverbal cues that help fill in the gaps of what customers may not be expressing in words but may be communicating through puzzled looks or blank stares, says Cockerell. "What a customer doesn't say can also speak volumes. When customers go from being talkative and inquisitive to silent and withdrawn, it's usually a sign that you're losing their interest and you'd better dig deeper to find out what they want."[36]

## Apologize and Accept Responsibility

The next step in dealing with dissatisfied customers is to apologize when things go wrong and accept responsibility for them. There's an old saying that "the customer is always right." Sometimes this is absolutely true; sometimes the customer may be flat-out wrong. Regardless, from a customer service perspective, it's advisable to offer an apology for the situation and for any inconvenience the issue at hand may have caused the customer.

It's also prudent not to try and shift blame or make excuses for why or how the issue happened. Instead, simply acknowledge the problem and accept responsibility for the fact that it happened in the first place. "It doesn't matter who's at fault," note Zemke and Anderson. "Customers want someone to acknowledge that a problem occurred and show concern for their disappointment. Saying, 'I'm sorry you have been inconvenienced this way' doesn't cost a dime, but it buys a barrel of forgiveness."[37]

## Offer to Make Restitution

In some situations, a simple "I'm sorry" will not be sufficient to make things right for unhappy or dissatisfied customers. An attraction may also need to provide some sort of compensation or restitution to make amends for the problems and inconveniences the guests have endured. Depending on the situation, this compensation can be as simple as a coupon for a free meal at the attraction's restaurant, a discount card for the gift shop, or a free pass for a future visit.

Keep in mind the purpose of offering compensation is not to try and buy the customer off, but "a way to provide a value-added touch to tell customers their business is important to you," explain Zemke and Anderson.[38] The ultimate goal is to make the guest leave the premises satisfied with how everything was resolved and willing to remain the attraction's customer.

## Track Online Comments and Issues

Some customer complaints can be addressed on-site at an attraction and quickly resolved in person. Others may not come to light until after-the-fact when they surface online on Facebook, Twitter, or customer review sites such as TripAdvisor or Yelp. To keep on top of this, attractions need to designate someone to keep a close watch on online platforms where customers may be likely to post comments. They also need to respond to these comments as quickly and diplomatically as possible.

"You'll be amazed at how a personal response changes the tenor of an online discussion," say authors Leonardo Inghilleri and Micah Solomon. "Get in there online and let your complainant know that you care, you're paying attention, and you're glad to clarify and assist." If the situation is handled properly, they say, "The complainant may alter the original posting if convinced by you that it's unfair."[39]

## Soliciting Customer Feedback

One way to build good guest relations and keep improving customer service is to regularly solicit feedback from attraction visitors. This feedback can be used to make adjustments to current policies and procedures. It may also prompt the development of new products and services attractions can offer guests based on their suggestions.

---

### Sample Customer Comment Card

⊙ Please evaluate the following as they relate to your experience with our attraction.

|  | Poor | Fair | Average | Good | Excellent |
|---|---|---|---|---|---|
| Parking | 1 | 2 | 3 | 4 | 5 |
| Dining areas | 1 | 2 | 3 | 4 | 5 |
| Rides/shows/exhibits | 1 | 2 | 3 | 4 | 5 |
| Grounds | 1 | 2 | 3 | 4 | 5 |
| Restrooms | 1 | 2 | 3 | 4 | 5 |

⊙ Please evaluate the following as they relate to your experience with our staff.

|  | Poor | Fair | Average | Good | Excellent |
|---|---|---|---|---|---|
| Professionalism | 1 | 2 | 3 | 4 | 5 |
| Attentiveness | 1 | 2 | 3 | 4 | 5 |
| Knowledge | 1 | 2 | 3 | 4 | 5 |
| Attitude | 1 | 2 | 3 | 4 | 5 |
| Responsiveness | 1 | 2 | 3 | 4 | 5 |

⊙ How would you rate your overall experience at our attraction? (circle one)

| Poor | Fair | Average | Good | Excellent |
|---|---|---|---|---|

⊙ Do you plan on returning?     ___ Yes  ___ No  ___ Maybe

Comments: _____

_____

_____

_____

## Make Feedback Easy

Although this may sound counterintuitive, Lee Cockerell recommends that organizations make it easy for their customers to complain. This encourages them to share their opinions about an attraction. "Think of it as preventative medicine: an ounce of complaint today is worth a pound of argument tomorrow," he says.[40]

One way to do this is through the use of comment cards strategically placed in locations such as onsite eateries and gift shops. Guests can easily pick them up, fill them out, and deposit them into suggestion boxes. Including space for an email address on the card gives the attraction a means to follow-up with a brief note, respond to the comments, and thank the customer for taking time to fill out the card.

## Use Data-Gathering Tools

Surveys and focus groups enable attractions to gather more in-depth information about customers' perceptions and opinions. Surveys are useful for collecting data from large groups of customers. They can be distributed on-site or sent in post-visit emails with links to online survey tools.

"Digital technology is changing the way attractions conduct market research," observes reporter Jim Futrell. "With services such as Survey Monkey or Zoomerang now commonplace, the ability to conduct consumer surveys is limited only by staff time and the number of e-mail addresses facilities can collect."[41]

Surveys should provide clear instructions and an explanation of how customers should go about completing them (check boxes, fill in the blanks, etc.). Questions should be fairly short and to the point to avoid confusing or frustrating customers. "A survey should reflect your most important questions about customer likes, dislikes, and needs," explain Inghilleri and Solomon.[42] While surveys are often used to collect quantitative data, it's recommended attractions also include some open-ended questions that allow guests to provide written comments.

Focus groups bring small groups of people together for in-depth discussions led by trained professionals. The focus group moderator guides participants through a series of questions that have been carefully crafted to elicit conversation about a specific topic. Futrell emphasizes that it's "important to use an experienced moderator to ensure the conversation remains focused and that all participants feel comfortable providing input."[43]

Focus groups are ideal when trying to solicit feedback about customer interest in future exhibits, rides, shows, or other components of an attraction. Because they can only accommodate limited numbers of people, however, focus groups are not necessarily reliable as standalone sources of information. An ideal way to make the most of focus group research is to use data gathered during a focus group to design questions that can then be incorporated into a survey and sent to a larger number of people.

Although not as reliable as more formal feedback tools, attractions can also use social media platforms to collect information in a relatively short period of time, says Futrell. "Many facilities cite Facebook not only as an important promotional tool, but also as a valuable research tool. While it has limitations for more detailed surveys, it has become an important way to obtain quick feedback."[44]

*Hire Mystery Shoppers*

Another way for attractions to collect customer service information is through a mystery shopper program. This involves hiring outside observers who come into an attraction and go through a routine day as though they were regular guests. While there, however, they observe and gather data about their experiences, which they later share with attraction managers.

Mystery shoppers use an attraction's facilities, interact with staff, and partake of guest services in an attempt to have the same experience as any paying customer. Depending on the type of attraction, they might check out special exhibits, go on rides, eat at an onsite restaurant, make a purchase in the gift shop, ask for directions, or take guided tours. While doing all of the above, they collect information about what they see, hear, and learn along the way.

Amusement Advantage in Arvada, Colo., is one of several companies that provide mystery shopper services to attractions. According to Miller, their shoppers "use mobile phones with cameras, digital voice recorders, PDAs, and digital cameras to document what they see. Some also have Wi-Fi access to report results back immediately."[45]

After gathering data, mystery shoppers compile reports and provide attractions with their findings. These reports may include photos and records of conversations with staff members. By engaging a mystery shopper for more than one site visit, it's possible to determine trends over time, says Heller.[46] Attractions can then use this information "to make changes in their facility and enhance their training and staff development initiatives."[47]

Sometimes, companies that hire mystery shoppers may get defensive when the results are negative. However, says Heller, "If you've contracted with a mystery shopper service, it behooves you to listen to what they have to say." If managers are open to the results, he says, a mystery shopper program can be a great asset to an attraction.[48]

## Conclusion

When customers visit an attraction, they come with certain expectations about what their experience should be like. Attractions can fulfill these expectations by creating a culture of service for customers that focuses on providing them with an ideal experience. This can be accomplished by properly training attraction staff and empowering them to make decisions that will help resolve customer issues. Accommodating special needs and thanking and rewarding customers for their business can contribute to this culture of service as well.

Attractions can provide added value to their customers by implementing programs and services designed to make their visits more memorable. Improved customer wait times, VIP tours, and accommodations for pets are a few examples of enhanced services attractions can offer their customers.

When visitors do have issues or problems, attraction staff should take steps to resolve them in a timely manner. Listening to customer complaints, apologizing when things go wrong, and offering to make restitution can go a long way in appeasing unhappy customers.

Attractions can also benefit from customer feedback that can be used to enrich future visits. Surveys and focus groups are useful tools for soliciting this feedback directly from customers. Mystery shopper programs can be valuable in gathering objective feedback about customer service.

Effective customer service springs from a well-prepared employee base. The next chapter will discuss the importance of developing an employee relations program, one that focuses on hiring, training, and recognizing the staff members that make an organization run.

## Notes

1. Carol Wain and Jay Conrad Levinson, *Guerrilla Tourism Marketing* (Lexington, KY: WINning Entrepreneur Press, 2012), 159.
2. Matt Heller, personal interview, December 9, 2013.
3. Ibid.
4. Ron Zemke and Kristin Anderson, *Delivering Knock Your Socks Off Service, 4th ed.* (New York: American Management Association, 2007), 13.
5. Heller, personal interview, December 9, 2013.
6. Ibid.
7. Lee Cockerell, *The Customer Rules: The 39 Essential Rules for Delivering Sensational Service* (New York: Crown Business, 2013), 9.
8. Wain and Levinson, *Guerrilla Tourism Marketing*, 154.
9. Cockerell, *The Customer Rules: The 39 Essential Rules for Delivering Sensational Service*, 129.
10. Shaun McKeogh, "Better Human Resources for the Attractions Industry: Creating a Coaching Culture," *Funworld*, May 2014, 86.
11. Cockerell, *The Customer Rules: The 39 Essential Rules for Delivering Sensational Service*, 55.
12. Alastair M. Morrison, *Hospitality & Travel Marketing, 4th ed.* (Clifton Park, NY: Delmar, 2010), 377.
13. Zemke and Anderson, *Delivering Knock Your Socks Off Service, 4th ed.*, 114.
14. Shaun McKeogh, "Better Human Resources for the Attractions Industry: Disability Awareness," International Association of Amusement Parks and Attractions, www.iaapa.org, http://www.iaapa.org/news/newsroom/news-articles/industry-report---february-2014.
15. Ibid.
16. Jodi Helmer, "How Attractions Meet the Needs of Guests with Food Allergies," International Association of Amusement Parks and Attractions, http://www.iaapa.org/news/newsroom/news-articles/how-attractions-meet-the-needs-of-guests-with-food-allergies.
17. See Keith Miller, "A Real Transformation," *Funworld*, April 2009, http://www.iaapa.org/news/newsroom/news-articles/a-real-transformation-funworld-april-2009.
18. See Jodi Helmer, "Saving Lives, One Bite at a Time," *Funworld*, April 2010, http://www.iaapa.org/news/newsroom/news-articles/saving-lives-one-bite-at-a-time-funworld-april-2010.
19. Zemke and Anderson, *Delivering Knock Your Socks Off Service, 4th ed.*, 125.
20. See, for example, Caesar's Total Rewards, http://www.totalrewards.com, and MGM Resorts International, http://www.mlife.com.
21. Hugo Martin, "Lines They Can Stand," *Los Angeles Times*, August 9, 2013, B1.
22. Ibid.
23. Juliana Gilling, "Why Wait?" *Funworld*, May 2014, 72.
24. Hugo Martin, "Theme Parks' Latest Thrill: VIP Treatment," *Los Angeles Times*, April 26, 2013, B1.
25. See Jodi Helmer, "The VIP Treatment," *Funworld*, November 2011, 135.
26. Martin, "Theme Parks' Latest Thrill: VIP Treatment," B1.
27. Ibid.
28. Helmer, "The VIP Treatment," 135.
29. Ibid.

30. Keith Miller, "Who Wants to Go to the Park?" *Funworld*, November 2013, 115.

31. Heller, personal interview, December 9, 2013.

32. Cockerell, *The Customer Rules: The 39 Essential Rules for Delivering Sensational Service*, 5.

33. Heller, personal interview, December 9, 2013.

34. Ibid.

35. Zemke and Anderson, *Delivering Knock Your Socks Off Service, 4th ed.*, 59.

36. Cockerell, *The Customer Rules: The 39 Essential Rules for Delivering Sensational Service*, 133.

37. Zemke and Anderson, *Delivering Knock Your Socks Off Service, 4th ed.*, 59.

38. Ibid., 162.

39. Leonardo Inghilleri and Micah Solomon, *Exceptional Service, Exceptional Profit* (New York: American Management Association, 2010), 117.

40. Cockerell, *The Customer Rules: The 39 Essential Rules for Delivering Sensational Service*, 157.

41. Jim Futrell, "Data Retrieval," *Funworld*, June 2013, 48.

42. Inghilleri and Solomon, *Exceptional Service, Exceptional Profit*, 75.

43. Futrell, "Data Retrieval," 49.

44. Ibid.

45. Keith Miller, "Industry Undercover," *Funworld*, November/December 2008, 90.

46. Heller, personal interview, December 9, 2013.

47. Scot Carson as quoted in "Experiences, Expectations, and Exploits," *InPark Magazine*, Summer 2006, 22.

48. Heller, personal interview, December 9, 2013.

# CHAPTER TEN

# Employee Relations

## Introduction

Employees are the heart and soul of any organization. As Matt Heller of Performance Optimist Consulting explains, in the attractions industry, "They're the ones who are running your business."[1] Just as a culture of service is ideal for promoting good customer relations, establishing what Victor Middleton, et al. call an "internal marketing" program is equally important for developing effective employee relations.

"Internal marketing…is a logical extension of the marketing mix considerations to recognize that the employees of an organization are stakeholders too. Marketing is as applicable to internal audiences within a company as to prospective customers and others outside it."[2] Management consultant Shaun McKeogh suggests that attractions should think of their employees as brand ambassadors because they serve as the face of an attraction's brand. "What your team members individually say and do while representing your attraction as your brand ambassadors is critical to your business success."[3]

Attractions need to ensure their employees serve as the best brand ambassadors they can possibly be. To achieve this, author Lee Cockerell recommends promoting a culture of inclusiveness, one where all employees feel appreciated and valued. "When everyone matters and everyone knows he or she matters, employees are happy to come to work, and they're eager to give you their energy, creativity, and loyalty."[4]

Ultimately, the goal of an attraction's employee relations efforts should be to promote enthusiastic, motivated, and productive employees who have a strong sense of commitment to their jobs and their employer. This can be accomplished by developing standards and establishing procedures for recruiting, training, motivating, rewarding, and communicating with employees. This chapter discusses what attractions can do to establish and promote good working relationships with their employees.

## Recruiting New Hires

A successful employee relations program begins with a well-planned recruitment strategy. Advertising, screening, and training a new employee can cost upwards of $4,500, according to reporter Jodi Helmer.[5] Therefore, it makes good financial sense to put some thought into the recruitment process to increase the chances of finding employees who will be a good organizational fit. In the long run, this can also reduce the potential for employee turnover.

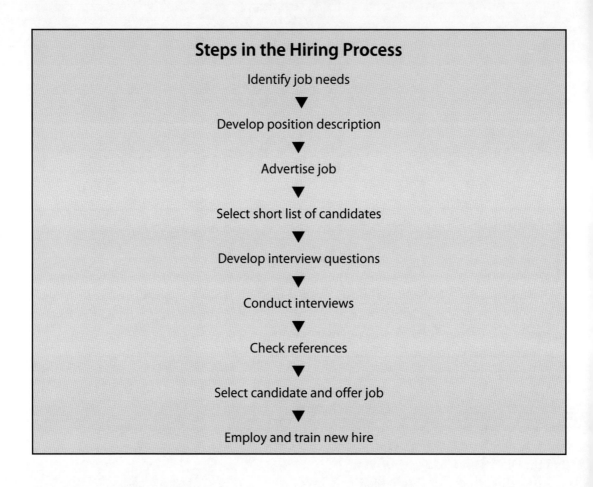

**Steps in the Hiring Process**

Identify job needs

▼

Develop position description

▼

Advertise job

▼

Select short list of candidates

▼

Develop interview questions

▼

Conduct interviews

▼

Check references

▼

Select candidate and offer job

▼

Employ and train new hire

### *Develop Recruitment Materials*

A place to start in the recruitment process is with a wish list of desired skills and qualifications for each potential staff member, says McKeogh.

> Identify a basic list of preferred qualities that would best allow an employee to fit into your organization. Make these qualities part of the selection criteria. Throughout the attractions industry, common recruitment qualities include confidence, friendliness, and possessing a genuine smile and desire to have and provide fun.[6]

Hiring managers can then use this list to create a position description. The description should be as specific as possible and tailored to fit the needs of the available job. If it is too general or vague, it may attract applicants who are not the best fit for the position.

Some attraction jobs are likely to be advertised and filled on an as-needed basis when existing positions are vacated or new ones created. Management positions, for instance, may be highly specialized and require a certain level of skill and experience. Recruitment for these jobs may best be done through national publications such as industry trade journals, or specialty publications and online resources managed by professional associations.

Attractions such as amusement and theme parks may need to hire large numbers of employees all at once to perform tasks such as operate rides, sell merchandise, clean facilities, etc. The best way to recruit for these types of positions is often through local job fairs in order to reach many applicants simultaneously.

Prior to the opening of the Shanghai Disney Resort, for example, the company launched a large-scale recruitment drive aimed at Chinese college graduates. The goal was to hire several thousand employees to fill positions in the resort's restaurants, retail stores, and hotels.[7]

No matter how an attraction chooses to recruit new hires, says author John Swarbrooke, its position announcements need to accurately reflect the nature of the jobs being advertised. They should also "give a good impression of the attraction to all those who see the advertisement; in other words, advertisements have a wider public relations role."[8]

## Use Social Media for Recruitment

Social media can also be a handy tool when recruiting staff. Some attractions hire high school and college-age students to fill many of their positions. Advertising these positions on social media sites where potential applicants are likely to be can increase the chances of attracting their attention. As far as which platforms to use for recruitment, says reporter Jennifer Salopek, "A valuable weapon in your arsenal is current employees. Use them to find out what social media channels and tools are hot right now, and engage them as online brand ambassadors."[9]

Attractions should also advertise positions on their own websites and use their social media platforms to drive traffic to the sites. McKeogh adds that an attraction's website can include detailed information about what to expect when working for the organization. "Many attractions have wisely chosen to start setting these expectations early on by communicating their vision, mission, and business values on their websites."[10]

In addition to social media, word of mouth can be a great way for attractions to recruit staff. According to an article in *Funworld* magazine, a study done by the University of Central Florida's Rosen College of Hospitality Management revealed that 33 percent of theme park employees found their jobs through referrals from someone already working at the park. This suggests that encouraging current employees to spread the word can often result in a positive outcome when hiring future employees.[11]

*View Internships as Screening Opportunities*

Internships are an effective way to jumpstart the recruitment process. Internships offer individuals the opportunity to gain hands-on experience, often while simultaneously earning college credit. They provide exposure to the day-to-day responsibilities of a job within a particular company. From an organizational perspective, internships give attractions a chance to see the performance of these individuals and assess them as possible candidates for future employment. In an article in *Funworld* magazine, one human resources manager characterized internships as "long-term interviews."[12]

Partnering with career centers at local universities is one way to find interns. Wild Adventures in Valdosta, Ga., recruits interns from nearby colleges and provides housing for them in the dorms. In the past, notes Helmer, when interns have shown long-term potential for leadership success, the company "has invited several of its interns to join the Leadership Mentoring Program…which has helped them secure management positions within the company."[13] To make an internship work, interns need to be integrated into the attraction's staff. "Treat them like valued team members," recommends Helmer, in hopes they will ultimately want to become a permanent part of the team.[14]

*Recruit Volunteers to Supplement Employees*

For nonprofit attractions, volunteers can be invaluable to supplement an organization's employee base. "A dedicated volunteer corps helps zoos, aquariums, and museums meet institutional objectives while enhancing the visitor experience without putting a strain on the operating budget," explains Helmer.[15] Many nonprofit attractions rely heavily on volunteers to make their organizations run. Some have formal recruitment and training programs to bring people in and prepare them for on-the-job success.

"Building a team of volunteers needs to be viewed as an essential investment…. Recruiting, training, and retaining volunteers often takes just as much effort as hiring staff," says Helmer. Attractions "with successful volunteer programs often use the same strategy to add volunteers and staff."[16]

---

### *Attraction Fun Fact*

The U.S. National Park Service has more than 22,000 employees and 2 million volunteers working at its 400+ sites.

---

## Integrating and Training Employees

Once employees have been successfully recruited, they need to be indoctrinated into an attraction's corporate culture and properly prepared for their specific positions. Much of this can be accomplished through an initial employee orientation and training program at the start of their jobs.

*Figure 10.1: Matt Heller of Performance Optimist Consulting believes leadership training can help employees succeed once they've been promoted.*
(Photo Credit: Photo courtesy of Matt Heller.)

## Explain Corporate Culture

Every organization, both large and small, has its own corporate culture. Thomas Atchison offers an explanation of what corporate culture means.

> An easy way to understand corporate culture is to compare it to the human personality. All humans have personalities. All organizations have cultures. But have you ever seen yours or anyone else's personality? No—because our personalities are intangible. Corporate culture is the most important intangible to the success of any organization.[17]

An organization's culture can be characterized by the stories that make up the company's history, the beliefs it adheres to, and the rituals it practices. The culture may also be directly rooted in the company's mission, which serves as a driving force for everything that is done on a day-to-day basis.

All of this needs to be communicated to new hires during employee orientation, emphasizes Heller, to "get them to understand what the company is all about, what they've signed up for. Give people expectations of what you're looking for, show people how to do it." If they walk away feeling like they're in the right place, he says, the attraction has done its job in hiring them.[18]

## Provide Basic Training

Employee orientation should include information about company policies and procedures as well as safety. It may also encompass detailed instruction about customer service and how to provide attraction visitors with an optimum experience.

Cockerell advises organizations to develop a script that typifies the ideal customer experience and share it with employees.

> Start by imagining the perfect experience for someone coming to your business, no matter what it is, from the moment they arrive…to the moment they leave, happy and content and eager to return…. Think through every detail and what you and your employees—the performers—have to do to make that perfect experience possible.[19]

Once employees begin their jobs, he says, they can develop their own scripts and tailor them to fit their individual roles in the company.

Many employees will also need to be trained to do their individual jobs. Heller recommends using what he calls a "funnel approach," starting with the big picture and then becoming more specific. When hiring individuals to run a gift shop cash register, for example, "Get them familiar with the entire area first, then teach them to run the register."[20] This provides employees with a greater sense of awareness of the overall operation of the attraction. Having this level of awareness can be extremely beneficial when employees are approached by customers and asked questions that go beyond the scope of their specific jobs.

## Promote Ongoing Training

While training may be necessary when employees first start their jobs, the opportunities for training should be ongoing. McKeogh suggests training be viewed as an opportunity for growth, one that should be embraced by all levels of employees including senior management. "In a culture that values training, managers should actively remind their team members of the importance of training."[21] He believes training can be promoted as a reward rather than an obligation. "Often this approach changes the perception team members might have toward training."[22]

Jim Covel, senior training manager at the Monterey Bay Aquarium, recommends what he calls "high-frequency" training, where employees are trained to perform new skills in short, intensive sessions, then given the immediate opportunity to use these skills. The philosophy behind this approach, he says, is that employees can often better retain what they've learned if they have a chance to practice it right away.

> At the Monterey Bay Aquarium our Guest Experience staff enjoys a daily three-to-five-minute "Quick Tip" that features new information or a key skill refresher. Staff members also attend one of three updates each day…. These updates are approximately 20 minutes long and focus on information about our animals, exhibits, and interpretive tips.[23]

As employees progress in their careers within an attraction, they may also require more advanced levels of training, says Heller. "As they move up the ladder, they need to be given skills to lead other people," as leadership is not always inherent. This is especially true when employees are promoted to positions where they are supervising people who have been their peers.

"Ninety percent of people can tell you the right thing to do," says Heller, but they often need a confidence boost to do it, especially when it comes to providing feedback to others. A leadership training program can "give them skills to build confidence, so they will want to do it."[24]

McKeogh suggests additional ways attractions can offer ongoing training for employees. These include providing online learning opportunities, encouraging job shadowing, tailoring development plans for individuals, and establishing mentoring programs.[25]

*Hire an Effective Trainer*

Perhaps the most crucial piece of a successful employee orientation and training program is a knowledgeable, competent trainer. An effective trainer should be someone who knows the operation but also has the skills and desire to communicate information patiently to others, explains Heller. The trainer also needs to recognize that people have different ways of processing information and present materials accordingly, he says.[26]

"The trainer should be passionate, have a command of the material, be able to adjust to the participants' needs, and be appropriately enthusiastic at the right times," adds McKeogh.[27] The skill level, attitude, and approach of the trainer can make or break the overall impact training will have on both new and seasoned employees. For this reason, it's essential for attractions to select appropriate individuals to conduct orientation and training sessions, so employees will feel like they've been well prepared to do their jobs.

## Motivating and Engaging Employees

Once an attraction has recruited and hired the right staff for the job, keeping them motivated and engaged becomes a key component of an employee relations program. Happy, fulfilled employees are generally also dedicated and productive employees, and this comes across to customers.

### Ways to Motivate Employees

- Financial incentives
- Time off
- Recognition and awards
- Job empowerment
- Bonuses
- Verbal praise
- Regular feedback
- Time to volunteer
- Training
- Promotion
- Thank-you notes
- Mentoring
- Social gatherings and events
- Comfortable working conditions
- Casual dress days
- Personal development
- Employee stock ownership
- Consistent communication
- Educational opportunities
- Designated break rooms
- Leadership opportunities
- Birthday/anniversary celebrations
- Interest shown in employees' lives
- Involvement in decision-making

Don MacPherson, president of Modern Survey says, "Employee engagement is the degree to which employees are psychologically motivated to contribute to the success of the organization. The benefits of having a highly engaged workforce are enormous. From increases in productivity and return on investment to customer satisfaction, engagement is a vital tool in building a successful organization."[28]

A common perception is that money is the primary motivating factor for most employees. In reality, studies have shown that while money *is* important, it is not necessarily the only factor that motivates people to do their jobs and do them well, says MacPherson. "Providing recognition/appreciation, giving employees a sense of personal accomplishment, offering career development opportunities, and giving employees a reason to believe in the future of their organization are even more effective methods of driving engagement than fiscal compensation."[29]

Heller adds that in many cases, what motivates employees is "feeling like you're part of something, understanding you bring value to the company, you are more than a paycheck."[30] To help employees feel valued, attractions can implement practices and programs designed to keep them engaged and enthusiastic on the job.

## One-on-One Meetings

Managers play a crucial role in motivating and engaging staff. Taking time to meet with individual staff members to find out what motivates them can mean a world of difference, says Heller. "Get to know the employee," he advises. Learn what their work preferences are, and listen to what they have to say. Show employees the organization cares about what they think and what they want from their individual jobs.[31]

Leadership coach Kimberly Paterson notes that many organizations hold exit interviews when employees leave a company. She recommends holding "stay interviews" with current employees to find out what is likely to make them stay on the job.

> People perform at their best when they are in an environment that reflects their values and style, doing work they enjoy with people they like and respect. Knowing what that looks like for each individual and consistently delivering it is the key to effective motivation.[32]

## Team-Building Activities

One approach to inspiring and motivating employees is to help them feel they are part of a team and that their contributions to the attraction as a whole mean far more than just their individual jobs. Managers can accomplish this by consistently communicating to employees the importance of these contributions to the overall success of the attraction. "The more your employees understand how their efforts directly translate into smiling faces at the turnstile, the more they'll be willing to put in the extra effort," says MacPherson.[33]

Organized team-building activities can be used to reinforce this level of commitment and build camaraderie among employees. According to Helmer, "Team-building activities can improve communication, develop leadership skills, facilitate creative problem solving, enhance conflict resolution, and boost teamwork within an organization."[34]

Team-building activities can be incorporated into employee retreats, training sessions, and regular staff meetings. One attractions manager recommends starting each day with "morning huddles," where managers gather employees as a group and brief them about the day's upcoming activities to ensure they have a sense of what's going on. This works well to "psych up" the team.[35]

Attractions can also organize team-building social activities that give employees a chance to interact across department lines. These may include picnics, movie nights, interdepartmental sports competitions, scavenger hunts, and other activities designed to bring employees together. Midwest-based Kalahari Resorts, for example, organizes a biannual Olympics for employees at its parks in Wisconsin and Ohio. The events are held mid-week when the attractions are less busy than on the weekends. Competitive games are scheduled throughout the day so staff members can participate before or after their shifts, allowing everyone a chance to take part in the activities.[36]

## Professional Development

Providing employees with opportunities for professional growth and development can also be a motivating force. Attractions can offer specialized classes to employees to help them develop new skills. They can pay for employees to attend outside workshops and conferences where they can interact with and learn from others in the industry. Attractions can also support higher education opportunities that go beyond the scope of the employees' day-to-day jobs.

At Luna Park in Sydney, Australia, for instance, "to encourage advanced education, the park…offers a tuition reimbursement program to team members enrolled in universities, colleges, and approved learning centers," notes Helmer.[37] This enables the attraction's employees to earn credentials that may qualify them for management and leadership positions within the organization. Luna Park's senior manager explains that the program "is aimed at creating cohesive teams, compelling cooperation, retaining valued employees, increasing productivity, and boosting overall pride in the organization."[38]

# Recognizing and Rewarding Employees

Acknowledging employee contributions and rewarding these efforts can also go a long way in sustaining a motivated and committed workforce. "Recognition/appreciation is one of the most powerful drivers of employee engagement. People want to know when they've done a good job, and they want to know their contributions are valued," says MacPherson.[39]

## Tie Rewards to Values

In designing an employee recognition program, Heller recommends, "whatever you're trying to reward should on some level tie back to your values."[40] He believes attractions need to make an effort to show the connection between employees' good work and the overall purpose and mission of the organization. The Atlantis water park in Dubai, for example, designed its

"Legends" employee recognition program to reflect the innovation and ingenuity of the residents of the lost continent for which the park is named, explains reporter Prasana William. "The program defines a "Legend of Atlantis" (in the modern sense) as an individual whose behavior is conducive to greatness, excellence, and perfection," he says. "The program ties the resort's core values, mission, and vision statement into 10 specific Legend qualities recognized each year."[41]

## Praise a Job Well Done

One of the simplest ways to recognize employees for their efforts is to let them know when they've done a good job. Tom Mehrmann is the CEO of Hong Kong's Ocean Park and a highly regarded leader in the attractions industry. When Mehrmann started his job in 2004, he began writing personal notes of acknowledgment to employees who received compliment cards from guests. According to reporter Jeremy Schoolfield, during his first year, he wrote 25 notes to his employees. Nearly 10 years later, Mehrmann was writing approximately 1,200 a year.[42]

Crealy Adventure Parks in Exeter, England, has a program called "Catch Me Doing it Right." Park managers are given numbered cards to hand out to employees when they see them doing something well. "The cards give employees entrance into a weekly drawing where those employees holding the right numbers win a prize."[43]

## Offer Awards and Bonuses

Formal awards programs are another way of recognizing employee contributions. These may be scheduled events where staff members are publicly honored for their achievements in front of their coworkers, managers, and even family members. Awards can be given for a variety of accomplishments such as outstanding customer service, creativity and innovation, safety and attendance records, etc.

Cockerell suggests organizations also make time for unscheduled employee recognition.

> Deserving employees should be recognized in front of their peers whenever it's appropriate. This not only enhances positive reinforcement but also motivates other employees to emulate the behavior that's being rewarded. It serves another function as well: It enables managers throughout the organization to learn about talented employees who might otherwise go undiscovered.[44]

In addition to formal awards, attractions can reward deserving employees with perks such as gift cards, time off, restaurant certificates, bonuses, and stock options.

---

### *Attraction Fun Fact*
The Walt Disney World Resort in Orlando, Fla., employs more than 70,000 workers.

# Communicating with Employees

Behind every effective employee relations effort is a strong commitment to communication. Keeping employees informed and providing them with an awareness of company activities reinforces an attraction's interest in and dedication to the success and well-being of its staff. "Truly engaging a company's employees—earning their trust, enabling their best work and inspiring their loyalty—is not a luxury but a business imperative," emphasizes Barbara Fagan-Smith, CEO of ROI Communication.[45]

## *Role of Communication*

Effective employee communication involves providing staff members with information that will help them do their jobs. In doing so, an attraction can offer employees an understanding of how they fit into the big picture of the organization. "People need to understand the collective goal they are working towards and to appreciate the difference they can make," explains Rebecca Clarke, research manager at the Chartered Institute of Personnel and Development.[46] If employees can see how their jobs relate to a company's goals, they are more likely to want to contribute to the success of these goals.

An employee communications program can also help build a sense of trust in an organization. If staff members trust their employers are committed to their best interests, they are likely to respond in kind. An article in *Communication World* reported on the Social Workplace Trust Study conducted by the International Association of Business Communicators and its partner organizations. Results indicated, "Building a culture of trust among employees pays specific, identifiable dividends, such as improved buzz about the company by its own employees and improved retention of workers."[47]

Ideally, attractions should strive to build a culture of open communication, says Fagan-Smith. In this type of environment, employees know they are receiving the information they need to do their jobs and have the freedom to express their ideas and opinions without fear of retribution.[48]

## *Resources for Employee Communication*

There are a number of ways attractions can communicate with employees. These include face-to-face meetings, social media channels, and traditional means such as newsletters and bulletin boards.

### Face-to-Face Communication
Even with the explosion of electronic communication, studies show that face-to-face is still the preferred method of communication between managers and employees.[49] Face-to-face communication provides for a more personal level of interaction between individuals. It offers an opportunity to see facial expressions and observe body language. It also gives employees a way to ask questions.

Staff members often prefer to get their news from their immediate supervisors, as these are the people with whom they have the most direct contact. Because of this, Heller says, it's essential for managers to check in with their employees on a regular basis. "Even a 15 minute one-on-one once a month can help communication," he explains.[50]

Regularly scheduled staff meetings offer another opportunity for face-to-face communication. They can be used to provide employees with updates on company happenings and other developments that may have an impact on their daily routines. When making company-wide announcements about policy changes or staff reorganizations, large-scale town hall meetings may be appropriate. Ideally, these meetings should allow employees the opportunity to ask questions about the information being shared.

### Interactive Communication

In today's tech-savvy world, two-way, interactive communication is almost a given. This carries over into the realm of employee communication, explains consultant Lee Smith.

> People expect content to be interactive. It's rare to consume media without being cajoled to interact in some way: to like, tweet, comment or share. Audiences also expect to be able to filter out what they don't find interesting. Both of these expectations apply at work as much as they do outside the office walls.[51]

Consequently, many organizations have started using their social media channels as part of their internal communications efforts. For example, Facebook groups can be used to connect individuals working on team projects. Twitter works well to publicize company-wide announcements. YouTube is an ideal medium for posting videos of employee events such as award ceremonies or company picnics.

Social media also helps promote transparency within an attraction. Reporter Catherine Skrzypinski says this is especially important when communicating breaking news. "Before the social media era, those responsible for internal communication used in-person meetings, memos, e-mail and interoffice mail to keep colleagues informed. Now, a single tweet or Facebook status update announcing a corporate change can cause an immediate ripple effect throughout a company."[52]

As a precaution against misuse of social media, some attractions have found it necessary to implement policies that outline the use of these sites. The purpose is to discourage employees from using them in a way that might be detrimental to the organization. The human resources director for the agency that runs the Oregon Zoo explains her organization's reason for such a policy. "Social media blurs the lines between personal and professional communication, and we felt that it was important to establish some guidelines for its use."[53]

### Additional Communication Media

There are many other tools that can be used to communicate with employees. Print or online newsletters are good vehicles for showcasing employee accomplishments through feature stories or profiles. Videoconferencing is effective for attractions that have more than one facility and want to hold system-wide staff meetings for employees in multiple locations. Email works well for sending short, quick messages to many employees at once. A corporate intranet can serve as a handy repository for documents and forms.

Cockerell even advocates the use of bulletin boards—"the old fashioned kind"—as a vehicle for connecting with employees. "It might sound antiquated in this electronic age, but if they're placed in the right location and kept fresh with interesting material, bulletin boards can be excellent communication tools."[54] The right location might be an employee cafeteria or break room where the boards will be highly visible to employees.

### Employee Feedback

Requesting feedback from employees is a valuable means of determining the overall effectiveness of an employee relations program. Chapter 9 discussed some of the tools that can be used to gather feedback from customers. Many of these same approaches are applicable when looking for ideas and suggestions from employees.

Surveys, focus groups, in-depth interviews, and suggestion boxes are all reliable methods of soliciting employee feedback. Attractions can take data gathered with these research tools and use the information to make adjustments to existing employee relations efforts. Asking for feedback is a way of showing employees their opinions are valued. Ultimately, it can also help an attraction enhance practices, programs, and communication channels that will be of value to both current and future employees.

## Conclusion

A well-managed attraction depends heavily on the employees who make it run. Employees serve as brand ambassadors for an attraction because they represent the organization through their actions and interactions with customers.

A successful employee relations program starts with the recruitment and hiring of staff members. Putting careful thought into the process will result in the hiring of employees who are a good fit for the attraction. Once employees are brought on board, they should be provided with information about the attraction's corporate culture as well as the expectations of their individual jobs.

Attraction managers need to devise ways to keep employees motivated and engaged on the job. This can be accomplished through monetary incentives, time off, team-building activities, recognition and reward programs, and professional development. Regular communication keeps staff informed of an attraction's activities. It can help foster a sense of trust and loyalty and give employees an understanding of how their jobs contribute to the overall success of the attraction.

Keeping employees informed is especially important during times of uncertainty or crisis. The next chapter will examine the impact an organizational crisis can have on an attraction and discuss how communication can facilitate the management of a crisis.

## Notes

1. Matt Heller, personal interview, December 9, 2013.
2. Victor T.C. Middleton, Alan Fyall, Michael Morgan, and Ashok Ranchhod, *Marketing in Travel and Tourism, 4th ed.* (Burlington, MA: Butterworth-Heinemann, 2009), 147.

3. Shaun McKeogh, "Four Critical Brand Ambassador Service Behaviors," International Association of Amusement Parks and Attractions, http://www.iaapa.org/news/newsroom/news-articles/human-resources---july-2013.

4. Lee Cockerell, *Creating Magic: 10 Common Sense Leadership Strategies from a Life at Disney* (New York: Doubleday, 2008), 35.

5. See Jodi Helmer, "Sustainable Staffing," *Funworld*, November 2013, 171.

6. Shaun McKeogh, "Better Human Resources for the Attractions Industry: Attracting and Recruiting the Right People," *Funworld*, October 2013, 74.

7. "Shanghai Disney Resort in Student Recruitment Drive," *Xinhua*, April 17, 2014, http://news.xinhuanet.com/english/china/2014-04/17/c_133270782.htm.

8. John Swarbrooke, *The Development and Management of Visitor Attractions, 2nd ed.*, (Burlington, MA: Elsevier Butterworth-Heinemann, 2005), 255.

9. Jennifer J. Salopek, "Hiring Through Social Media," International Association of Amusement Parks and Attractions, http://www.iaapa.org/news/newsroom/news-articles/digital-world-hiring-through-social-media.

10. McKeogh, "Better Human Resources for the Attractions Industry: Attracting and Recruiting the Right People," 74.

11. "Study of Hourly Park Employees Yields Intriguing Results," *Funworld*, June 2013, 16.

12. Bethany Painter quoted in Andrew Hyde, "Internships: Why They Are Good for Business," *Funworld*, June 2013, 59.

13. Jodi Helmer, "Will Work for Experience," *Funworld*, April 2014, 69.

14. Ibid.

15. Jodi Helmer, "The Value of Volunteers," *Funworld*, November 2012, 137.

16. Ibid.

17. Thomas A. Atchison, "What Is Corporate Culture?" *Trustee*, April 2002, 11.

18. Heller, personal interview, December 9, 2013.

19. Lee Cockerell, *The Customer Rules: The 39 Essential Rules for Delivering Sensational Service* (New York: Crown Business, 2013), 44.

20. Heller, personal interview, December 9, 2013.

21. Shaun McKeogh, "Establish Standards and Train to Them," *Funworld*, November 2013, 214.

22. Ibid.

23. Jim Covel, "The Benefits of 'High-Frequency' Training for Employees," *Funworld*, March 2013, 76.

24. Heller, personal interview, December 9, 2013.

25. See McKeogh, "Establish Standards and Train to Them," 217.

26. Heller, personal interview, December 9, 2013.

27. McKeogh, "Establish Standards and Train to Them," 217.

28. Don MacPherson, "Keep Employees Focused," International Association of Amusement Parks and Attractions, http://www.iaapa.org/news/newsroom/news-articles/special-report-keep-employees-focused.

29. Ibid.

30. Heller, personal interview, December 9, 2013.

31. Ibid.

32. Kimberly Paterson, "How Motivated and Engaged Are Your People?" *Rough Notes*, February 2012, 40.

33. MacPherson, "Keep Employees Focused," http://www.iaapa.org/news/newsroom/news-articles/special-report-keep-employees-focused.

34. Jodi Helmer, "Play Hard, Work Hard," *Funworld*, November 2011, 131.

35. See Mike Bederka, "Employee Development: Help Keep FEC Staff for the Long Run," *Funworld*, March 2013, 72.

36. See Helmer, "Play Hard, Work Hard," 132.

37. Jodi Helmer, "Sustainable Staffing," *Funworld*, November 2013, 171.

38. Brad Loxley quoted in Helmer, "Sustainable Staffing," 171.

39. MacPherson, "Keep Employees Focused," http://www.iaapa.org/news/newsroom/news-articles/special-report-keep-employees-focused.
40. Heller, personal interview, December 9, 2013.
41. Prasana William, "Standout Qualities of Award-Winning HR Programs," *Funworld*, June 2014, 92.
42. Jeremy Schoolfield, "Ocean Park CEO Tom Mehrmann: 'Be Disruptive,'" *Funworld*, January 2013, 77.
43. See "Crealy Reaches for Gold Through Employee Magic," *Funworld*, August 2012, 13.
44. Cockerell, *Creating Magic: 10 Common Sense Leadership Strategies from a Life at Disney*, 197.
45. Barbara Fagan-Smith, "The Value of Trust," *Communication World*, June 2013, 22.
46. Rebecca Clarke, "How to Improve Staff Communication," *People Management*, July 15, 2010, 33.
47. Edward K. Moran and Francois Gossleaux, "How Employee Trust Affects the Bottom Line," *Communication World*, June 2013, 18.
48. See Fagan-Smith, "The Value of Trust," 22.
49. See, for example, Karina R. Jensen, "Cooperative Efforts," *Communication World*, October 2013, 15.
50. Heller, personal interview, December 9, 2013.
51. Lee Smith, "The Growing Pains of Employee Communicators," *Communication World*, July 2013, 24.
52. Catherine Skrzypinski, "Communicating with Weapons of Mass Distraction," Society for Human Resource Management, www.shrm.org.
53. Mary Rowe quoted in Jodi Helmer, "Attractions Share New HR Policies Regarding Social Media," International Association of Amusement Parks and Attractions, http://www.iaapa.org/news/newsroom/news-articles/attractions-share-new-hr-policies-regarding-social-media.
54. Cockerell, *Creating Magic: 10 Common Sense Leadership Strategies from a Life at Disney*, 136.

# CHAPTER ELEVEN

# Crisis Communications

## Introduction

No matter how well managed an attraction may be, there is always a possibility that something can go terribly wrong. Accidents, natural disasters, and scandals can all turn a perfectly normal day at an attraction into one mired in chaos, uncertainty, and, occasionally, tragedy. When that happens, marketing communicators may suddenly need to become crisis communicators.

An organizational crisis is an unexpected occurrence that causes major disruption and upheaval to normal operations of a business. Crises usually occur very suddenly and may take a fair amount of time and energy to resolve, as authors David Guth and Charles Marsh explain.

> The difference between a problem and a crisis is a matter of scope. Problems are commonplace occurrences and fairly predictable. They usually can be addressed in a limited time frame, often without arousing public attention or without draining an organization's resources. On the other hand, crises tend to be less predictable. They require a considerable investment of time and resources to resolve and often bring unwanted public attention.[1]

Additionally, if a crisis is not handled properly from a communications standpoint, the aftermath of the crisis may linger long after the issue itself has been resolved.

This chapter looks at the different kinds of crises that can affect tourism attractions. It examines the impact a crisis can have on an attraction and offers tips on how those in communications roles can successfully manage and weather the storm.

## Types of Crises

Within the attractions industry, there are any number of crises that can occur, as evidenced by past events at a variety of attractions. In 2007, for instance, a guest at the San Francisco Zoo was killed after a tiger leaped out of its enclosure and attacked him.[2] Accidents at theme parks can happen when rides malfunction or when something goes awry. At Six Flags Magic Mountain in Valencia, Calif. in 2014, a roller coaster derailed when a pine tree crashed onto the track, causing minor injuries and leaving 22 riders stranded for several hours.[3]

Natural disasters are often the cause of crisis. A 9.0 magnitude earthquake in Japan in 2011 caused major upheaval throughout the country and affected many of Japan's tourism attractions, including Tokyo Disneyland. The park was closed for five weeks while repairs were made.[4] Hurricane Sandy took a significant toll on attractions in the seaside towns along the coast of New Jersey and New York in 2012. The storm destroyed amusement piers, rides, and retail outlets, requiring significant repair and restoration.[5] These are only a few examples of the kinds of crises that can affect the attractions industry at any time.

---

### Crises That Can Affect Tourism Attractions

| | |
|---|---|
| Ride accidents | Onsite illness or death |
| Natural disasters | Toxic fumes |
| Animal escapes or attacks | Sewage spills |
| Robberies or thefts | Fire |
| Building collapses | Food poisoning |
| Transportation accidents | Epidemics and diseases |
| Computer hackings | Terrorist threats |
| Equipment defects | Severe weather |
| Employee strikes | Organized protests |
| Sexual predators | Political instability |
| Child abductions | Explosion or bomb scare |

Source: Adapted from Victor C. Middleton and Jackie Clarke, *Marketing in Travel and Tourism*, 3rd ed.

---

## Crisis Management

Because of the potential for the many different crisis scenarios that can occur, attractions need to anticipate this and accept the inevitable, explain authors Timothy Coombs and Sherri Holladay.

> Management must be prepared for the time when a crisis eventually hits an organization. No organization is immune from a crisis and no management should delude themselves into believing they are crisis resistant. Preparation allows for a more effective crisis management effort that protects constituents and the organization from undue harm.[6]

Although every crisis is different, there are typically three stages associated with the evolution of an organizational crisis. The preplanning stage is the time before a crisis actually happens when organizations prepare for what could possibly occur. The response period occurs during the unfolding of the crisis and encompasses the organization's process in responding and resolving it. The recovery period is the aftermath of the crisis, when the company attempts to return to a sense of normalcy and resume business as usual. If the first two stages are not handled properly, however, the third stage can sometimes be an arduous process for an organization from a reputation management standpoint.

Crisis preparation involves fully understanding the stages of a crisis and taking steps to address them when they happen. Preparation also means comprehending what a crisis means to an organization's various publics and recognizing why communication with these publics is so critical.

## Crisis Communications

When crises happen, people have many questions. They want to know what happened, how it happened, why it happened, and who is ultimately responsible. In times of crisis, a number of questions may come from the media who show up to report on the events and who will ask these and many other questions related to the situation. As the media serve as a conduit to the general public, it is in an organization's best interests to try to answer as many of these questions as possible under the circumstances.

"The most effective crisis communicators are those who provide prompt, frank, and full information to the media in the eye of the storm…. When information gets out quickly, rumors are stopped and nerves are calmed," says author Fraser Seitel.[7] Another factor to consider in crisis management and communications is the impact electronic communication can have on an organization during a crisis, says Lisa Rau, director of publicity and public relations for Herschend Family Entertainment.

> It doesn't seem long ago that those in the PR industry would say that the first 24 hours of an incident are critical. Just a decade ago, they would reference the first three days. Now, however, social media can turn a message into a speeding viral bullet within seconds and reputations can be tainted or broken, created or built almost in an instant.[8]

In fact, an attraction's reputation can be directly affected by how well or how poorly its leaders and managers react and respond during a crisis. It is often up to those working in a communications capacity for an organization to help these individuals understand how the management and communications response to a crisis can affect the attraction's reputation in the long run. "Poor handling of events…can cripple an organization's reputation and cause it enormous monetary loss," explains Seitel. "On the other hand, thinking logically and responding thoughtfully and quickly in a crisis…can cement a positive reputation and establish enormous goodwill for an organization."[9]

# Crisis Pre-Planning

Attractions can do a great deal to mitigate the impact of a crisis by anticipating what could potentially happen and how best to respond, explains communication consultant Gerard Braud. "You cannot predict the hour or the day, but you can predict likely scenarios."[10] Individuals working in other areas of tourism know to anticipate the kinds of crises that could impact their businesses. Airlines, for example, need to plan for the potential of airplane crashes. Hotels and restaurants must have contingency plans for the impact of fire or food-borne illnesses.

Attractions can also assess the kinds of issues that have the potential to reach crisis elevations. This can help in the planning of how to respond if and when these incidents actually occur. Braud suggests this evaluation be done in what he calls a vulnerability assessment. Early in the process, leaders and managers need to identify the kinds of potential crises that are likely to affect the organization.

Braud encourages managers to make this exercise a formal process, one involving people from all different areas of the attraction. "Use a facilitator to help these employees list and discuss everything that could go wrong, from the likely to the bizarre. The resulting list may exceed 100 possibilities, from an explosion to executive misbehavior," he says.[11]

## Form a Crisis Management Team

Once this list has been compiled, a crisis management team should be formed. The individuals on this team will be responsible for developing a crisis management and communications plan and for implementing it should a crisis occur. Ideally, members of a crisis management team will include individuals who are intimately familiar with the inner-workings of the organization. It should also include key communicators who can help draft the plan. In the event of a crisis, members of the crisis management team should be fully prepared to spring into action.

## Develop a Crisis Communications Plan

An attraction's crisis communications plan should spell out the steps needed to communicate with the organization's publics during a crisis. The plan should include detailed information about the communications process and the assignment of communication responsibilities during the crisis.

### Designate a Spokesperson

A key element of the plan should be the designation of a spokesperson who can disseminate information to the media during a crisis. The spokesperson should be a seasoned communications professional who has experience in working with the media and speaking in public. "The more serious the crisis, the higher up the organizational ladder you go to identify the appropriate spokesperson," says Seitel.[12] The spokesperson should be the main contact for communications with the press and public. "Other employees should be instructed to refer media to this person. This ensures that the company is giving a consistent story based on facts," advise authors Philip Kotler et al.[13]

# What to Include in a Crisis Communications Plan

- Names and contact information of crisis management team members.

- Location of crisis command center. This should be a place where crisis communicators can work without being in the spotlight. It should be equipped with telephones, computers, radios, and televisions and should have adequate cell phone reception and Internet access.

- Process for designating a spokesperson. The specific individual selected to be the spokesperson may vary depending on the nature of the crisis.

- List of key stakeholders to notify about the crisis. These can include employees, members of the board of directors, members of the media, shareholders, community leaders, customers, union officials, vendors, and government officials, among others.

- Location of media center where reporters can go to receive information about the situation. This location can be used for media briefings and press conferences.

- Policy that includes guidelines on who can respond to media inquiries and when and how material should be disseminated to the press and public. This policy should also include guidelines for the appropriate use of social media during a crisis.

- Templates for press releases, media advisories, and other relevant documents. These should include basic information that can be tailored to fit a specific crisis.

- System for notifying key publics. This may be through an attraction's website and/or Facebook page, press conference, media releases, etc.

- List of emergency personnel to notify about the crisis such as police, fire officials, health department, and government officials.

- System for maintaining a log that can be used to track all incoming media requests. This log should include caller name, telephone number, date, time, request, information provided, and information about any needed follow-up.

- Steps for evaluating the crisis response once the crisis has been resolved.

The crisis communications plan should include the names, job titles, and contact information of every member of the crisis management team, says Braud. This ensures that when something happens, these individuals can be contacted immediately and kept apprised of information as the situation unfolds.

## Prepare Materials in Advance

A crisis communications plan should also contain templates for press releases, media advisories, and other materials that can be drafted, tailored to a specific crisis, and disseminated to the press as quickly as possible. "Crisis managers can anticipate the basic messages needed in a particular crisis," explain Coombs and Holladay.[14] As more facts emerge about a situation, these can be updated to keep the media informed.

Marketing professional Dimitris Zotos says, "Preparing your responses and all the proper content (images, press release templates, documents with social responsibility actions, etc.) is a time management practice that will enable you to focus on high priority tasks. Time is crucial during crisis and you can't afford being slow."[15]

Guidelines for holding press conferences as needed should be incorporated into the crisis communications plan. The plan should also address strategies for the dissemination of information through social media and a process for monitoring online communications for any hint of information that could be potentially harmful to the attraction in the long run.

In addition, say crisis management specialists Oliver Schmidt and Dianne Chase, "Your company's crisis communications should definitely include an employee communications component…. Processes, responsibilities, channels and recurring training should be determined and a framework established that encompass employee communication."[16]

### Accommodate the Media

A crisis communications plan may also identify a specific area within the attraction that can serve as a media center during a crisis. This might be a conference room, cafeteria, or other area that has sufficient space to accommodate those who show up at the attraction when the crisis occurs. It can also be used for press conferences as needed. Media who arrive on the scene should be directed to this location and encouraged to remain there. This reduces the chances of reporters wandering throughout the facility unaccompanied, trying to gather information from random employees or customers.

An attraction's crisis communications plan should be updated regularly throughout the year. Guth and Marsh also advise that the plan be thought of as a reference tool, not an ironclad document. "Although the organization should be guided by its crisis communications plan, its responses should not be dictated by it. As is the case with all plans, it should be flexible enough to address unanticipated circumstances."[17]

## Crisis Response

When a crisis occurs, no matter what the scope, an attraction's crisis management team should immediately go into response mode. At the same time, the attraction's communications professionals will begin to implement the steps of the crisis communications plan. "Every crisis is different, but the steps you need to take to communicate never change," says Braud. "From the onset, you must (1) gather the facts about the incident, (2) notify and confer with members of your crisis management team, and (3) issue your first statement about the event."[18]

### Respond Quickly

In the event of a crisis, it is in an organization's best interests to work with the media as cooperatively as possible, advise Kotler et al.

> When a crisis does occur, good communication with the press can reduce the impact of negative publicity…. The company should notify the press when a crisis does occur and keep the press updated. The media will learn about the event, so it is best that they find out from the company.[19]

The initial crisis communications response needs to be "quick, accurate, and consistent," advise Coombs and Holliday.[20] The initial statement should acknowledge what has happened and offer as much information as possible about what is known about the situation. This is especially important when the crisis involves injuries or loss of life. The organization should also inform the public of any known risks that may still exist. "The first statement should be the same for all audiences, including the media, employees and stakeholders," says Braud.[21]

The initial communication also needs to make it clear that the attraction is doing everything possible to address and rectify the situation, says Seitel. "Letting people know that the organization has a plan and is implementing it helps convince them that you are in control," he says. "Defining the issues means both having a clear sense internally of what the focus of action should be and communicating that action into the marketplace to reach key constituents."[22]

If people have been harmed or inconvenienced by the incident, the attraction should issue an apology through a formal statement to the media and public. The statement can be posted on the organization's website and social media sites. Depending on the severity of the crisis, the attraction's CEO or someone else in a leadership position might also want to deliver this apology in person during a press conference.

## Keep Everyone Informed

Press conferences are a routine part of crisis communications, says Braud. They offer attractions a venue to provide information to many reporters at the same time and give them an opportunity to ask questions. "If the crisis brings out the media, you should hold a live news conference within an hour of the incident. As the news conference begins, simultaneously post the same statement to your official website and send it via email to all employees," he says.[23] In addition, Braud advises, "Send out a public relations person who has been trained to speak to the media for the first news conference. Select a subject matter expert who has been through media training for a subsequent news conference."[24]

Social media should also play a key role in an attraction's crisis communications efforts. According to the International Association of Amusement Park and Attractions' (IAAPA) crisis communications guide, "Your most loyal customers, fans, and members of the media will naturally look to your social media outlets for information. It is important to either post your official statement directly to your blog, Facebook, and Twitter sites or provide links to the information."[25]

The IAAPA guide suggests that employees be regularly updated on the crisis as the situation develops. As part of this update, employees need to be informed about the organization's policy on speaking to the media. "Employees should expressly know NOT to speak to the media and should direct any inquiries to the public relations department or person on staff trained to respond to the press."[26]

## Update and Monitor Information

In the early stages of a crisis, there is a high probability there will still be a great deal that is unknown. However, it is never advisable to issue a statement of "no comment" to the media. It's better to offer to provide updates as soon as more information is available than simply refuse to answer questions. Otherwise, reporters are likely to go looking for answers to their questions from other sources such as employees or guests.

It's also advisable to stick to the facts and not speculate on a situation, says Rau. "Understand that the news people, or your social media audiences, are seeking information to share—with the public or via Internet channels. You must be very focused on stating the situation using only the facts, not speculation or what 'might' be."[27] Speculation leads to rumors, which could ultimately be more harmful to the attraction than the crisis itself.

As indicated in the crisis communications plan, during the crisis someone from the organization should be assigned to monitor the Internet and keep a close watch on social media channels to see what's being said about the attraction, Zotos says.

> Monitoring what people say about your brand should be added in your daily routine. Search your brand on Google, on forums, on review websites, on blogs, and on any online media related to your industry....
> It is also important to heavily monitor what users say on social networks and respond.[28]

## Crisis Recovery

Eventually, the worst of the crisis will be over, and everyone at the attraction will want to get back to business as usual. From a communications standpoint, much of this return to normalcy will depend on how the crisis was handled and how much this handling has affected the organization's reputation. As Guth and Marsh explain, "Some crises cast organizations in the role of victim. In other crises, organizations may be seen as the villain. And in a few cases, well-prepared organizations have emerged from crises in the role of hero."[29] In the recovery phase of a crisis, communications professionals may be called upon to assess which of these roles the media and public have designated to the attraction.

### Attraction as Victim

If forces of nature such as an earthquake or hurricane have impacted an attraction, it may come off looking like a victim, garnering sympathy from the public. The National Corvette Museum in Bowling Green, Ky., was thrown into turmoil in early 2014 when a giant sinkhole opened up and swallowed eight of the museum's cars. Although no one was injured, the disaster threatened the attraction's future existence.

---

### *Attraction Fun Fact*

The world's largest museum collection is at the Vatican Museums complex in Italy.

---

The curious nature of the incident, however, prompted compassion and interest from the public. "Security camera footage showing the floor's collapse [was] viewed nearly 8.3 million times on YouTube," notes reporter Bruce Schreiner.[30] This resulted in a 66% increase in museum attendance and 71% revenue increase, as well as a spike in museum memberships and merchandise sales.

"What started as a tragedy has turned into an opportunity to lure more people off a nearby interstate to visit the museum, which struggled in prior years to keep its doors open," notes Schreiner.[31] As a result of positive public response, the museum's board of directors even considered leaving part of the sinkhole intact—along with several submerged Corvettes—as a permanent part of the museum's attractions.[32] Although the idea was eventually abandoned because of costs and safety factors, the entire situation illustrates how a crisis does not always need to end badly, even for a small attraction.

*Figure 11.1:   The National Corvette Museum in Bowling Green, Ky., successfully recovered from a crisis that resulted when a sinkhole swallowed up eight of the museum's prized cars.*
(Photo Credit: Photo courtesy of the National Corvette Museum.)

## Attraction as Villain

As Guth and Marsh suggest, if the public and the media perceive an organization as having done something inappropriate or unethical, it may emerge from the crisis as a villain. This could be potentially damaging to an attraction's long-term reputation and could take years to repair. On Christmas Day 2007, a female Siberian tiger leaped out of her enclosure at the San Francisco Zoo, killed a 17-year-old boy, and injured two others. Although an investigation into the incident suggested the teens may have provoked the tiger, the zoo was ultimately blamed for the attack after it was determined the height of its animal enclosure did not meet federal safety standards.[33]

According to reporter Stephanie Lee, "The attack transformed the zoo, once popular and respected, into an international joke. It was criticized for its safety lapses and slow response, and it risked losing accreditation."[34] Following the attack, the zoo's director resigned from his position. The zoo also saw a drop in attendance and donations, and it was forced to layoff employees and cut back programs. While some of this was attributed to a weak economy, the memory of the tiger attack in the minds of the public did not help matters.[35]

Under the guidance of a new director, Tanya Peterson, over the next six years the zoo was able to slowly restore its public image. According to an article in *Funworld*, "The zoo apologized and moved forward; it embraced the incident rather than trying to hide from it, by committing to become the best tiger breeding program in the world, among other new initiatives."[36]

### Attraction as Hero

If an attraction has done an excellent job of keeping its publics informed through all available channels of communication, it may emerge from a crisis unscathed and looking like a hero. Likewise, an organization's proactive efforts in rebounding from a crisis can also earn it high praise.

In response to the devastation caused by Hurricane Sandy in 2012, Coney Island's Luna Park organized a relief effort to restore the area's damaged boardwalk attractions and nearby residences. Park staff recruited volunteers using word-of-mouth, email, and social media, says journalist Prasana William. "More than 300 volunteers from all over the world showed up Nov. 10–11, 2012, and cleared four parks and playgrounds, overhauled nine homes, cleared the boardwalk of sand, and donated hundreds of dollars worth of food, clothing, and supplies."[37]

The project reflected the park's determination to let the world know of its plans to move forward as quickly as possible after the storm. It also showed how a planned communication effort could help achieve this. "The integration element that was most successful contained PR outreach, an event, a design concept, and online communications on the website, Facebook, and e-mail," notes Luna Park brand manager Nichole Purmal.[38]

According to William, the number of likes on Luna Park's Facebook page increased by 77.97% in the three months following the project. As a result of the cleanup efforts, the park and other nearby Coney Island attractions were able to open on schedule to great fanfare the following spring.[39]

## Long-Term Reputation Management

Even after a crisis has passed, it's crucial for an attraction to continue to monitor what's being said online and to respond to it, explains Zotos. "Maintain the reputation monitoring efforts and continue publishing positive information about the organization. For a reasonable period, the communication efforts should have one objective: to disconnect your brand name from the crisis event."[40]

Although the circumstances may not be ideal, organizational crises often provide opportunities for attractions to take stock of their overall reputation with the public, as author Steven Fink explains.

> We often use the phrase reservoirs of goodwill, and part of your proactive crisis management and crisis communications strategies should be to measure the depth of your goodwill reservoir and see what you can do to increase it. The more goodwill you have in the bank or reservoir, the more your public will tend to trust you and believe you when your crisis hits, and the more you can draw on it to tide you over.[41]

In the aftermath of a crisis, attractions can use interviews, surveys, focus groups, and other evaluation tools to solicit feedback from stakeholders about their post-crisis impressions of the organization's overall image.[42] If it becomes clear that the public's perception is less than stellar, attraction leadership may need to think about making adjustments to company practices to rectify this.

"Wherever you are perceived as weak, play to your strengths and devise a strategy to bolster your image. Do this in deeds, not just in words," says Fink. "Improving your reputation is good for business in general, but in a crisis it can spell the difference between success and failure."[43] When an attraction is able to show through its actions that its business practices are reputable and well intentioned, it can successfully prepare itself to survive future crises.

> ### *Attraction Fun Fact*
> New Orleans has more historic districts than any other U.S. city.

## Conclusion

Even the most well-run attraction can be susceptible to an unforeseen event or crisis. When a crisis occurs, those working in a communications capacity need to be prepared to deal with it. There are many different types of crises that can affect tourism attractions. Among these are ride accidents, natural disasters, and animal attacks, to name just a few.

A crisis generally has three stages: the preplanning stage, the crisis itself, and the recovery period. Advanced crisis planning can help attraction managers and marketers prepare for the inevitable. This includes forming a crisis management team and developing a crisis communications plan.

This communications plan should designate someone as an official spokesperson during a crisis. It should include templates for press releases and media advisories that can be used to disseminate information. During a crisis, communicators should get the word out using both traditional and electronic media. They should also respond to inquiries from the press as quickly as possible.

The long-term reputation of an attraction may depend on how a crisis is managed from a communications perspective. If a crisis is handled properly, everything should eventually return to normal. Until this occurs, attraction marketers need to monitor comments posted online about their organizations for a period of time after the crisis subsides.

Effective crisis management and communication reflect an attraction's commitment to responsible business practices. There are many other ways attractions can demonstrate this commitment. The final chapter of this book will discuss the concepts of social responsibility and sustainability. It will illustrate how these practices contribute to an attraction's overall promotion and marketing efforts.

# Notes

1. David W. Guth and Charles Marsh, *Public Relations: A Values-Driven Approach, 4th ed.* (Boston, MA: Pearson, 2009), 377.
2. "Tiger Attack Documents Released," *Contra Costa Times*, February 13, 2011, A3.
3. Jenna Chandler, "Roller Coaster Derailment Under Investigation," *Los Angeles Register*, July 9, 2014, http://www.losangelesregister.com/articles/ride-601916-one-coaster.html.
4. See Doug Meigs, "Aftershock," *Funworld*, November 2011, 49; and Keith Miller, "Nature's Fury," *Funworld*, February 2012, 20.
5. See Jeremy Schoolfield, "Recovery Effort," *Funworld*, February 2013, 36; and Mike Bederka, "The Road Back," *Funworld*, November 2013, 88.
6. W. Timothy Coombs and Sherry J. Holladay, *PR Strategy and Application: Managing Influence* (Malden, MA: Wiley-Blackwell, 2010), 241.
7. Fraser P. Seitel, *The Practice of Public Relations, 11th ed.* (Upper Saddle River, NJ: Prentice Hall, 2011), 390.
8. Lisa Rau, "Manage the Message! Crisis Management in a 'Mediaholic' World," *Park World*, March 2014, 40.
9. Seitel, *The Practice of Public Relations, 11th ed.*, 385.
10. Gerard Braud, "Anticipate Risks," *Communication World*, November/December 2012, 14.
11. Ibid.
12. Seitel, *The Practice of Public Relations*, 11th ed., 387.
13. Philip Kotler, John T. Bowen, and James C. Makens, *Marketing for Hospitality and Tourism, 5th ed.* (Boston, MA: Pearson, 2010), 410.
14. Coombs and Holladay, *PR Strategy and Application: Managing Influence*, 242.
15. Dimitris Zotos, "How to Use Social Media for Crisis Management," Webseo Analytics, http://www.webseoanalytics.com/blog/how-to-use-social-media-for-crisis-management.
16. Oliver S. Schmidt and Dianne L. Chase, "Communicating Inside and Out," *Communication World*, December 2013, 14.
17. Guth and Marsh, *Public Relations: A Values-Driven Approach, 4th ed.*, 397.
18. Braud, "Anticipate Risks," 14.
19. Kotler, Bowen, and Makens, *Marketing for Hospitality and Tourism, 5th ed.*, 410.
20. Coombs and Holladay, *PR Strategy and Application: Managing Influence*, 243.
21. Braud, "Anticipate Risks," 14.
22. Seitel, *The Practice of Public Relations, 11th ed.*, 388.
23. Braud, "Anticipate Risks," 14.
24. Ibid.
25. "IAAPA's Quick Guide: Crisis Communication," International Association for Amusement Parks and Attractions, http://www.iaapa.org/resources/tools/crisis-communications.
26. Ibid.
27. Rau, "Manage the Message! Crisis Management in a 'Mediaholic' World," 41.
28. Zotos, "How to Use Social Media for Crisis Management," http://www.webseoanalytics.com/blog/how-to-use-social-media-for-crisis-management.
29. Guth and Marsh, *Public Relations: A Values-Driven Approach, 4th ed.*, 377-78.
30. Bruce Schreiner, "Corvette Museum Board Decides to Fill in Entire Sinkhole That Swallowed 8 Prized Sports Cars," *Associated Press*, August 30, 2014.
31. Bruce Schreiner, "Corvette Museum Likely to Keep Part of Sinkhole," *Associated Press*, June 25, 2014.
32. Earl Allen, "National Corvette Museum to Leave Part of Sinkhole Visible to Public," *McClatchy-Tribune Business News*, July 8, 2014.
33. "Tiger Attack Documents Released," A3.
34. Stephanie Lee, "Former Corporate Attorney Turns Talents to Bringing S.F. Zoo Back," *San Francisco Chronicle*, December 11, 2011.

35. See Ben Worthen, "San Francisco Zoo Tries to Claw Back to Prosperity," *Wall Street Journal*, January 20, 2010.

36. "San Francisco Zoo Rebuilds its Image," *Funworld*, May 2014, 37.

37. Prasana William, "A Different Storm Story," *Funworld*, June 2014, 88.

38. Nichole Purmal quoted in William, "A Different Storm Story," 88.

39. See Joe Jackson, "Coney Island's Rides Reopen," *Wall Street Journal*, March 25, 2013, A21; Ivan Pereira, "Summer Comes Early at Coney," *AM New York*, March 25, 2013, 7; and Mark Morales, "Isle Be Back," *Newsday*, May 17, 2013, 34.

40. Zotos, "How to Use Social Media for Crisis Management," http://www.webseoanalytics.com/blog/how-to-use-social-media-for-crisis-management.

41. Steven Fink, *Crisis Communication: The Definitive Guide to Managing the Message* (New York: McGraw Hill, 2013), 230.

42. See Martha Muzychika, "Minimize the Damage," *Communication World*, April 2014, 24.

43. Ibid., 234.

# CHAPTER TWELVE

# Social Responsibility and Sustainability

## Introduction

In today's globally conscious society, many companies have begun adopting practices that reflect a commitment to corporate social responsibility (CSR) and sustainability. This involves implementing measures that can potentially have widespread implications for an organization and its customers. According to authors Timothy Coombs and Sherry Holladay, "CSR initiatives may focus on people and/or the natural environment. CSR initiatives can impact both simultaneously."[1]

Within the attractions industry, being socially responsible can encompass implementing philanthropic projects, supporting local nonprofit organizations, and developing educational programs for the public, among other activities. From a sustainability perspective, it may involve the creation of practices designed to conserve energy, reduce waste, and contribute to the long-term health of the environment.

Just as an organization's handling of a crisis can have an impact on its public image, as noted in the previous chapter, an attraction's approach to business can also influence how the public perceives the organization. "A corporation with a strong positive reputation for CSR initiatives can distinguish itself from the crowd of competitors," note Coombs and Holladay.[2] While this should not be the driving force behind a company's commitment to social responsibility and sustainability, it can be integrated into the attraction's communications efforts.

This chapter looks at different ways attractions can develop socially responsible and sustainable business practices designed to benefit their communities and the environment. It also addresses various means of communicating these actions to the public.

# Corporate Social Responsibility

Corporate social responsibility is a means for an attraction to use its resources to contribute to the well-being of the local community and to society as a whole. When an attraction makes a public commitment to social responsibility, it conveys a message that its priorities go beyond simply making a profit for shareholders. "The CSR philosophy encourages businesses to use their expertise and other resources to improve society."[3]

An attraction's CSR efforts need to be compatible with the organization's mission. They also need to be realistic in terms of the resources available to implement them. Following are examples of CSR practices that have proven successful for attractions.

---

## Socially Responsible Practices

- Employee volunteerism
- Matching gift programs
- Scholarships and grants
- Fundraising events
- Discounted admission
- Educational programs
- Food and clothing drives
- Event sponsorship
- Volunteer grants
- Ethical marketing
- Fair labor practices
- Charitable donations
- Social marketing seminars
- Employee perks and programs
- Disaster relief assistance

---

## Corporate Philanthropy

Corporate philanthropy is a way for an attraction to give back to the community that supports it. Philanthropy includes "all of the ways in which companies achieve a positive social impact through strategic and generous use of finances, employee time, facilities or their own products and services, to help others in the community and support beneficial causes."[4]

While some philanthropy may come in the form of monetary donations, other activities can include the donation of time by employees who volunteer their services to local nonprofit groups. In this way an organized philanthropy program can ideally involve people working in all areas of an attraction.

### Charitable Donations

Attractions can make financial gifts or donations of admission tickets to local community groups part of their philanthropic efforts. Large corporate attractions with multiple sites often have the resources to give away significant amounts of money every year. However, an attraction's philanthropy practices don't need to be limited by size or scope.

California's Santa Cruz Beach Boardwalk, for example, "has an aggressive community relations program that donates more than $500,000 annually to regional charities," notes reporter Jim Futrell. Woodland Park in Amarillo, Tex., donates "5,000 to 6,000 passes annually for charitable raffles, auctions, and giveaways," he says.[5]

"Sometimes community support takes a nonfinancial angle," adds Futrell. Del Grosso's Amusement Park in Tipton, Pa., "has constructed a Christmas float featuring horses from its antique carousel. The park sends the float out to about a dozen parades annually."[6] Not only does the donation help the local communities hosting the parades, it also helps maintain awareness of the park in the off-season.

## Comped Admission

Some attractions sponsor philanthropic programs tailored for specific groups or nonprofit organizations. El Rollo is a water park in Tlaquiltenango, Mexico, that attracts more than 400,000 visitors a year. The park opens its gates to children and their sponsors from a local home for orphaned and abandoned children each year. The park offers free admission to the children and discounted group rates for their sponsors. El Rollo also has special programs for school groups, notes reporter Jane Di Leo.

> The park gives 50 percent of its ticket sales from school groups back to the school, much like a fundraising mechanism that schools may use to help drum up much-needed income. The money goes to help local schools with such projects as upkeep, improvements, school supplies, and sports equipment.[7]

## Matching Gifts and Volunteer Grants

Matching gift programs are "charitable giving programs set up by corporations in which the company matches donations made by employees to eligible nonprofit organizations."[8] Attractions can develop their own policies on how the programs should be set up, as noted by the organization Double the Donation. "Some companies will match the donation, 1:1, and others might even triple the donation."[9]

Matching gift programs not only help local organizations, they also generate a sense of employee pride and goodwill, notes writer Ryan Scott. "When a company offers matching contributions for every donation an employee makes, the message the company sends to the employee is: 'I care about what you care about.'"[10] This can go a long way in building company loyalty among employees.

Volunteer grants are similar to matching gifts and are another way of getting employees involved with an attraction's philanthropic activities. In this case, organizations make donations to nonprofit organizations or charitable causes based on the number of hours their employees spend volunteering for these organizations or causes.[11]

## Employee Volunteer Programs

Attractions can go one step further in supporting employee volunteer efforts by creating their own programs to promote staff volunteerism. Many employees may already be contributing to their communities by volunteering, while others might be interested but not know how to go about getting started. An organized program can engage employees while at the same time help the local community. A successful employee volunteer program depends upon a vested interest from staff members, notes Scott.

> Before deciding to partner with a specific organization, reach out to your team members to identify their interests. Many people might already be engaged with a particular non-profit or campaign, and, if so, they will be more enthusiastic about participating in your program if it supports a cause which they already support. Distributing a survey or questionnaire is an easy way to gather information about existing community involvement within your company. You might also encourage employees to nominate a cause.[12]

Once an attraction decides on the recipient of the volunteer efforts, it needs to determine how it will allocate staff members the time to participate. One approach is to dedicate a finite period of time—such as a day or weekend—to accomplish a specific task for an organization. This works well when organizing a food drive or participating in a telethon, for instance.

Another option is to give employees time off from their jobs to volunteer with the selected organization on an ongoing basis. "Employee volunteer programs provide excellent opportunities for businesses to create a positive corporate image, establish friendly relations among staff members and, most importantly, do something good for the community," notes Scott.[13]

## Cause Promotion and Marketing

Both cause promotion and cause marketing involve raising money to support specific social issues or causes. In the case of cause promotion, an attraction might sponsor an event or activity and then donate the money it raises from the activity to that cause. With a cause marketing effort, an attraction donates a portion of its profits to a specific cause.

---

### *Attraction Fun Fact*
Approximately 80% of adult travelers partake of a cultural activity when traveling.

---

### Event Promotions

Organized events are ideal means of generating funds for charitable causes. West Midland Safari & Leisure Park in Bewdley, Worcestershire, England, for example, sponsored a Fun Run in 2012 to raise money to support animal conservation efforts. Twenty-nine employees from throughout the park participated in the run, which raised more than $3,000. An article in *Funworld* notes, "The run was an opportunity for them to show their commitment to conservation at the same time as having fun."[14]

In some cases an attraction might design a promotion to raise funds for a specific organization as part of its cause promotion efforts. A popular beneficiary for the attractions industry is a charity in central Florida called Give Kids the World. The organization is dedicated to providing theme park experiences for children with life-threatening illnesses.[15]

Give Kids the World has attracted corporate sponsors such as Walt Disney World, SeaWorld, and Universal Orlando, and has been the beneficiary of events sponsored by organizations like the Jacksonville Zoo. In addition, the International Association of Amusement Parks and Attractions (IAAPA) holds annual events to support the nonprofit's mission in conjunction with its annual expo each November. These events include a golf tournament, fun run, and motorcycle ride and are open to individuals from the attractions industry attending the expo. In 2013, IAAPA raised more than $115,000 for Give Kids the World.[16]

*Figure 12.1:  Some attractions sponsor events to raise money for Give Kids the World, a Florida-based nonprofit that provides a theme park experience for children with life-threatening illnesses.*
(Photo Credit: Photos courtesy of Give Kids the World.)

### Discounted Admission Promotions
Some cause promotions get customers actively involved in the cause by offering them discounts for their support. Six Flags Mexico, for example, sponsors a program called "Feed Your Fun," explains Di Leo. "The park collects rice and bean packages from patrons for the local food bank in exchange for a ticket discount."[17] Similar promotions encourage customers to bring canned foods or toys to an attraction in exchange for discounted admission. These products are used to support food or toy drives for local organizations.

## *Education and Social Marketing*

One way for attractions to show an interest in the well-being of the communities they serve is by sponsoring and supporting educational programs and activities. These programs might offer visitors information related to an attraction, raise awareness about specific social causes or issues, or provide support for educational pursuits.

### Educational Programs
Theme and amusement parks in particular have found educational programs to be beneficial for both the public and the attractions themselves, explains reporter Juliana Gilling. "From an educator's point of view, parks are helping to demystify subjects like science and math, making them accessible and enjoyable for children." At the same time, she notes, "For park operators, educational programs are a way of filling up the attractions in the low season, reaching new audiences, and enhancing their reputations."[18]

Quassy Amusement Park in Middlebury, Conn., for instance, offers a variety of on-site workshops and classes for local schoolchildren during the fall, winter, and spring when the park is closed for the season. Students have an opportunity to learn about physics by studying roller coasters, take a class about the history of the park, or learn how to report and write news stories through a journalism class called "ABCs About News."[19]

Tivoli Gardens in Copenhagen, Denmark, started its educational offerings with online courses that teachers could download and use in their own classrooms. The park progressed to offering an on-site event for local schools called "Climate and Energy Days," explains Gilling. "The event's success led Tivoli to create annual Academic Days, with four-week courses for children ages 10–13 in the spring and for teenagers (13–18 years old) in the autumn."[20]

## Social Marketing Seminars

Attractions can also use educational programs and activities as a means of raising awareness and informing visitors about social causes and issues. Nutrition, tolerance, and diversity are all examples of topics that can become the focus of programs designed to help people think about and take action on certain issues.

In 2013, for example, The Children's Museum of Indianapolis sponsored a Bullying Prevention Summit for 350 local schoolchildren and their teachers. The seminar was tied to an exhibit called "The Power of Children" and featured a keynote speaker and interactive breakout sessions. The purpose was "to encourage children and their families to be tolerant of others and inspire them to be strong, no matter what obstacles may confront them."[21] Other attractions such as Six Flags New England and the Newport Aquarium in Kentucky have sponsored similar anti-bullying activities.[22]

## Scholarships, Grants, and Awards

Attractions can also promote and support education by offering scholarships, grants, and awards. These can enable visitors to conduct research at an attraction's facilities, fund individual educational pursuits, or reward students and educators for their work. The Field Museum in Chicago, for example, offers scholarships and fellowships to scientists and graduate students who want to study the museum's collection of historical and scientific artifacts through on-site research. The museum also sponsors residency programs for science educators and high school students interested in studying genetics.[23]

The Grammy Museum in Los Angeles gives out the Jane Ortner Education Award each year to teachers who use music as a means of teaching educational curriculum. Those honored receive tickets to the Grammy Awards, as well as museum admission and transportation for their classes.[24]

## Employee Perks

Corporate social responsibility efforts don't need to be limited to doing charitable work for outside organizations. Attractions can also be socially responsible by developing programs and practices designed to enhance the well-being of their own staff members. Each year *Fortune* magazine publishes a list of the "100 Best Companies to Work For" in conjunction with the Great Places to Work Institute.[25] Many of these organizations make the list because of their commitment to enhancing the lives of their employees by providing them with perks such as on-site childcare, flextime, employee workout rooms, and subsidized meals, to name just a few.

All of these can contribute to the overall welfare and satisfaction of an attraction's staff members. They also serve the organization well when recruiting new employees, as author

Jeffrey Pfeffer observes. "Just as green companies enjoy reputational benefits that help in brand building and product differentiation…companies with better records of human sustainability could enjoy benefits in attracting and retaining employees and also in building a reputation that could attract additional consumer demand."[26]

## Sustainability

Part of being a socially responsible attraction means maintaining a commitment to environmental sustainability. In recent years, the expression "going green" has become a familiar catchphrase for many different organizations attempting to beef up their sustainability efforts. Within the attractions industry, the term can have a variety of interpretations, notes journalist Lisa Anderson Mann.

---

### Attraction Tips for "Going Green"

#### Facilities
Provide recycle bins throughout the facility
Use energy-efficient light bulbs
Install solar panels

#### Transportation
Promote carpooling
Provide bike racks for employees
Use alternative fuel in company vehicles

#### Natural Resources
Install drought-resistant plants
Use reclaimed water for irrigation
Adjust thermostat settings

#### Waste Reduction
Reuse boxes and envelopes
Recycle printer cartridges
Refurbish old equipment or furniture

#### Food and Beverage
Sell recyclable cups at concession stands
Donate leftover food when feasible
Compost food scraps

#### Marketing Materials
Replace print publications with online options
Use recycled paper for marketing materials
Print double-sided when copying documents

---

Going green can cover a wide range of activities—from recycling, energy conservation, and reducing water use; to serving organic food, reducing chemical use or oil consumption, and cutting CO2 emissions. Initiating green policies, likewise, encompass a huge range of investments. Some policies are quite easy and inexpensive; others require significant upfront costs but recoup their investments; and still others may help the environment but never recoup costs.[27]

As with CSR, part of a viable sustainability effort is to ensure that it is genuine. Attempting to make the organization look like it is implementing environmentally sound practices when these efforts are only superficial is known as greenwashing, note Coombs and Holladay. "Essentially corporations attempt to create the impression that they care about the environment without demonstrating the underlying commitment to the environment."[28] This is not only unethical but can ultimately damage the organization's overall reputation.[29] Following are examples of different practices attractions can implement as part of a reputable sustainability program.

## Recycling Programs

One popular option for attractions is the implementation of a recycling program. According to reporter Jennifer Salopek, "Beverage bottle recycling is possibly the easiest, most accessible way for your…attraction to participate in environmental sustainability—and it's something your guests probably expect."[30] Recycling can also include aluminum, paper, cardboard, and food waste.

Recycling bins should be adorned with eye-catching graphics that clearly indicate what should be placed where—cans, bottles, paper products, etc. They can be strategically placed throughout the facility, says Salopek, "near entrances, food concessions, restrooms, and attractions that tend to have long lines."[31] Prominently placed signage helps direct guests to the bins. Universal Studios Singapore, for instance, posts messages throughout its park to encourage guests to recycle.[32]

Recycling programs don't need to be limited to products used by attraction visitors. At the Oregon Zoo, for example, recycling encompasses "construction waste, computer and copier cartridges, kitchen cooking oil, electronics, polystyrene, bubble wrap, and yard debris," notes Keith Miller.[33]

Other attractions have also found ways to recycle that go beyond bottles and cans. Hong Kong's Ocean Park "recycles more than 222,000 pounds of food waste per year," says reporter Jodi Helmer.[34] SeaWorld sells its beverages in plant-based recyclable plastic cups.[35] The St. Louis Zoo donates leftover food from large-scale on-site events to local food banks.[36] Attractions can even sponsor recycling drives by encouraging visitors to bring empty beverage containers in exchange for discounted admission.[37]

## Resource Conservation

Some attractions have taken measures that help conserve natural resources throughout their facilities. These include the installation of solar power panels and energy-saving light bulbs, water-saving measures, and the use of alternative vehicle fuel.

At the Cincinnati Zoo & Botanical Gardens, for example, visitors park their vehicles under a canopy of solar panels that stretches over four acres, says reporter John Morell. Since their installation, the panels have generated nearly 20% of the zoo's power. In addition, he says, "Using the zoo's parking lot for the panels solves two problems simultaneously. It turns a one-use area into a multi-use area, and it provides an added benefit for guests in summer: shade that keeps their cars out of the baking sun while they enjoy visiting the exhibits."[38]

Making the switch to solar power has an added benefit for nonprofit attractions such as zoos, aquariums, and museums. Their nonprofit status often makes them eligible for government grants that help subsidize installation costs, explains Morell. Organizations also have the option to "partner with a solar company or utility that is hoping the visibility of the project will add to its profile."[39]

Other energy saving options are available for attractions that don't want to go the solar route. The National Liberty Museum in Philadelphia switched out its fluorescent lighting for more energy-efficient bulbs. "The new eco-friendly light bulbs not only last longer, but they use less energy, so the museum ends up saving money," according to *Tourist Attractions & Parks* magazine.[40]

The Shedd Aquarium in Chicago replaced 600 light bulbs in the facility's chandeliers with LED bulbs, for an estimated $7,000 annual electricity bill savings. The organization also installed meters on "everything from lighting systems to chillers so it can track and analyze how and when energy is being used," says reporter Julie Wernau. "From there it can determine which systems could safely be powered down without harming the animals or causing a disruption to patrons."[41]

Another example of a natural resource conservation effort is Legoland California's installation of drought-resistant plants to reduce the need for watering, as well as the park's use of reclaimed water for irrigation purposes. Attractions are also finding ways to use more eco-friendly sources of fuel in their company vehicles. "The steam locomotives were the largest consumer of diesel fuel at Disneyland before being converted to biodiesel—a move that saved 150,000 gallons of diesel fuel each year while greatly reducing emissions," says Mann.[42] Likewise, the Toronto Zoo now relies on electric power rather than gasoline to fuel its Zoomobile train, golf karts, and passenger vans.[43]

## Transit Alternatives

Attractions can also implement programs intended to garner support from their employees and get them involved in the sustainability effort when they come to work. The Chester Zoo, for example, sponsors an employee commute program called the Green Travel Reward Scheme, explains Gilling. The program offers incentives for employees willing to leave their cars at home when commuting to work—by taking the train or bus, carpooling, bicycling, or walking.

"Staff use a monthly worksheet to record their green commutes. Each month they are entered into a drawing to win £60 ($93) of shopping vouchers. Around a third of the zoo's 300 staff regularly participate in the scheme," says Gilling.[44] The zoo offers its employees discounts on tickets for local rail and bus operators. It also provides free bike repair workshops for employees in conjunction with local vendors.

*Community Cooperation*

Another way attractions can be environmentally proactive is by encouraging members of the community to be part of their commitment to sustainability. The Oregon Zoo, for instance, "discourages its vendors from using wasteful packaging and asks school-group visitors to pack low-waste lunches," says Miller. "Also, with a Portland MAX light rail system station at the zoo's entrance, visitors are encouraged to use the system and are given a $1.50 discount on zoo admission if they do."[45]

The Aquarium of the Pacific in Long Beach, Calif., launched a venture called Seafood of the Future (SFF) in conjunction with local restaurants. The purpose was to encourage diners to select meal choices of seafood that had been caught and produced in a manner that minimized harm to the marine environment.

> SFF evaluates what seafood items it sees as being harvested responsibly and then puts its logo on the menu next to the items that meet the qualifications. To help foster the support of the consumer, the program offers discount tickets to the aquarium for any customer who chooses a SFF-approved item from the menus of the 10 or so partner restaurants that participate in the ticket program.[46]

## Communicating CSR and Sustainability

Once an attraction has put its CSR and sustainability efforts into place, the next step is to let people know about them. According to Coombs and Holladay, attractions should "develop a plan that outlines the stakeholders to be addressed, channels (media) to be used to reach them, and primary messages to be sent to each stakeholder group."[47] For attractions, stakeholders may include customers, media, local community members, shareholders, and employees, to name just a few.

*Channels of Communication*

Attractions can use a variety of channels to communicate with their stakeholders. Some organizations designate areas of their websites to showcase their CSR and sustainability activities. Website links to online resources such as videos and slideshows can provide valuable information as well about specific CSR and sustainability projects.

A best practices study conducted by the International Association of Business Communicators revealed that "stakeholder groups prefer to find CSR information within one click from the company home page; they prefer to consult videos or interactive maps for more in-depth information; and they appreciate concrete facts about the CSR efforts impact, budget and external audit as well as detailed information about activities."[48]

Some attractions produce annual reports for shareholders and donors that summarize their yearly CSR and sustainability efforts. For more timely communication, press releases and social media channels can be used to promote these activities as they happen, note Coombs and Holladay. "Given the nature of social media, periodic CSR messages will not appear to overpromote. Stakeholders expect regular blog entries, tweets, and posts to Facebook."[49]

The authors also stress the need to include employees as part of the communication effort, especially when they are actively engaged in an attraction's CSR or sustainability efforts. "Employees can provide a valuable communication channel for CSR if they are well informed on the subject. Their personal involvement and investment in CSR activities often make them highly credible and enthusiastic supporters of the initiatives."[50]

---

### Attraction Fun Fact

More than 6,000 songs are performed at the Grand Ole Opry every year.

---

*Recognition Through Certification*

Finally, one way to have an attraction's social responsibility and sustainability practices publicly acknowledged is by seeking certification that officially validates the organization's efforts. Certification involves meeting a certain set of standards and criteria established by an outside organization. The National Wildlife Federation, for example, grants certified wildlife habitat status to attractions that designate areas of their facilities where creatures such as birds and butterflies can flourish. These can include gardens, parks, or green areas near entrances or parking lots.

"A wildlife certification is an easy-to-understand way for a business to demonstrate to guests its concern for the environment," explains reporter Kim Button. "Having a wildlife friendly habitat lends a business extra credibility when seeking funding or connections among a community that values eco-friendly practices."[51] Attractions that receive certification can publicize this status as part of their overall promotional efforts, providing added visibility for the organization.

## Conclusion

Tourism attractions have the ability to go beyond entertaining audiences and make a difference in the communities they serve. They can achieve this by implementing practices that reflect a commitment to social responsibility and sustainability.

Attractions are socially responsible when they use their resources to help others. This can be done through a variety of philanthropic activities such as charitable donations, matching gifts, and employee volunteer programs. Attractions can also offer educational programs that benefit their communities and implement practices that enrich the lives of their employees.

Many attractions have begun implementing sustainability measures designed to conserve and protect natural resources. Among these are recycling, energy conservation, waste reduction, and alternative transit programs.

Attractions can incorporate the communication of their social responsibility and sustainability practices into their promotion and marketing activities. Company websites and annual reports are ideal for communicating information about these practices. As with many of the topics discussed in this book, this communication can contribute to the overall promotion and marketing efforts used to showcase the best of an attraction.

# Notes

1. W. Timothy Coombs and Sherry J. Holladay, *Managing Corporate Social Responsibility: A Communication Approach* (Malden, MA: Wiley-Blackwell, 2012), 20.

2. Ibid., 36.

3. Ibid., 6.

4. "What Is Corporate Philanthropy?" *Truist*, August 5, 2013, http://truist.com/what-is-corporate-philanthropy.

5. Jim Futrell, "Beneficial to All: Giving Back to the Community Is Good Business," International Association of Amusement Parks and Attractions, http://www.iaapa.org/news/newsroom/news-articles/giving-back-to-the-community-is-good-business.

6. Ibid.

7. Jane Di Leo, "The Giving Tide," *Funworld*, November 2012, 165.

8. "Defining Corporate Philanthropy," Double the Donation, https://doublethedonation.com/blog/2013/09/defining-corporate-philanthropy.

9. Ibid.

10. Ryan Scott, "The Best Gift You Can Give Your Employees," *Forbes.com*, June 26, 2012, http://www.forbes.com/sites/causeintegration/2012/06/26/the-best-gift-you-can-give-your-employees.

11. Ibid.

12. Ryan Scott, "6 Tips for Creating Employee Volunteer Programs," *Causecast*, December 15, 2011, http://www.causecast.com/blog/bid/102826/5-Tips-for-Creating-an-Employee-Volunteer-Program.

13. Ibid.

14. "Safari Park Staff Shows Conservation Efforts Can Be Playful," *Funworld*, October 2012, 14.

15. See "About Us," Give Kids the World, http://www.gktw.org/about.

16. Keith Miller, "$115,000 raised for GKTW During Expo," *Funworld*, January 2014, 81.

17. Jane Di Leo, "Corporate Responsibility," International Association of Amusement Parks and Attractions, http://www.iaapa.org/news/newsroom/news-articles/corporate-responsibility.

18. Juliana Gilling, "New Way of Learning," International Association of Amusement Parks and Attractions, http://www.iaapa.org/news/newsroom/news-articles/new-way-of-learning.

19. E. Jones, "Quassy Educational Programs," WTNH News8, http://wtnh.com/2014/08/24/quassy-educational-programs.

20. Gilling, "New Way of Learning," http://www.iaapa.org/news/newsroom/news-articles/new-way-of-learning.

21. Jeffrey Patchen quoted in Keith Miller, "Attractions Become Vocal Messengers Against Bullying," *Funworld*, March 2014, 62.

22. Ibid.

23. See "Research Scholarships and Grants," The Field Museum, http://www.fieldmuseum.org/about/careers/research-scholarships-and-grants.

24. See "The Jane Ortner Education Award," Grammy Museum, http://www.grammymuseum.org/education/for-teachers/the-jane-ortner-educating-through-music-curriculum-awards.

25. See "Fortune Best Companies," *Fortune.com*, http://fortune.com/best-companies, and Great Places to Work Institute, http://www.greatplacetowork.com/best-companies/100-best-companies-to-work-for.

26. Jeffrey Pfeffer, "Companies Emphasize the Environment Over Employees," in Margaret Haerens and Lynn M. Zott, eds., *Corporate Social Responsibility* (Farmington Hills, MI: Greenhaven Press, 2014), 98.

27. Lisa Anderson Mann, "What Does Green Mean?" International Association of Amusement Parks and Attractions, http://www.iaapa.org/news/newsroom/news-articles/what-does-green-mean.

28. Coombs and Holladay, *Managing Corporate Social Responsibility: A Communication Approach*, 74.

29. Ibid., 76.

30. Jennifer Salopek, "Low-Hanging Fruit: Beverage Bottle Recycling Is an Easy—and Potentially Profitable—Way to Kick Off Your Green Initiative," International Association of Amusement Parks and Attractions, http://www.iaapa.org/news/newsroom/news-articles/beverage-bottle-recycling-is-an-easy-way-to-start-going-green.

31. Ibid.
32. See Jeremy Schoolfield, "What Does Green Mean to You?" *Funworld*, February 2011, http://www.iaapa.org/news/newsroom/news-articles/what-does-green-mean-to-you-feb-2011.
33. Keith Miller, "Oregon Zoo: Sustainability Done for the Right Reasons," *Funworld*, February 2012, 42.
34. Jodi Helmer, "One Man's Trash," International Association of Amusement Parks and Attractions, http://www.iaapa.org/news/newsroom/news-articles/turning-scraps-into-cash.
35. "Sea World Introduces Reusable Cup for Park Guests," *Tampa Tribune Online*, July 10, 2014, http://tbo.com/news/business/seaworld-introduces-reusable-cup-for-park-guests-20140710.
36. "Waste Not, Want Not: How Zoos and Aquariums are Reducing Food Waste," *Tourist Attractions & Parks*, March 1, 2013, http://tapmag.com/2014/03/01/waste-not-want-not-how-zoos-and-aquariums-are-reducing-food-waste.
37. Salopek, "Low-Hanging Fruit: Beverage Bottle Recycling Is an Easy—and Potentially Profitable—Way to Kick Off Your Green Initiative," http://www.iaapa.org/news/newsroom/news-articles/beverage-bottle-recycling-is-an-easy-way-to-start-going-green.
38. John Morell, "Zoo Power: How Zoos and Aquariums are Embracing and Profiting from Solar Energy," International Association of Amusement Parks and Attractions, http://www.iaapa.org/news/newsroom/news-articles/maintenance-zoos-and-aquariums-are-embracing-and-profiting-from-solar-energy.
39. Ibid.
40. "The Greening of Museums," *Tourist Attractions & Parks*, January 16, 2011, http://tapmag.com/2011/01/16/the-greening-of-museums-an-environmentally-friendly-approach-to-art-science-and-history-institutions.
41. Julie Wernau, "Shedd Aims to Cut Whale of Power Bill," *Chicago Tribune*, January 26, 2013, 1.
42. Mann, "What Does Green Mean?" http://www.iaapa.org/news/newsroom/news-articles/what-does-green-mean.
43. See James Careless, "Toronto Zoo: Green Makes Economic Sense, Too," *Funworld*, February 2012, 40.
44. Juliana Gilling, "Chester Zoo: Green Light for Travel," *Funworld*, February 2012, 35.
45. Miller, "Oregon Zoo: Sustainability Done for the Right Reasons," 42.
46. "Aquarium of the Pacific Promotes Responsible Seafood Consumption," *Funworld*, May 2012, 14.
47. Coombs and Holladay, Managing Corporate Social Responsibility: A Communication Approach, 110.
48. Silvia McCallister Castillo, Laura Illia, and Belén Rodriguez-Canovas, "When CSR Clicks," *Communication World*, September/October 2012, 32.
49. Coombs and Holladay, *Managing Corporate Social Responsibility: A Communication Approach*, 128.
50. Ibid., 123.
51. Kim Button, "'Wild' Additions Promote Environmental Concern," *Funworld*, November 2013, 199.

# Suggested Readings

## Books

### Advertising and Marketing

Kotler, Philip, John T. Bowen, and James C. Makens. *Marketing for Hospitality and Tourism, 6th ed.* Boston, MA: Pearson, 2013.

Middleton, Victor T.C., and Jackie Clarke. *Marketing in Travel and Tourism, 3rd ed.* Oxford, England: Butterworth-Heinemann, 2001.

Middleton, Victor T.C., Alan Fyall, Michael Morgan, and Ashok Ranchhod. *Marketing in Travel and Tourism, 4th ed.* Burlington, MA: Butterworth-Heinemann, 2009.

Morrison, Alastair M. *Hospitality & Travel Marketing, 4th ed.* Clifton Park, NY: Delmar, 2010.

Shimp, Terence A. *Advertising, Promotion, and Other Aspects of Integrated Marketing Communications, 8th ed.* Mason, OH: South-Western Cengage Learning, 2010.

Shoemaker, Stowe, Robert C. Lewis, and Peter C. Yesawich. *Marketing Leadership in Hospitality and Tourism, 4th ed.* Upper Saddle River, NJ: Pearson, 2007.

Wain, Carol, and Jay Conrad Levinson. *Guerrilla Tourism Marketing.* Lexington, KY: WINning Entrepreneur Press, 2012.

### Crisis Communications

Coombs, W. Timothy. *Ongoing Crisis Communication: Planning, Managing, and Responding, 4th ed.* London, United Kingdom: Sage Publications, 2015.

Fearn-Banks, Kathleen. *Crisis Communications: A Casebook Approach.* New York: Routledge, 2011.

Fink, Steven. *Crisis Communication: The Definitive Guide to Managing the Message.* New York: McGraw Hill, 2013.

Henderson, Joan C. *Managing Tourism Crises.* Burlington, MA: Butterworth Heinemann, 2007.

Laws, Eric, and Bruce Prideaux, eds. *Tourism Crises: Management Responses and Theoretical Insight.* New York: Routledge, 2012.

Walker, Bill. *Crisis Communication in the 24/7 Social Media World: A Guidebook for CEOs and Public Relations Professionals.* Ithaca, NY: Paramount Market Publishing, 2014.

## Employee Relations

Andersen, Erika. *Growing Great Employees: Turning Ordinary People into Extraordinary Performers.* New York: Penguin Group, 2006.

Cowan, David. *Strategic Internal Communication: How to Build Employee Engagement and Performance.* London, United Kingdom: Kogan Page Limited, 2014.

Diamond, Harriet, and Linda Eve Diamond. *Perfect Phrases for Motivating and Rewarding Employees: Hundreds of Ready-to-Use Phrases for Encouraging and Recognizing Employee Excellence, 2nd ed.* New York: McGraw-Hill, 2010.

Heller, Matt. *The Myth of Employee Burnout: What It Is. Why It Happens. What To Do About It.* Sarasota, FL: The Peppertree Press, 2013.

## Entertainment Studies

Gottdiener, Mark. *The Theming of America.* Boulder, CO: Westview Press, 2001.

Lieberman, Al, and Patricia Esgate. *The Definitive Guide to Entertainment Marketing: Bringing the Moguls, the Media, and the Magic to the World, 2nd ed.* Upper Saddle River, NJ: Pearson Education, 2014.

Moss, Stuart, ed. *The Entertainment Industry: An Introduction.* Oxfordshire, United Kingdom: CABI, 2010.

Sayre, Shay. *Entertainment Promotion and Communication: The Industry and Integrated Campaigns.* Dubuque, IA: Kendall Hunt Publishing, 2010.

Sayre, Shay, and Cynthia King. *Entertainment and Society: Impacts, Influences, and Innovations, 2nd ed.* New York: Routledge, 2010.

Stein, Andi, and Beth Bingham Evans. *An Introduction to the Entertainment Industry.* New York: Peter Lang Publishing, 2009.

Stein, Andi. *Why We Love Disney: The Power of the Disney Brand.* New York: Peter Lang Publishing, 2011.

## Guest Relations and Customer Service

Cockerell, Lee. *The Customer Rules: The 39 Essential Rules for Delivering Sensational Service.* New York: Crown Business, 2013.

Ford, Robert C., Michael C. Sturman, and Cherrill P. Heaton. *Managing Quality Service in Hospitality.* Clifton Park, NY: Cengage Learning, 2012.

Inghilleri, Leonardo, and Micah Solomon. *Exceptional Service, Exceptional Profit.* New York: American Management Association, 2010.

Kinni, Theodore. *Be Our Guest: Perfecting the Art of Customer Service.* New York, NY: Disney Enterprises, 2011.

Lucas, Robert W. *Please Every Customer.* New York: McGraw-Hill, 2011.

Zemke, Ron, and Kristin Anderson. *Delivering Knock Your Socks Off Service, 4th ed.* New York: American Management Association, 2007.

## Management and Leadership

Attractions Management. *Attractions Management Handbook 2013–2014: The Global Resource for Attractions Professionals,* http://www.attractionshandbook.com.

Barrett, Deborah J. *Leadership Communication, 4th ed.* Boston, MA: McGraw Hill/Irwin, 2013.

Cockerell, Lee. *Creating Magic: 10 Common Sense Leadership Strategies from a Life at Disney.* New York: Doubleday, 2008.

Evans, Nigel, David Campbell, and George Stonehouse. *Strategic Management for Travel and Tourism.* Oxford, England: Butterworth-Heinemann, 2003.

Fyall, Alan, Brian Garrod, Anna Leask, and Stephen Wanhill. *Managing Visitor Attractions, 2nd ed.* Burlington, MA: Butterworth-Heinemann, 2008.

Leask, Anna, and Alan Fyall, eds. *Managing World Heritage Sites.* New York: Routledge, 2011.

Swarbrooke, John. *The Development and Management of Visitor Attractions, 2nd ed.* Burlington, MA: Elsevier Butterworth-Heinemann, 2005.

## Museums

French, Ylva, and Sue Runyard. *Marketing and Public Relations for Museums, Galleries, Cultural and Heritage Attractions.* New York: Routledge, 2011.

Kotler, Neil G., Philip Kotler, and Wendy I. Kotler. *Museum Marketing and Strategy: Designing Missions, Building Audiences, Generating Revenue and Resources.* San Francisco, CA: Jossey-Bass, 2008.

Rentschler, Ruth, and Anne-Marie Hede. *Museum Marketing.* New York: Routledge, 2011.

## Public Relations

Coombs, W. Timothy, and Sherry J. Holladay. *PR Strategy and Application: Managing Influence.* Malden, MA: Wiley-Blackwell, 2010.

Guth, David W., and Charles Marsh. *Public Relations: A Values-Driven Approach, 5th ed.* Boston, MA: Pearson, 2012.

Howard, Carole M., and Wilma K. Mathews. *On Deadline: Managing Media Relations.* Long Grove, IL: Waveland Press, Inc., 2013.

Phillips, Brad. *The Media Training Bible.* Washington, D.C.: SpeakGood Press, 2013.

Seitel, Fraser P. *The Practice of Public Relations, 12th ed.* Upper Saddle River, NJ: Prentice Hall, 2013.

Wilcox, Dennis L., Glen T. Cameron, Bryan H. Reber, and Jae-Hwa Shin. *Think Public Relations, 2nd ed.* Boston, MA: Pearson, 2013.

## Social Media

Kolb, Jeremy. *Social Media Marketing That Works.* Roundeux Publishing, 2013.

Macarthy, Andrew. *500 Social Media Marketing Tips: Essential Advice, Hints and Strategy for Business: Facebook, Twitter, Pinterest, Google+, YouTube, Instagram, LinkedIn, and More!* CreateSpace Independent Publishing Platform, 2014.

Schaefer, Mark W. *Social Media Explained.* Schaefer Marketing Solutions, 2014.

Scott, David Meerman. *The New Rules of Marketing & PR.* Hoboken, NJ: John Wiley & Sons, 2013.

## Social Responsibility

Beal, Brent D. *Corporate Social Responsibility: Definition, Core Issues, and Recent Developments.* Thousand Oaks, CA: Sage Publications Inc., 2014.

Chandler, David, and William Werther, Jr. *Strategic Corporate Social Responsibility.* Thousand Oaks, CA: Sage Publications Inc., 2014.

Coombs, Timothy W., and Sherry J. Holladay. *Managing Corporate Social Responsibility: A Communication Approach.* Malden, MA: Wiley-Blackwell, 2012.

Haerens, Margaret, and Lynn M. Zott, eds. *Corporate Social Responsibility.* Farmington Hills, MI: Greenhaven Press, 2014.

## Special Events

Allen, Johnny, William O'Toole, Robert Harris, and Ian McDonnell. *Festival & Special Event Management.* Queensland, Australia: John Wiley & Sons Australia Ltd., 2011.

Getz, Donald. *Event Management & Event Tourism, 2nd ed.* New York: Cognizant Communication Corporation, 2005.

Mallen, Cheryl, and Lorne J. Adams, eds. *Event Management in Sport, Recreation and Tourism, 2nd ed.* New York: Routledge, 2013.

O'Toole, William, and Phyllis Mikolaitis. *Corporate Event Project Management.* New York: John Wiley & Sons, 2002.

Preston, C.A. *Event Marketing: How to Successfully Promote Events, Festivals, Conventions, and Expositions.* Hoboken, NJ: Wiley & Sons, 2012.

Shone, Anton, and Bryn Parry. *Successful Event Management: A Practical Handbook, 3rd ed.* Hampshire, United Kingdom: Cengage, 2010.

## Sustainability

Esty, Daniel C., and P.J. Simmons. *The Green to Gold Business Playbook: How to Implement Sustainability Practices for Bottom-Line Results in Every Business Function.* Hoboken, NJ: John Wiley & Sons, 2011.

Weybrecht, Giselle. *The Sustainable MBA: A Business Guide to Sustainability, 2nd ed.* Chicester, West Sussex, United Kingdom: John Wiley & Sons, 2014.

Young, Scott T., and K. Kathy Dhanda. *Sustainability: Essentials for Business.* Thousand Oaks, CA: Sage Publications Inc., 2013.

## Theme Parks

Clavé, S. Anton. *The Global Theme Park Industry.* Oxfordshire, United Kingdom: CABI Press, 2007.

Hillman, Jim. *Amusement Parks.* Oxford, United Kingdom: Shire General, 2013.

Lukas, Scott A. *Theme Park.* London, United Kingdom: Reaktion Books Ltd., 2008.

## Travel and Tourism

Cook, Roy A., Cathy H.C. Hsu, and Joseph J. Marqua. *Tourism: The Business of Hospitality and Travel.* Boston, MA: Pearson, 2014.

Goeldner, Charles R., and J.R. Brent Ritchie. *Tourism: Principles, Practices, Philosophies, 12th ed.* Hoboken, NJ: John Wiley & Sons, Inc., 2012.

Lennon, John, and Malcolm Foley. *Dark Tourism: The Attraction of Death and Disaster.* London: United Kingdom: Continuum, 2000.

Page, Stephen J. *Tourism Management, 4th ed.* Burlington, MA: Butterworth-Heinemann, 2011.

Weaver, David, and Laura Lawton. *Tourism Management, 5th ed.* Milton, Queensland: John Wiley & Sons Australia Ltd., 2014.

# Trade Magazines

*Amusement Today*
www.amusementtoday.com

*Attractions Management*
www.attractionsmanagement.com

*Casino Journal*
www.casinojournal.com

*Connect Magazine*
www.aza.org/azapublications

*Dimensions Magazine*
astc.org/pubs/dimensions.htm

*Funworld*
www.iaapa.org/news/funworld

*Gaming Floor*
www.gamingfloor.com

*Global Gaming Business Magazine*
ggbmagazine.com

*ICOM News Magazine*
icom.museum/media/icom-news-magazine

*InPark Magazine*
www.inparkmagazine.com

*InterPark Magazine*
www.interpark.co.uk

*Museum Magazine*
www.aam-us.org/resources/publications/museum-magazine

*Museums & Heritage Advisor*
www.museumsandheritage.com/advisor

*Museums Journal*
www.museumsassociation.org/museums-journal

*National Parks Magazine*
www.npca.org/news/magazine

*Parks & Recreation Magazine*
www.parksandrecreation.org

*Parkworld Magazine*
www.parkworld-online.com

*Shopping Center Business*
www.shoppingcenterbusiness.com/index.php/magazine

*Shopping Centers Today*
www.icsc.org/sct/sct-usa

*ShowTime Magazine*
www.oaba.org/showtime-magazine

*Special Events Magazine*
specialevents.com

*Sports Travel Magazine*
sportstravelmagazine.com

*Tactics Magazine*
tacticsmagazine.com

*Tourist Attractions & Parks Magazine*
www.tapmag.com

*Venues Today*
www.venuestoday.com/magazine

# Attraction Fun Fact Sources

Bakken, http://www.bakken.dk/english.

City of Las Vegas, http://www.lasvegasnevada.gov/factsstatistics/funfacts.htm.

Empire State Building, http://www.esbnyc.com/fun-facts?page=1.

Fact Sheet, Walt Disney World News, http://wdwnews.com/fact-sheets.

Google Cultural Institute, http://www.google.com/culturalinstitute/about/artproject.

Grand Ole Opry, http://www.opry.com/sites/default/files/Opry_fun_facts.pdf.

The Hollywood Sign, http://www.hollywoodsign.org/the-history-of-the-sign.

*HuffingtonPost.com*, http://www.huffingtonpost.com/2012/12/14/wall-drug-south-dakota-billboard-photos_n_2296122.html.

International Association of Amusement Parks and Attractions, http://www.iaapa.org.

Legends of America, http://www.legendsofamerica.com/66-facts.html.

Mall of America, http://www.mallofamerica.com/about/moa/facts.

MDG Advertising, http://www.mdgadvertising.com/blog/vacationing-the-social-media-way-infographic.

Metropolitan Museum of Art, http://www.metmuseum.org/collection/the-collection-online/search/501788.

Olympic Movement, http://www.olympic.org/ancient-olympic-games.

*Reader's Digest*, http://www.readersdigest.ca/travel/tips/13-things-you-didnt-know-about-worlds-greatest-tourist-attractions.

Smithsonian Institution, http://newsdesk.si.edu/factsheets/facts-about-smithsonian-institution-short.

Tidbit Fun, http://tidbitfun.com/07/15/zoo-fun-facts.

U.S. National Park Service, http://www.nps.gov.

*Venere Travel Blog*, http://www.venere.com/blog/top-15-fun-facts-new-orleans.

Walt Disney Family Museum, http://www.waltdisney.org/storyboard/walt-disneys-oscars%C2%AE.

# INDEX